KIOWA, COMANCHE, APACHE, FORT SILL APACHE, WICHITA, CADDO AND DELAWARE INDIANS BIRTH AND DEATH ROLLS 1924-1932

TRANSCRIBED BY
JEFF BOWEN

NATIVE STUDY
Gallipolis, Ohio
USA

Originally published:
Signal Mountain, Tennessee
1996

Santa Maria, California
2019

Reprinted by:

Native Study LLC
Gallipolis, Ohio
www.nativestudy.com

Library of Congress Control Number: 2022906552

ISBN: 978-1-64968-162-1

Made in the United States of America.

Other Books and Series by Jeff Bowen

Compilation of History of the Cherokee Indians and Early History of the Cherokees by Emmet Starr with Combined Full Name Index
(Hardbound & Softbound)

1901-1907 Native American Census Seneca, Eastern Shawnee, Miami, Modoc, Ottawa, Peoria, Quapaw, and Wyandotte Indians (Under Seneca School, Indian Territory)

1932 Census of The Standing Rock Sioux Reservation with Births And Deaths 1924-1932

Kiowa, Comanche, Apache, Fort Sill Apache, Wichita, Caddo and Delaware Indians Birth and Death Rolls 1924-1932

Census of The Blackfeet, Montana, 1897- 1901 Expanded Edition

Eastern Cherokee by Blood, 1906-1910, Volumes I thru *XIII*

Choctaw of Mississippi Indian Census 1929-1932 with Births and Deaths 1924-1931   Volume I
Choctaw of Mississippi Indian Census 1933, 1934 & 1937, Supplemental Rolls to 1934 & 1935 with Births and Deaths 1932-1938, and Marriages 1936-1938 Volume II

Eastern Cherokee Census Cherokee, North Carolina 1930-1939 Census 1930-1931 with Births And Deaths 1924-1931 Taken By Agent L. W. Page Volume I
Eastern Cherokee Census Cherokee, North Carolina 1930-1939 Census 1932-1933 with Births And Deaths 1930-1932 Taken By Agent R. L. Spalsbury   Volume II
Eastern Cherokee Census Cherokee, North Carolina 1930-1939 Census 1934-1937 with Births and Deaths 1925-1938 and Marriages 1936 & 1938 Taken by Agents R. L. Spalsbury And Harold W. Foght Volume III

Seminole of Florida Indian Census, 1930-1940 with Birth and Death Records, 1930-1938

Texas Cherokees 1820-1839 A Document For Litigation 1921

Starr Roll 1894   (Cherokee Payment Rolls) Districts: Canadian, Cooweescoowee, and Delaware Volume One
Starr Roll 1894 (Cherokee Payment Rolls) Districts: Flint, Going Snake, and Illinois   Volume Two
Starr Roll 1894 (Cherokee Payment Rolls) Districts: Saline, Sequoyah, and Tahlequah; Including Orphan Roll   Volume Three

Cherokee Intruder Cases Dockets of Hearings 1901-1909 Volumes I & II

Other Books and Series by Jeff Bowen

Indian Wills, 1911-1921 Records of the Bureau of Indian Affairs
Books One thru *Seven*
Native American Wills & Probate Records 1911-1921

Turtle Mountain Reservation Chippewa Indians 1932 Census with Births & Deaths, 1924-1932

Chickasaw By Blood Enrollment Cards 1898-1914 Volume I thru *V*

Cherokee Descendants East An Index to the Guion Miller Applications Volume I
Cherokee Descendants West An Index to the Guion Miller Applications Volume II (A-M)
Cherokee Descendants West An Index to the Guion Miller Applications Volume III (N-Z)

Applications for Enrollment of Seminole Newborn Freedmen, Act of 1905

Eastern Cherokee Census, Cherokee, North Carolina, 1915-1922, Taken by Agent James E. Henderson   *Volume I (1915-1916)*
                                        Volume II (1917-1918)
                                        Volume III (1919-1920)
                                        Volume IV (1921-1922)

Complete Delaware Roll of 1898

Eastern Cherokee Census, Cherokee, North Carolina, 1923-1929, Taken by Agent James E. Henderson   *Volume I (1923-1924)*
                                        Volume II (1925-1926)
                                        Volume III (1927-1929)

Applications for Enrollment of Seminole Newborn Act of 1905 Volumes I & II

North Carolina Eastern Cherokee Indian Census 1898-1899, 1904, 1906, 1909-1912, 1914   Revised and Expanded Edition

1932 Hopi and Navajo Native American Census with Birth & Death Rolls (1925-1931) Volume 1 - Hopi
1932 Hopi and Navajo Native American Census with Birth & Death Rolls (1930-1932) Volume 2 - Navajo

Western Navajo Reservation Navajo, Hopi and Paiute 1933 Census with Birth & Death Rolls 1925-1933

Cherokee Citizenship Commission Dockets 1880-1884 and 1887-1889 Volumes I thru *V*

Applications for Enrollment of Chickasaw Newborn Act of 1905 Volumes I thru *VII*

Other Books and Series by Jeff Bowen

Cherokee Intermarried White 1906 Volume I thru *X*

Applications for Enrollment of Creek Newborn Act of 1905
Volumes I thru *XIV*

Applications for Enrollment of Choctaw Newborn Act of 1905 Volumes I thru *XX*

Choctaw By Blood Enrollment Cards 1898-1914 Volumes I thru *XX*

Oglala Sioux Indians Pine Ridge Reservation 1932 Census Book I
Oglala Sioux Indians Pine Ridge Reservation Birth and Death Rolls 1924-1932
Book II

Census of the Sioux and Cheyenne Indians of Pine Ridge Agency
1896 - 1897 Book I
Census of the Sioux and Cheyenne Indians of Pine Ridge Agency
1898 - 1899 Book II

Northern Cheyenne Tongue River, Montana 1904 - 1932 Census
1904-1916 Volume I
Northern Cheyenne Tongue River, Montana 1904 - 1932 Census
1917-1926 Volume II

Identified Mississippi Choctaw Enrollment Cards 1902-1909 Volumes I, II & III

Sac & Fox - Shawnee Estates 1885-1910 (Under Sac & Fox Agency)
Volumes I-VIII
Sac & Fox - Shawnee Estates 1920-1924 (Under The Sac & Fox Agency,
Oklahoma) & Wills 1889-1924 Volume IX
Sac & Fox - Shawnee Deaths, Cemetery, Births, & Marriage Cards (Under The Sac
& Fox Agency, Oklahoma) 1853-1933 Volume X
Sac & Fox - Shawnee Marriages, Divorces, Estates Log Books Volumes 1 & 2, Log
Book Births & Deaths (Under Sac & Fox Agency, Oklahoma)1846-1924 Volume XI
Sac & Fox - Shawnee Guardianships Part 1 (Under Sac & Fox Agency, Oklahoma)
1892-1909 Volume XII
Sac & Fox - Shawnee Guardianships, Part 2 (Under The Sac & Fox Agency,
Oklahoma) 1902-1910 Volume XIII
Sac & Fox - Shawnee Guardianships, Part 3 (Under The Sac & Fox Agency,
Oklahoma) 1906-1914 Volume XIV

Census of the Pima, Tohono O'odham (Papago), and Maricopa Indians of the Gila
River, Ak Chin & Gila Bend Reservations 1932 with Birth and Death Rolls 1924-
1932

Visit our website at **www.nativestudy.com** to learn more about these
and other books and series by Jeff Bowen

This book is dedicated to
Mario Nick Klimiades
Thank you for the inspiration
in getting this book started and
the great work you do.

Author's Note

Please be sure you read the Introduction. You will find not only new updated and interesting tribal information, but also **blood quantum** requirements for some of the tribes. You will find within these pages a combination of each tribe's general history, as well as present-day data.

TABLE of CONTENTS

INTRODUCTION

The original printing of this book was done in 1996. The book itself has been reformatted to a smaller version rather than the old uncomfortable 8.5x11" format where folks were just buying a bound Xerox copy of the materials. Every effort has been made to ensure that the individual can not only feel good about searching for their Native heritage, but also enjoy what they are holding in their hands and putting on their shelves. Hopefully with the new format we've saved a few trees along the way and still remain informative. A simple key can be found at the top of each page explaining the layout of the information.

Several sources have been used for this introduction along with a few pieces used from the original introduction. It will give brief histories for the seven tribes along with present day tribal information; where able blood quantum requirements are given. The only thing to remember not all blood requirements remain the same, circumstances change along with policies. Every one of the Birth and Death Rolls within these pages comes from the jurisdictions of the Wichita and Kiowa Reservations of Oklahoma 1924-1932.

The source material used for this census comes from National Archives microfilm [Indian Census Rolls, 1885-1940, Series M-595, Roll number 220] listing over 2500 names. Each entry lists surname and given name, degree of blood, date of birth or death. On most of the death entries the cause of death or disease is shown. Great care has been taken to transcribe the names and dates exactly as shown on the original records.

"**Kiowa** (/ˈkaɪəwə, -wɑː, -weɪ/) people are a Native American tribe and an indigenous people of the Great Plains. They migrated southward from western Montana into the Rocky Mountains in Colorado in the 17th and 18th centuries, and finally into the Southern Plains by the early 19th century. In 1867, the Kiowa were moved to a reservation in southwestern Oklahoma. Today, they are federally recognized as Kiowa Tribe of Oklahoma with headquarters in Carnegie, Oklahoma. As of 2011, there were 12,000 members. The Kiowa language (Cáuijògà), part of the Tanoan language family, is still spoken today. The Kiowa Tribe of Oklahoma is headquartered in Carnegie, Oklahoma. Their tribal jurisdictional area includes Caddo,

Comanche, Cotton, Grady, Kiowa, Tillman, and Washita Counties. Enrollment in the tribe requires a minimum blood quantum of ¼ Kiowa descent."[1]

"Little is known of the prehistoric origin of the Kiowa, but they have a story that tells how a trickster led the people out of a dark lower world into this one by climbing up a hollow cottonwood log. A pregnant woman got stuck and could not get out, though, blocking the way for the rest; they say this is why there are not many people in the tribe. Scholars disagree whether they migrated south to the Montana mountains sometime after the glaciers melted or moved north in more recent times. Over the years, they moved to southwestern Oklahoma. Spanish sources note that the Kiowa were on the Plains in 1732. They may have become mounted buffalo hunters a few years earlier, obtaining horses from other tribes."[2]

One of the most famous Comanche leaders in their history was Quanah Parker. The product of a white woman, (Cynthia Ann Parker), who was captured as a child and a Comanche warrior. An excellent book that portrays their personal history is *Empire of the Summer Moon*, you won't want to put it down.

"The **Comanche** /kə'mæntʃi/ (Comanche: *Numunuu*) are a Native American nation from the Great Plains whose historic territory consisted of most of present-day northwestern Texas and adjacent areas in eastern New Mexico, southeastern Colorado, southwestern Kansas, western Oklahoma, and northern Chihuahua. The Comanche people are federally recognized as the **Comanche Nation,** headquartered in Lawton, Oklahoma. Their tribal jurisdictional area is located in Caddo, Comanche, Cotton, Grady, Jefferson, Kiowa, Stephens, and Tillman Counties. Membership of the tribe requires a 1/8 blood quantum (equivalent to one great-grandparent). Decimated by European diseases, warfare, and encroachment by Americans on Comancheria, the Comanche were defeated by the United States army in 1875 and confined to a reservation in Oklahoma. In the 21st century, the Comanche Nation has 17,000 members, around 7,000 of whom reside in tribal jurisdictional area around Lawton, Fort Sill, and the surrounding areas of southwestern Oklahoma."[3]

---

[1] Kiowa, Wikipedia

[2] Indian Nations of North America, Kiowa, Pg. 182, Para. 1

[3] Comanche, Wikipedia

The Comanche coming from west of the Rocky Mountains around the fifteenth century lived in an arid territory. Moving into the huge plains territories these nomadic travelers were soon to become a changed people. They realized skills that were not only natural for them but would make them master hunters and horseman usually unmatched by any other. "No tribe's way of life was more dramatically reshaped by the horse than that of the Comanche, a group with no previous connection to the Plains. Before 1700 the Comanche were an impoverished Shoshonean-speaking group of hunter-gatherers living in the mountains of western Colorado. Then they acquired horses. Mounted Comanches descended from the Rockies, rapidly evolving as superb horsemen and buffalo hunters. The Comanche, a white plainsman said, believed that 'the Great Spirit had created horses especially for them.'"[4] The Comanche practiced limited farming and were known as fierce warriors and skilled desert survivors. They lived in tepees. Tribal members wore buckskins, with fur hats during the winter. Though they met defeat surely by numbers, power, persistence and disease the Comanche were a formidable people in their prime.

"The **Apache** (/əˈpætʃi/) are a group of culturally related Native American tribes in the Southwestern United States, which include the Chiricahua, Jicarilla, Lipan, Mescalero, Salinero, Plains and Western Apache. Distant cousins of the Apache are the Navajo, with which they share the Southern Athabaskan languages. There are Apache communities in Oklahoma, Texas, and reservations in Arizona and New Mexico. Apache people have moved throughout the United States and elsewhere, including urban centers. The Apache Nations are politically autonomous, speak several different languages and have distinct cultures.

"Historically, the Apache homelands have consisted of high mountains, sheltered and watered valleys, deep canyons, deserts, and the southern Great Plains, including areas in what is now Eastern Arizona, Northern Mexico (Sonora and Chihuahua) and New Mexico, West Texas, and Southern Colorado. These areas are collectively known as Apacheria. The Apache tribes fought the invading Spanish and Mexican peoples for centuries. The first Apache raids on Sonora appear to have taken place during the late 17th century. In 19th-century confrontations during the

---

[4] The Buffalo Hunters, Time-Life Books, Pg. 28, Para. 3

American-Indian wars, the U.S. Army found the Apache to be fierce warriors and skillful strategists. The Plains Apache are located in Oklahoma, headquartered around Anadarko, and are federally recognized as the Apache Tribe of Oklahoma."[5]

Like the Comanche the Apache were adept in desert survival. Most families lived in wickiups, dome shaped brush huts, or lived in buffalo-hide tepees erected by the women. Religion was a fundamental part of Apache life.

"Known historically as the Ka-ta-ka, the members of the Apache Tribe of Oklahoma are descendants of the Athabascan-speaking Eastern Apache groups who have inhabited the Plains since the 15th century. However, because of their alliance with the more numerous Kiowa tribe, the Plains Apache were commonly referred to as the Kiowa Apache. Reservation lands were opened for allotment during the late 19th century, with most passing into non-Indian hands.

"This reservation land is jointly held by the Comanche Nation and the Kiowa Indian Tribe of Oklahoma. Today, tribal members work in a variety of professions in the Anadarko and Fort Cobb areas, and tribal identity and tradition continue to flourish."[6]

Fort Sill, Oklahoma, is likely the most well-known because of Geronimo being taken there where he made a home even though a prisoner. Eventually when he died in 1909 he was buried among family. The move to Fort Sill in 1894 brought a better life for the Apache prisoners of war since they were living in hardship while being looked for. Homes were built for them, they received cattle, hogs, turkeys and chickens, along with agricultural assistance.

"The **Fort Sill Apache Tribe** is the federally recognized Native American tribe of Chiricahua Warm Springs Apache in Oklahoma. The Fort Sill Apache Tribe is headquartered in Apache, Oklahoma. Tribal member enrollment, which requires a 1/16 minimum blood quantum (equivalent to one great-great-grandparent), stands at 650. The tribe continues to maintain close connections to the Chiricahua Apache who were moved to the Mescalero Apache Reservation in the late 19th century. The tribal jurisdictional area, as opposed to a reservation, spans Caddo, Comanche, and Grady

---

[5] Apache, Wikipedia
[6] Indian Nations of North America, Kiowa, Pg. 149-150, Para. 3-5

Counties in Oklahoma. A private landholder returned four acres of sacred land in Cochise County, Arizona to the tribe, and it is included in their trust lands.

"In 2011, the tribe won the right to establish a reservation in New Mexico. They now control 30 acres (12 ha) near Deming, New Mexico. The Fort Sill Apache Tribe is composed of Chiricahua Apache, who were made up of 4 bands:

- Chihende (*Chinde, Chihenne* – 'Red Painted People', known as Warm Springs Apache Band or Gila Apaches, Eastern Chiricahua)
- Chukunende (*Chokonende, Chokonen* – 'Ridge of the Mountainside People', known as Chiricahua Band, proper or Central Chiricahua)
- Nde'ndai (*Ndénai, Nednai, Ndé'ndai* – 'Enemy People', 'People who make trouble', sometimes known as Pinery Apache Band, known as Sierre Madre Apaches, Southern Chiricahua)
- Bidánku (*Bedonkohe* – 'In Front of the End People', *Bi-da-a-naka-enda* – 'Standing in front of the enemy', sometimes known as Bronco Apache Band, known as Mogollon Apaches or Gila Apaches, Northeastern Chiricahua)

"The Apache are southern Athabaskan-speaking peoples who migrated many centuries ago from the subarctic to the southwestern region of what would become the United States. The Chiricahua settled in southeastern Arizona, southwestern New Mexico of the present-day United States, and northern Sonora, and northern Chihuahua of present-day Mexico. By the late 19th century, the Chiricahua Apache territory encompassed an estimated 15 millions acres.

"In 1886 to break up the Apache Wars and resistance to European-American settlement, the US federal government took the Chiricahua into custody as prisoners of war and seized their land. The Army forcibly removed 400 members of the tribe from the Fort Apache and San Carlos Reservations in present-day Arizona, and transported them to U.S. Army installations in Alabama and Florida. Some warriors were held at Fort Pickens in Florida. Their ledger drawings are held in a collection by the Smithsonian Institution. "Many of the Apache Scouts who serve in the capture of Geronimo were arrested by the order of General Miles forced on the same train as Geronimo was on, the Apache Scouts came from the Tonto, Pinal, Aravaipa, Apache Pecks, Chiricahua, San Carlos, White Mountain Apache bands, some of the Apache Scouts where also Apache chiefs were from different Apache bands. "In 1894, the US Congress passed a special provision to allow the Chiricahua to be relocated to

Indian Territory. They were the last Indian tribe to be relocated into what is now Oklahoma. When the Chiricahua arrived at Fort Sill, they had been promised the lands surrounding the fort as theirs to settle. Local non-Indians resisted Apache settlement, and the tribe was pressured to leave. Many wanted to return to their traditional lands in the Southwest, and the Mescalero Apache offered them land on their reservation.

"A third of the Chiricahua stayed in Indian Territory, demanding that the US fulfill its promise to give them the Fort Sill lands. As a compromise, the government gave the remaining Chiricahua land which it had classified as surplus after allotment of tribal lands to individual households under the Dawes Act, on the nearby Kiowa-Comanche-Apache Reservation. In 1914, the US government finally released 84 individuals from prisoner status and granted them household allotment lands around Fletcher and Apache, Oklahoma.

"The Fort Sill Apache struggled for survival in the ensuing years in the economically depressed areas of southwestern Oklahoma. The tribe seized the opportunity afforded by Oklahoma Indian Welfare Act of 1936. Persevering through the difficulty of satisfying documentation requirements for tribal continuity, they were recognized by the federal government (Department of Interior) as a tribe in 1976."[7]

The **Wichita** tribe is one of Oklahoma's oldest living communities with the French discovering a village in the early 1700's. They were also the object of the earliest missionary work done among the Plains Indians.

"The Wichitas and Caddos adapted to reservation life fairly easily. A settled folk who had farmed part-time for centuries, they built thatch roofed houses and planted corn.

"The chief federal agent in Texas, Robert Neighbors, saw that something had to be done. A man of principle, Neighbors doubted the federal government could keep its commitment to protect the reservation dwellers in the face of mounting pressure, and he persuaded authorities to resettle them in safer environs-the western part of present-day Oklahoma. In the summer of 1859, Neighbors and four companies of soldiers escorted 1,112 Wichitas and Caddos and 384 Comanches

---

[7] Ft. Sill Apache Tribe, Wikipedia

northward, marching them away from the reservations in such haste that much of their livestock had to be left behind."[8]

"The **Wichita people or Kitikiti'sh** are a confederation of Southern Plains Native American tribes. Historically they spoke the Wichita language and Kichai language, both Caddoan languages. They are indigenous to Oklahoma, Texas, and Kansas.

"Today, Wichita tribes, which include the Kichai people, Yscani, Waco, Taovaya, Tawakoni, and the Wichita proper (or Guichita or Kanoatino), are federally recognized as the **Wichita and Affiliated Tribes (Wichita, Keechi, Waco and Tawakoni)**.

"The Wichita and Affiliated Tribes are headquartered in Anadarko, Oklahoma. Their tribal jurisdictional area is in Caddo County, Oklahoma. The Wichitas are a self-governance tribe, who operate their own housing authority and issue tribal vehicle tags.

"The Wichita language is one of the Caddoan languages. They are related by language and culture to the Pawnee, with whom they enjoy close relations.

"The Wichita lived in fixed villages notable for their large, domed-shaped, grass-covered dwellings, sometimes up to 30 feet in diameter. The Wichita were successful hunters and farmers and skilled traders and negotiators. Their historical homelands stretched from San Antonio, Texas in the south to as far north as Great Bend, Kansas. A semi-sedentary people, they occupied northern Texas in the early 18th century. They traded with other Southern Plains Indians on both sides of the Red River and as far south as Waco.

"Historically, for much of the year, the Wichita lived in huts made of forked cedar poles covered by dry grasses. In the winter, they followed American bison (buffalo) in a seasonal hunt and lived in hunting camps. Wichita hunters used all parts of the bison—for clothing, food and cooking fat, winter shelter, leather supplies, sinew, and medicine. Each spring, Wichita families to their villages for another season of cultivating crops.

---

[8] Tribes of the Southern Plains, Time-Life Books, Pg. 149-150, Para. 1 and 2

"Wichita people wore clothing from tanned hides, which the women prepared and sewed. They often decorated their dresses with elk canine teeth. Both men and women tattooed their faces and bodies with solid and dotted lines and circles. The Wichita tribes call themselves **Kitikiti'sh / Kirikirish** ("raccoon-eyed people"), because of the historical practice of tattooing marks around their eyes. The kindred Pawnee called them Kírikuuruks / Kírikuruks ("bear-eyed people") and the Arikara referred to them as Čirikuúnux (a reference to the Wichita practice of tattoos). The Kiowa knew them as Thoe-Khoot ("tattoo faces")."[9]

"The Spanish explorer Hernando de Soto made contact with the Caddo in the early 1540s. In the 17th century, the French ventured south on the Mississippi River into Caddo territory. Being good traders, bartering furs and salt for European finished goods, the Caddo were able to maintain relative stability despite these early encroachments. Contact with the American settlers migrating westward following the Louisiana Purchase in 1803 brought conflict. During the 1830s, Texans dispossessed the Caddo of their lands, which lay within the Texas Republic."[10]

When left alone the **Caddo** thrived by planting corn for hundreds of years prior to their forced migration. They originally were a sedentary agricultural people who dwelled along the Red River area of Louisiana and Arkansas. They lived in cone-shaped dwellings of thatched grass over poles. Groups of the dwellings were usually surrounded by Temple Mounds as mentioned below.

"The **Caddo Nation** is a confederacy of several Southeastern Native American tribes. Their ancestors historically inhabited much of what is now East Texas, Louisiana, and portions of southern Arkansas and Oklahoma. They were descendants of the Caddoan Mississippian culture that constructed huge earthwork mounds at several sites in this territory. In the early 19th century, Caddo people were forced to a reservation in Texas; they were removed to Indian Territory in 1859.

"Today, the **Caddo Nation of Oklahoma** is a federally recognized tribe with its capital at Binger, Oklahoma. Descendants of the historic Caddo tribes, with

[9] Wichita People, Wikipedia
[10] Indian Nations of North America, Caddo Reservation, Pg. 150-151, Para. 2-3

documentation of at least $\frac{1}{16}$ ancestry, are eligible to enroll as members in the Caddo Nation. The several Caddo languages have converged into a single language.

"The Caddo Nation was previously known as the Caddo Tribe of Oklahoma. The tribal constitution provides for election of an eight-person council, with a chairperson, that is based in Binger, Oklahoma.

"The tribe operates its own housing authority and issues its own tribal vehicle tags. It also operates an administrative center, dance grounds, several community centers, the Caddo Nation Heritage Museum, and an active NAGPRA office, located south of Binger. As of 2012, 5,757 people are enrolled in the nation, with 3,044 living within the state of Oklahoma. Individuals are required to document at least 1/16 Caddo ancestry in order to enroll as citizens."[11]

The **Delaware** depended primarily on agriculture, along with hunting and fishing as important additions to their economy. They were grouped into three clans based on maternal descent; these were in turn divided into linages, whose members generally lived together in a longhouse. A council of lineage chiefs and other distinguished men decided public affairs of the community. The eldest woman of the lineage appointed and dismissed the chiefs.

"The Delaware Tribe of Oklahoma descends from the eastern woodland Delaware Indians, an Algonquian-speaking tribe of the Delaware and Hudson River Valleys in what is now southern New York and northern New Jersey. They called themselves Lenni Lenape, or 'original people,' and were called 'grandfathers' by other tribes, most likely because of their longtime existence prior to European contact and for their reputations peacekeepers.

"The Delaware were forced into what is now Pennsylvania by waves of European immigrants seeking new lives and land in the emerging colonies. By the time of the American Revolution, the Delaware were residing as far west as present-day Ohio. American colonists referred to the Delaware as 'friendly' Indians because of their cooperation in treaty negotiations; loyal to the fledgling United States, the Delaware served as scouts and soldiers.

---

[11] Caddo, Wikipedia

"One band of Delawares branched off in 1793 and settled in present-day Missouri. Referred to as the Absentee Delaware, this band became the ancestors of the modern Delaware Tribe of Oklahoma. The Absentee Delaware received a land grant from the Spanish government in 1820 and relocated to what is now East Texas. In 1854, Texas settlers drove them off their land. Five years later, several Delaware families settled at the Wichita Agency in Indian Territory (Oklahoma). The Wichita Agency was largely allotted following the Jerome Agreement of 1890, and the Absentee Delaware were allotted as either Caddo or Wichita. Since members were not designated as Delaware on any census between 1895 and 1930, organization under the 1934 Indian Reorganization Act presented a struggle for the tribe. They eventually organized under the Oklahoma Indian Welfare Act in 1936. Thereafter, the tribe worked to rebuild after centuries of cultural dislocation and forced relocation. During the 1950s, the tribe filed joint claims with the Indian Claims Commission and received a small settlement in 1977. The tribe also gained joint ownership of trust lands with the Caddo and Wichita tribes."[12]

"The **Delaware Nation**, also known as the **Delaware Tribe of Western Oklahoma** and sometimes called the **Absentee** or **Western Delaware**, based in Anadarko, Oklahoma is one of three federally recognized tribes of Delaware Indians in the United States, along with the Delaware Indians based in Bartlesville, Oklahoma and the Stockbridge-Munsee Community of Wisconsin. Communities also reside in Canada. The Delaware Nation had 1,440 enrolled members in 2011, of which 859 lived in Oklahoma. Members must have a minimum blood quantum of 1/8 to join the tribe.

"The Delaware Nation's tribal complex is located two miles (3 km) north of Anadarko, Oklahoma on Highway 281. Their tribal jurisdictional area is located within Caddo County, Oklahoma. They operate their own housing authority and issue tribal vehicle tags."[13]

It was noticed that 23 years ago this author along with his inexperience in transcription work needed to make a few corrections, three to be exact. The text now is an exact transcription of the microfilm used even though the older book stated the

---

[12] Indian Nations of North America, Delaware Reservation, Pg. 166-167, Para. 1-4
[13] Delaware Nation, Wikipedia

same terms it wasn't exactly as the film showed.   First, the word, "Full" for blood quantum, was used in the first book rather than 4/4 as it shows on the original film. Second, the dates typed in the initial book were in the form of a numbers-slash format rather than being spelled out as the film showed and have been corrected.   Third, the diseases or cause of death in many places were abbreviated rather than spelled out as the film showed and are all now corrected.

Jeff Bowen
Gallipolis, Ohio
NativeStudy.com

KIOWA INDIAN AGENCY
Kiowa Reservation
Oklahoma
1925

BIRTH ROLL
**Kiowa, Comanche, Apache and
Fort Sill Apache Indians –**

State __Oklahoma__ Reservation __Kiowa__ Agency or Jurisdiction __Kiowa__
Office of Indian Affairs Births Occurring Between the Dates of July 1, 1924 and
June 30, 1925 to Parents Enrolled at Jurisdiction

KEY: 1925 Census Roll Number; Surname and Given Name; Date of Birth; Live Birth (Yes or No); Sex; Tribe; Ward (yes or no); Degree of Father's blood; Degree of Mother's blood; Degree of Child's blood; At Jurisdiction Where Enrolled (yes or no); [If "no", where, if given]

1927   105;   AHTONE, Ruth; 1925; yes; F; Kiowa; yes; 4/4; 4/4; 4/4; yes

1925   1715;   AITSON, Radburg; 1925-Jan-25; yes; M; Kiowa; yes; 4/4; 4/4; 4/4; yes

1925   1570;   APEKAUM, Paul J; 1925-June-13; yes; M; Kiowa; yes; 4/4; 4/4; 4/4; yes

1925   19;   ASENAP, Rhoda Coleen; 1924-Nov-9; yes; F; Kiowa; yes; 4/4; 4/4; 4/4; yes

1925   779;   ASEPERMY, Fern; 1925-Jan-30; yes; F; Kiowa; yes; 4/4; 4/4; 4/4; yes

1925   1179;   ASETAMY, Frank; 1925-Feb-24; yes; M; Comanche; yes; 4/4; 4/4; 4/4; yes

1925   1276;   ASEWAYAH, Geneice; 1925-Jan-23; yes; F; Comanche; yes; 4/4; 4/4; 4/4; yes

1925   219;   AUNKO, Ralph; 1924-Sept-12; yes; M; Kiowa; yes; 4/4; 4/4; 4/4; yes

1926   1716;   AUTAUBO, Ruby; 1924-July-19; yes; F; Kiowa; yes; 4/4; 4/4; 4/4; yes

1925   1617;   BEARTRACK, Clay Clifton; 1924-Dec-9; yes; M; Kiowa; yes; 4/4; 4/4; 4/4; yes

See #
1925   173;   BOINTY, Baby; 1925-Apr-18; yes; F; Kiowa; yes; 4/4; 4/4; 4/4; yes

1925   1111;   BOSIN, Jack Wesley; 1924-Dec-28; yes; M; Kiowa; yes; 4/4; 4/4; 4/4; yes

1925   1176;   BROWN, May; 1924-Aug-18; yes; F; Kiowa; yes; 4/4; 4/4; 4/4; yes

1926   1599;   CADDO, Bennie Leonard; 1925-June-4; yes; M; Comanche; yes; 4/4; 4/4; 4/4; yes

1925   658;   CARNEY, James Virgil; 1924-Aug-25; yes; M; Comanche; yes; 4/4; 4/4; 4/4; yes

3

State __Oklahoma__ Reservation __Kiowa__ Agency or Jurisdiction __Kiowa__
Office of Indian Affairs Births Occurring Between the Dates of July 1, 1924 and
June 30, 1925 to Parents Enrolled at Jurisdiction

1925   178;   CATO, Phil; 1924-Dec-24; yes; M; Comanche; yes; 4/4; 4/4; 4/4; yes

1925   1079;   CLARK, Mary Pache; 1924-Aug-20; yes; F; Comanche; yes; 4/4; 4/4; 4/4; yes

1925   70;   CLEVELAND, Ruby May; 1924-Dec-1; yes; F; Kiowa; yes; 4/4; 4/4; 4/4; yes

1925   1589;   DIETRICH, Betty Ruth; 1924-Nov-2; yes; F; Comanche; yes; 4/4; 4/4; 4/4; yes

1926   1612;   DIETRICH, Wm Edw; 1924-Feb-11; yes; M; Comanche; yes; 4/4; 4/4; 4/4; yes

1926   1639;   ELMS; 1925-June-4; yes; M; Comanche; yes; W; 1/4; 1/8; yes

          See #
1925   219;   ESADOOAH, Fred; 1925-Jan-1; yes; M; Comanche; yes; 4/4; 4/4; 4/4; yes

1925   991;   EVANS, Billie Carl; 1924-July-20; yes; M; Comanche; yes; 4/4; 4/4; 4/4; yes

1925   863;   FAWBUSH, Wanda; 1925-May-3; yes; F; Kiowa; yes; 4/4; 4/4; 4/4; yes

2436   281;   GONZOLES, Geneva; 1925-Jan-1; yes; F; Kiowa; yes; 4/4; 4/4; 4/4; yes

1925   89;   GEIMAUSADDLE, Irene; 1924-July-13; yes; F; Kiowa; yes; 4/4; 4/4; 4/4; yes

1926   1351;   GEIOGAMAH, Winona; 1925-Apr-23; yes; F; Kiowa; yes; 4/4; 4/4; 4/4; yes

1925   1139;   GOODIN, Teddy Parker; 1925-Feb-12; yes; F; Comanche; yes; 4/4; 4/4; 4/4; yes

1924   301;   HAMILTON, Enosta Viola; 1924-July-19; yes; F; Kiowa; yes; 4/4; 4/4; 4/4; yes

4

State __Oklahoma__ Reservation __Kiowa__ Agency or Jurisdiction __Kiowa__
Office of Indian Affairs Births Occurring Between the Dates of July 1, 1924 and
June 30, 1925 to Parents Enrolled at Jurisdiction

KEY: 1925 Census Roll Number; Surname and Given Name; Date of Birth; Live Birth (Yes or No); Sex; Tribe; Ward (yes or no); Degree of Father's blood; Degree of Mother's blood; Degree of Child's blood; At Jurisdiction Where Enrolled (yes or no); [If "no", where, if given]

1925   495;   HAUZYSTA, Albert, Jr; 1924-Aug-10; yes; M; Kiowa; yes; 4/4; 4/4; 4/4; yes

1925   886;   HEATH, Marietta; 1925-Mar-17; yes; F; Comanche; yes; 4/4; 4/4; 4/4; yes

1926   837;   HENRY, Leo Horace; 1924-Oct-29; yes; M; Kiowa; yes; 4/4; 4/4; 4/4; yes

See #
1925   993;   HIGHWALKER, Nettie; 1925-Mar-28; yes; F; Kiowa; yes; 4/4; 4/4; 4/4; yes

1925   1725;   HORSE, David Livingston; 1924-Aug-29; yes; M; Kiowa; yes; 4/4; 4/4; 4/4; yes

1925   262;   HOVAKAH, Christie; 1924-Nov-20; yes; F; Kiowa; yes; 4/4; 4/4; \ 4/4; yes

1925   3;   KADAYSO, LeRoy; 1924-Sept -5; yes; M; Apache; yes; 4/4; 4/4; 4/4; yes

1926   1691;   KAPADDY, Virginia Mae; 1925-June-11; yes; F; Kiowa; yes; 4/4; 4/4; 4/4; yes

1925   122;   KASSAWAVOID, Samuel, Jr; 1924-Sept-22; yes; M; Comanche; yes; 4/4; 4/4; 4/4; yes

1925   618;   KAULAY, Pearl; 1925-Apr-1; yes; F; Kiowa; yes; 4/4; 4/4; 4/4; yes

1926   339;   KAULAITY, Violet May; 1925; yes; F; Kiowa; 4/4; 4/4; 4/4; yes

1925   12;   KAUDLE KAULE, Daisy; 1924-Sept-26; yes; F; Apache; yes; 4/4; 4/4; 4/4; yes

1925   739;   KODASEET, Wanada May; 1925-Mar-30; yes; F; Kiowa; yes; 4/4; 4/4; 4/4; yes

1925   1629;   KOMAH, Lester; 1925-Apr-2; yes; M; Comanche; yes; 4/4; 4/4; 4/4; yes

State __Oklahoma__ Reservation __Kiowa__ Agency or Jurisdiction __Kiowa__
Office of Indian Affairs Births Occurring Between the Dates of July 1, 1924 and
June 30, 1925 to Parents Enrolled at Jurisdiction

KEY: 1925 Census Roll Number; Surname and Given Name; Date of Birth; Live Birth (Yes or No); Sex; Tribe; Ward (yes or no); Degree of Father's blood; Degree of Mother's blood; Degree of Child's blood; At Jurisdiction Where Enrolled (yes or no); [If "no", where, if given]

1925   1531;   KOTAY, Lillie Bettie; 1925-May-26; yes; F; Kiowa; yes; 4/4; 4/4;
4/4; yes

1925   141;   KOMARDLEY, Morris; 1925-Mar-23; yes; M; Apache; yes; 4/4; 4/4;
4/4; yes

1925   207;   KOWENO, Marjorie Eleanor; 1924-Aug-8; yes; F; Comanche; yes;
4/4; 4/4; 4/4; yes

1925   65;   LeBARRE, Lolita; 1925-Jan-18; yes; F; Apache & Come; yes; 4/4;
4/4; 4/4; yes

1925   1439;   LITTLE CHIEF, Caroline; 1925-Jan-17; yes; F; Kiowa; yes; 4/4; 4/4;
4/4; yes

1925   36;   LOCO, Ralph; 1925-Feb-21; yes; M; Apache; yes; 4/4; 4/4; 4/4; yes

       See #
1926   1367;   MAHSETHY, Leighton; 1925; yes; M; Comanche; yes; 4/4; 4/4; 4/4;
yes

1925   583;   MAUCHAHTY, Arthur; 1925; yes; M; Kiowa; yes; 4/4; 4/4; 4/4; yes

1925   1427;   MIHECOBY, Pernell; 1924-July-8; yes; M; Comanche; yes; 4/4; 4/4;
4/4; yes

1925   1347;   MONATOBAY, Geraldine; 1924-Dec-9; yes; F; Comanche; yes; 4/4;
4/4; 4/4; yes

1925   669;   NAHOUADDY, Nathan; 1925-Apr-11; yes; M; Comanche; yes; 4/4;
4/4; 4/4; yes

1925   643;   NAUNI, Velma; 1925-Mar-17; yes; F; Comanche; yes; 4/4; 4/4; 4/4;
yes

1925   1424;   NEMSIE, Mary Virginia; 1925-May-31; yes; F; Comanche; yes; 4/4;
4/4; 4/4; yes

1926   156;   NEWOOKOHHER, Leroy; 1925-Apr; yes; M; Apache; yes; 4/4; 4/4;
4/4; yes

State __Oklahoma__ Reservation __Kiowa__ Agency or Jurisdiction __Kiowa__
Office of Indian Affairs Births Occurring Between the Dates of July 1, 1924 and
June 30, 1925 to Parents Enrolled at Jurisdiction

1925   1240;   NOYOBAD, Rachel; 1925-Oct-1; yes; F; Comanche; yes; 4/4; 4/4; 4/4; yes

1925   462;   OTIPPOBY, Lucile; 1925-May-16; yes; F; Comanche; yes; 4/4; 4/4; 4/4; yes

1925   971;   PAHCODY, Roxie; 1925-Jan-29; yes; F; Comanche; yes; 4/4; 4/4; 4/4; yes

1925   1155;   PAHCHEKA, Priscilla; 1925-May-27; yes; F; Comanche; yes; 4/4; 4/4; 4/4; yes

See #
1925   444;   PAHDOCONY, Kenneth; 1924-Nov-17; yes; M; Comanche; yes; 4/4; 4/4; 4/4; yes

1925   1082;   PAHDINGKER, Christina; 1924-Sept-23; yes; F; Kiowa; yes; 4/4; 4/4; 4/4; yes

1925   23;   PARKER, Cynthia Joy; 1924-Dec-21; yes; F; Kiowa; yes; 4/4; 4/4; 4/4; yes

1925   31;   PARKER, Elmer Thos; 1925-Apr-25; yes; M; Comanche; yes; 4/4; 4/4; 4/4; yes

1925   1282;   PARKER, Harold; 1925-Jan-21; yes; M; Comanche; yes; 4/4; 4/4; 4/4; yes

See #
1925   1055;   PAYWETOWAUP, Pearl; 1924-Dec-5; yes; F; Comanche; yes; 4/4; 4/4; 4/4; yes

1925   132;   PEBEAHSY, Hugh; 1924-Nov-1; yes; M; Comanche; yes; 4/4; 4/4; 4/4; yes

1925   1087;   PERMAMSU, Barbara June; 1925-June-17; yes; F; Comanche; yes; 4/4; 4/4; 4/4; yes

1925   928;   PERMAMSU, Benson; 1925-Apr-24; yes; M; Comanche; yes; 4/4; 4/4; 4/4; yes

State __Oklahoma__ Reservation __Kiowa__ Agency or Jurisdiction __Kiowa__
Office of Indian Affairs Births Occurring Between the Dates of July 1, 1924 and
June 30, 1925 to Parents Enrolled at Jurisdiction

KEY: 1925 Census Roll Number; Surname and Given Name; Date of Birth; Live Birth (Yes or No); Sex; Tribe; Ward (yes or no); Degree of Father's blood; Degree of Mother's blood; Degree of Child's blood; At Jurisdiction Where Enrolled (yes or no); [If "no", where, if given]

1925   1047;   PORTILLO, Baby; 1925-May-19; yes; F; Comanche; yes; Mex; Mex; Mex; yes

1926   1056;   PRENTISS, Frederick; 1925-May-31; yes; M; Comanche; yes; 4/4; 4/4; 4/4; yes

1925   867;   PUEBLO, Corine; 1924-Nov-5; yes; F; yes; Comanche; yes; 4/4; 4/4; 4/4; yes

1925   431;   QUETONE, Wm Wayne; 1924-Nov-9; yes; M; Kiowa; yes; 4/4; 4/4; 4/4; yes

1925   1580;   RED ELK, William, Jr; 1925-Feb-15; yes; M; Kiowa; yes; 4/4; 4/4; 4/4; yes

1925   1323;   RHODES, Eleanor Mathe[sic]; 1924-Dec-7; yes; F; Kiowa; yes; 4/4; 4/4; 4/4; yes

1925   1510;   RIVAZ, Pia; 1925-May-5; yes; F; Comanche; yes; 4/4; 4/4; 4/4; yes

1925   862;   ROSCOE, Charley; 1925-Feb-24; yes; M; Kiowa; yes; 4/4; 4/4; 4/4; yes

1925   26;   SAHDINGKEI, Rush; 1924-Aug-16; yes; M; Kiowa; yes; 4/4; 4/4; 4/4; yes

1923   1212;   SAHMAUNT, Daniel Evans; 1924-Dec-10; yes; M; Kiowa; yes; 4/4; 4/4; 4/4; yes

1925   756;   SAMONE, Marjorie; 1924-Oct-26; yes; F; Kiowa; yes; 4/4; 4/4; 4/4; yes

1923   200;   SAUPITTY, Conny Coffee; 1924-Sept-3; yes; F; Comanche; yes; 4/4; 4/4; 4/4; yes

1925   863;   SAUPITTY, Kelley; 1924-Sept-1; yes; M; Kiowa; yes; 4/4; 4/4; 4/4; yes

See #
1925   342;   SEAHMER, Burke; 1925-Jan-3; yes; M; Kiowa; yes; 4/4; 4/4; 4/4; yes

State __Oklahoma__ Reservation __Kiowa__ Agency or Jurisdiction __Kiowa__
Office of Indian Affairs Births Occurring Between the Dates of July 1, 1924 and
June 30, 1925 to Parents Enrolled at Jurisdiction

KEY: 1925 Census Roll Number; Surname and Given Name; Date of Birth; Live Birth (Yes or No); Sex; Tribe;
Ward (yes or no); Degree of Father's blood; Degree of Mother's blood; Degree of Child's blood; At Jurisdiction
Where Enrolled (yes or no); [If "no", where, if given]

	See #	
1925	103;	SPOTTED CROW, Susie; 1924-Nov-24; yes; F; Apache; yes; 4/4; 4/4; 4/4; yes
1925	201;	STUMBLING BEAR, Clifton; 1924-Oct-16; yes; M; Kiowa; yes; 4/4; 4/4; 4/4; yes
1925	1459;	SUANNY, May; 1925-May-11; yes; F; Comanche; yes; 4/4; 4/4; 4/4; yes
1925	1607;	TABBYTITE, La Rue; 1925-Feb-23; yes; F; Comanche; yes; 4/4; 4/4; 4/4; yes
1925	591;	TABBYTOSOVIL, Buntin; 1925-Feb-21; yes; M; Kiowa; yes; 4/4; 4/4; 4/4; yes
1925	42;	TAHMAHKERA, Franklin Page; 1925-Apr-7; yes; M; Comanche; yes; 4/4; 4/4; 4/4; yes
1923	1017;	TAHPAY, Clarence; 1924-July-29; yes; M; Comanche; yes; 4/4; 4/4; 4/4; yes
1925	102;	TAICYPOKEDOOAH, Johanna; 1924-Nov-29; yes; F; Comanche; yes; 4/4; 4/4; 4/4; yes
1925	1250;	TAKEWAHPOOW, Clara Alice; 1925-Mar-11; yes; F; Kiowa; yes; 4/4; 4/4; 4/4; yes
1926	918;	TALLAMONTS, Barbara; 1924-Sept-29; yes; F; Kiowa; yes; 4/4; 4/4; 4/4; yes
1926	175;	TANEDOOVAH, Lavina Inez; 1925-June-6; yes; F; Kiowa; yes; 4/4; 4/4; 4/4; yes
1925	1485;	TAPPAH, Naoma; 1924-Nov-30; yes; F; Kiowa; yes; 4/4; 4/4; 4/4; yes
1926	283;	TAYLOR, Betty Ann; 1925-Mar-28; yes; F; Kiowa; yes; 4/4; 4/4; 4/4; yes
1925	580;	TEHAUNO, Vernan Tabbytosovit; 1924-Oct-15; yes; M; Kiowa; yes; 4/4; 4/4; 4/4; yes

State __Oklahoma__ Reservation __Kiowa__ Agency or Jurisdiction __Kiowa__
Office of Indian Affairs Births Occurring Between the Dates of July 1, 1924 and
June 30, 1925 to Parents Enrolled at Jurisdiction

KEY: 1925 Census Roll Number; Surname and Given Name; Date of Birth; Live Birth (Yes or No); Sex; Tribe; Ward (yes or no); Degree of Father's blood; Degree of Mother's blood; Degree of Child's blood; At Jurisdiction Where Enrolled (yes or no); [If "no", where, if given]

1926   1551;   TEE, Erwin; 1925-May-27; yes; M; Kiowa; yes; 4/4; 4/4; 4/4; yes

1925   709;   THOMAS, Frederick Headley; 1924-Aug-28; yes; M; Kiowa; yes; 4/4; W; 1/2; yes

1925   132;   THOMPSON, Fannie; 1924-Oct-14; yes; F; Kiowa; yes; 4/4; 4/4; 4/4; yes

1927   912;   TOEHAY, Edgar Stephen; 1925-June; yes; M; Kiowa; yes; 4/4; 4/4; 4/4; yes

1925   303;   TOMAH, Lawrence, Jr; 1925-Feb-24; yes; M; Kiowa; yes; 4/4; 4/4; 4/4; yes

1926   934;   TOMAHSAH, Henry; 1925-May-15; yes; M; Kiowa; yes; 4/4; 4/4; 4/4; yes

1925   126;   TOWHO, Bennie; 1925-Mar-12; yes; M; Apache; yes; 4/4; 4/4; 4/4; yes

1925   1502;   TREVIOR, Marie Louisa; 1925-Jan-26; yes; F; Comanche; yes; 4/4; 4/4; 4/4; yes

1926   1431;   TSATOKE, Rita Elizabeth; 1925-June-20; yes; F; Kiowa; yes; 4/4; 4/4; 4/4; yes

1926   663;   TSONETAKOY, Olivia; 1925-Feb-9; yes; F; Kiowa; yes; 4/4; 4/4; 4/4; yes

1925   656;   TUSTURY, William; 1924-July-7; yes; M; Kiowa; yes; 4/4; 4/4; 4/4; yes

1925   485;   WAHAHKINNY, Charlie; 1924-Oct-6; yes; M; Comanche; yes; 4/4; 4/4; 4/4; yes

1925   479;   WAHAHKINNEY, Russell; 1925-Jan-29; yes; M; Comanche; yes; 4/4; 4/4; 4/4; yes

        See #
1923   1030;   WALLACE, Winifred Wanda; 1924-Aug-6; yes; F; Comanche; yes; 4/4; 4/4; 4/4; yes

State __Oklahoma__ Reservation __Kiowa__ Agency or Jurisdiction __Kiowa__
Office of Indian Affairs Births Occurring Between the Dates of July 1, 1924 and
June 30, 1925 to Parents Enrolled at Jurisdiction

1925   1482;   WERHEVAHWERMY, Fred; 1925-Jan-1; yes; M; Comanche; yes; 4/4; 4/4; 4/4; yes

1925   254;   WERMY, Gloria; 1924-Sept-7; yes; F; Kiowa; yes; 4/4; 4/4; 4/4; yes

1925   730;   WHITE WOLF, Edwin; 1925-Feb-11; yes; M; Comanche; yes; 4/4; 4/4; 4/4; yes

1925   1753;   WILLIAMS, Mary Anna; 1925-Apr-30; yes; F; Comanche; yes; 4/4; 4/4; 4/4; yes

1926   1947;   WOODARD, Marvin Allen; 1925-Jan-12; yes; M; Kiowa; yes; 4/4; 4/4; 4/4; yes

1925   1133;   YACKESCHI, June; 1925-June-4; yes; F; Comanche; yes; 4/4; 4/4; 4/4; yes

1925   1578;   YEAHQUO, Samuel Tiedle; 1924-Aug-13; yes; M; Kiowa; yes; 4/4; 4/4; 4/4; yes

1925   717;   YELLOWFISH, Wiley, Jr; 1924-Aug-28; yes; M; Comanche; yes; 4/4; 4/4; 4/4; yes

1925   49;   ZUREGA, Thelma Jennie; 1924-Oct-22; yes; F; Apache; yes; 4/4; 4/4; 4/4; yes

11

KIOWA INDIAN AGENCY
Kiowa Reservation
Oklahoma
1926

BIRTH ROLL
Kiowa, Comanche, Apache and Fort Sill Apache Indians.

State ___Oklahoma___ Reservation ___Kiowa___ Agency or Jurisdiction ___Kiowa___
Office of Indian Affairs Births Occurring Between the Dates of July 1, 1925 and
June 30, 1926 to Parents Enrolled at Jurisdiction

1926   1466;   AHHAITTY, Blossom; 1926-May-3; yes; F; Kiowa; yes; 4/4; 4/4; 4/4; yes

1926   719;   AHPEAHTONE, Oscar, Jr; 1926-Mar-8; yes; M; Kiowa; yes; 4/4; 4/4; 4/4; yes

1926   1668;   AKO, Mildred; 1926-May-21; yes; F; Kiowa; yes; 4/4; 4/4; 4/4; yes

1926   366;   APAUTY, Joanna May; 1925-July-13; yes; F; Kiowa; yes; 4/4; 4/4; 4/4; yes

1926   1647;   ASANEHIDDLE, Spencer; 1926-May-26; yes; M; Kiowa; yes; 4/4; 4/4; 4/4; yes

1926   232;   ATCHHAVIT, Amelia; 1926-Feb-28; yes; F; Comanche; 4/4; 4/4; 4/4; yes

1926   382;   ATETEWATHTAKEWA, Lillie May; 1926-Mar-8; yes; F; Comanche yes; 4/4; 4/4; 4/4; yes

         See #
1926   1718-;   ATTOCKNIE, Theodore; 1926-Feb-15; yes; M; Comanche; yes; 4/4; 4/4; 4/4; yes

1926   1782;   AUNKO, Carrie; 1926-May-22; yes; F; Kiowa; yes; 4/4; 4/4; 4/4; yes

1927   335;   AUTAUBO, Adam; 1926-Jan-30; yes; M; Kiowa; yes; 4/4; 4/4; 4/4; yes

1926   24;   BITSEEDY, Allene; 1926-Apr-29; yes; F; Comanche; yes; 4/4; 4/4; 4/4; yes

1926   144;   BLACKBEAR, Emerson; 1926-Feb-6; yes; M; Apache; yes; 4/4; 4/4; 4/4; yes

1926   818;   BLACKSTAR, Thos, Jr; 1925-Sept-18; yes; M; Comanche; yes; 4/4; 4/4; 4/4; yes

1926   1441;   BOINTY, Thelma Mae; 1926-Mar-18; yes; F; Kiowa; yes; 1/2; 4/4; 3/4; yes

Office of Indian Affairs Births Occurring Between the Dates of July 1, 1925 and
June 30, 1926 to Parents Enrolled at Jurisdiction

KEY: 1926 Census Roll Number; Surname and Given Name; Date of Birth; Live Birth (Yes or No); Sex; Tribe; Ward (yes or no); Degree of Father's blood; Degree of Mother's blood; Degree of Child's blood; At Jurisdiction Where Enrolled (yes or no); [If "no", where, if given]

1926   139;   BOINTY, Vincent Horace; 1925-Dec-10; yes; M; Kiowa; yes; 1/2; 4/4; 3/4; yes

See #
1926   1659;   BOSIN, Alvin Blackbear; 1925-Aug-5; yes; M; Comanche; yes; 4/4; 4/4; 4/4; yes

See #
1925   525;   BURGESS, LaVera; 1925-Aug-9; yes; F; Comanche; yes; 4/4; 4/4; 4/4; yes

1926   525;   BURNS, Willie; 1925-Sept-11; yes; M; Kiowa; yes; 4/4; 4/4; 4/4; yes

1926   295;   CABLE, Theresa Mae; 1926-Mar-9; yes; F; Comanche; yes; 3/4; yes; 4/4; 7/8; yes

1926   1084;   CERDAY, Edgar Lun; 1925-July-7; yes; M; Comanche; yes; 4/4; 4/4; 4/4; yes

1925   150;   CHAHSENAH, John Harold; 1925-Apr-25; yes; M; Comanche; yes; 4/4; 4/4; 4/4; yes

1926   191;   CHAHSENAH, Forrest; 1925-July-21; yes; M; Comanche; yes; 4/4; 4/4; 4/4; yes

1926   81;   CHEBAHTAH, Cleo; 1925-Dec-21; yes; F; Comanche; yes; 4/4; 4/4; 4/4; yes

1926   1584;   CONOVER, William; 1926-Apr-21; yes; M; Comanche; yes; Mex & White; 1/4; 1/8; yes

1926   6;   COONIE, LeRoy; 1926-May-14; yes; M; Apache & Wichita; yes; 4/4; 4/4; 4/4; yes

1926   1364;   COOSEWOON, Emma; 1925-Nov-1; yes; F; Kiowa; yes; 4/4; 4/4; 4/4; yes

1926   1288;   COONYWERDY, Gladys; 1925-Nov-21; yes; F; Comanche; yes; 4/4; 4/4; 4/4; yes

1926   1509;   DOYETO, Betty; 1926-June-5; yes; F; Kiowa; yes; 4/4; 4/4; 4/4; yes

State __Oklahoma__ Reservation __Kiowa__ Agency or Jurisdiction __Kiowa__
Office of Indian Affairs Births Occurring Between the Dates of July 1, 1925 and
June 30, 1926 to Parents Enrolled at Jurisdiction

KEY: 1926 Census Roll Number; Surname and Given Name; Date of Birth; Live Birth (Yes or No); Sex; Tribe; Ward (yes or no); Degree of Father's blood; Degree of Mother's blood; Degree of Child's blood; At Jurisdiction Where Enrolled (yes or no); [If "no", where, if given]

1926 61; EMTADDLE, Thelma; 1925-Aug-28; yes; F; Kiowa; yes; 4/4; 4/4; 4/4; yes

1926 1675; ERKOBITTY, Joanne; 1925-Sept-30; yes; F; Kiowa; yes; 4/4; 4/4; 4/4; yes

[Blank] FRANKLIN, Ruby Ellen; 1925-Dec-17; yes; F; Kiowa; yes; 4/4; 1/2; 3/4; yes

See #
1926 798; FRYUAR, Juanita; 1926; yes; F; Comanche; yes; White; W & Mex; W & Mex; yes

1926 882; GEARY, George Klera; 1926-May-11; yes; M; Kiowa; yes; 4/4; 4/4; 4/4; yes

1926 1755; GEIONETY, Ruby; 1925-Aug-4; yes; F; Kiowa; yes; 4/4; 4/4; 4/4; yes

1926 1678; GONZALES, Ramon Palmer; 1926-Jan-25; yes; M; Comanche; yes; Mex & White; Mex & White; Mex & White; yes

1926 1064; GOODAY, Bob; 1926-Jan-17; yes; M; Comanche; yes; 4/4; 3/4; 7/8; yes

1927 2645; GOOMBI; Josephine Gladys; 1926-June-10; yes; F; Comanche; yes; 4/4; 4/4; 4/4; yes

1927 982; HADLEY, Marhta[sic]; 1926-May-24; yes; F; Kiowa; yes; 4/4; 4/4; 4/4; yes

1926 29; HAOZONS, Marjorie; 1926-May-9; yes; F; Apache & Wich; yes; 4/4; 4/4; 4/4; yes

1926 1639; HAUNGOOAH, Chester; 1925-Aug-10; f[sic]; Kiowa; yes; 4/4; 4/4; 4/4; yes

1926 1642; HAUNGOOAH, Velma Charlotte; 1925-Sept-16; yes; F; Kiowa; yes; 4/4; 4/4; 4/4; yes

1926 154; HEINASY, Charles Ross; 1926-Apr-27; yes; M; Comanche; yes; 4/4; 4/4; 4/4; yes

17

State __Oklahoma__ Reservation __Kiowa__ Agency or Jurisdiction __Kiowa__
Office of Indian Affairs Births Occurring Between the Dates of July 1, 1925 and
June 30, 1926 to Parents Enrolled at Jurisdiction

KEY: 1926 Census Roll Number; Surname and Given Name; Date of Birth; Live Birth (Yes or No); Sex; Tribe; Ward (yes or no); Degree of Father's blood; Degree of Mother's blood; Degree of Child's blood; At Jurisdiction Where Enrolled (yes or no); [If "no", where, if given]

[Blank]   HENRY, Frank Vincent; 1926-Jan-24; yes; M; Kiowa; yes; 4/4; 4/4; 4/4; yes

1926   1447;   HOPKINS, John Washington; 1926-Apr-22; yes; M; Comanche; yes; W; 4/4; 1/2; yes

1926   1009;   HOWRY, Theodore; 1925-Oct-13; yes; M; Kiowa; yes; 4/4; 4/4; 4/4; yes

1926   585;   HUMMINGBIRD, Gladys; 1925-July-3; yes; F; Kiowa; yes; 4/4; 4/4; 4/4; yes

1926   581;   HUMMINGBIRD, Vern; 1926-Apr-2; yes; M; Kiowa; yes; 4/4; 4/4; 4/4; yes

1927   1198;   HUNT, Julia Given; 1926-June-6; yes; F; Kiowa; yes; 4/4; 4/4; 4/4; yes

1926   1353;   HYDE, Wanda Hope; 1926-May-3 or July; yes; F; Comanche; yes; White; 4/4; 1/2; yes

1927   154;   JACKSON, Evaline; 1925-Sept-29; yes; F; Kiowa; yes; 4/4; 4/4; 4/4; yes

1926   1183;   JAY, Cleo; 1925-July-30; yes; F; Kiowa; yes; 4/4; 4/4; 4/4; yes

1926   1187;   JONES, Frank Rogers; 1926-Jan-29; M; Kiowa; yes; 3/4; 3/4; 3/4; yes

1926   33;   KAMESALADDLE, Lavona; 1925-July-21; yes; F; Kiowa; yes; 4/4; 4/4; 4/4; yes

1926   119;   KASSANAVOID, Bruce; 1925-Dec-12; yes; M; Comanche; yes; 4/4; 4/4; 4/4; yes

1926   1779;   HAUBIN, Henley Adam; 1925-Aug-26; yes; M; Kiowa; yes; 4/4; 4/4; 4/4; yes

1927   1316;   KAULAY, Ruby Naomi; 1926-May-16; yes; F; Kiowa; yes; 4/4; 4/4; 4/4; yes

18

State __Oklahoma__ Reservation __Kiowa__ Agency or Jurisdiction __Kiowa__
Office of Indian Affairs Births Occurring Between the Dates of July 1, 1925 and
June 30, 1926 to Parents Enrolled at Jurisdiction

KEY: 1926 Census Roll Number; Surname and Given Name; Date of Birth; Live Birth (Yes or No); Sex; Tribe; Ward (yes or no); Degree of Father's blood; Degree of Mother's blood; Degree of Child's blood; At Jurisdiction Where Enrolled (yes or no); [If "no", where, if given]

1926   622;   KAULAY, Tom Boles; 1925-July-23; yes; M; Kiowa; yes; 4/4; 4/4; 4/4; yes

1926   41;   KAULAITY, Francis; 1925-July-4; yes; M; Kiowa; yes; 4/4; 4/4; 4/4; yes

1926   1585;   KAUYEDAUTY, Geraldine; 1926-Jan-9; yes; F; Kiowa; yes; 4/4; 4/4; 4/4; yes

1927   1377;   KEAHBONE, Alecia; 1926-Apr-30; yes; F; Apache; yes; 4/4; 4/4; 4/4; yes

1926   1201;   KEITHTAHCOCO, Betty; 1925-Aug-8; yes; F; Comanche; yes; 4/4; 4/4; 4/4; yes

1926   192;   KLINEKOLE, Wm Buntin; 1925-Nov-15; M; Apache; yes; 4/4; 4/4; 4/4; yes

1926   1781;   KODASEET, Wilbur Mae; 1926-June-17; yes; F; Kiowa; yes; 4/4; 4/4; 4/4; yes

1926   211;   KOWENO, Lewis; 1926-Mar-31; yes; M; Comanche; yes; 4/4; 4/4; 4/4; yes

1926   1251;   LAMENZANA, Josephine; 1926-Apr-16; yes; F; Comanche; yes; Mex; 3/4; 3/8; yes

1926   1426;   LITTLE ELK, Gilbert; 1925-Nov-27; yes; M; Kiowa; yes; 4/4; 4/4; 4/4; yes

1926   834;   LOCKE, Iva Geneva; 1926-Apr-11; yes; F; Comanche; yes; W; 1/2; 1/4; yes

1926   952;   LOOKING GLASS, Frank; 1926-Mar-21; yes; M; Kiowa; yes; 4/4; 4/4; 4/4; yes

1927   2742;   LUNA, George; 1926-Jan-18; yes; M; Comanche; yes; Mex; 3/4; 3/8; yes

1926   999;   MADDOX, Henry Wm; 1925-Oct-11; yes; M; Comanche; yes; 4/4; 4/4; 4/4; yes

19

State Oklahoma Reservation Kiowa Agency or Jurisdiction Kiowa
Office of Indian Affairs Births Occurring Between the Dates of July 1, 1925 and
June 30, 1926 to Parents Enrolled at Jurisdiction

KEY: 1926 Census Roll Number; Surname and Given Name; Date of Birth; Live Birth (Yes or No); Sex; Tribe; Ward (yes or no); Degree of Father's blood; Degree of Mother's blood; Degree of Child's blood; At Jurisdiction Where Enrolled (yes or no); [If "no", where, if given]

1926   136;   MAYNAHOMA, Kosope; 1925-July-23; yes; M; Apache; yes; 4/4; 4/4; 4/4; yes

1925   942;   MAUSAPE, Mildred; 1925-Feb-10; yes; F; Kiowa; yes; 4/4; 4/4; 4/4; yes

1926   1776;   MAUSANAP, Dorothy May; 1926-May-30; yes; F; Kiowa; yes; 4/4; 4/4; 4/4; yes

1926   1736;   MISESAUH, Wanda; 1925-Nov-4; yes; F; Comanche; yes; 4/4; 4/4; 4/4; yes

1926   18;   MITHLO, Thurman Lee; 1926-Apr-11; yes; M; Apache; yes; 4/4; 4/4; 4/4; yes

1926   623;   MORA, Caroline; 1925-Dec-31; yes; F; Comanche; yes; 4/4; 4/4; 4/4; yes

1926   779;   MULLIN, Sammie Lilliam[sic]; 1925-Sept-28; yes; F; Comanche; yes; 4/4; W; 1/2

1926   773;   NAHNO, Berdenia; 1925-July-7; yes; F; Comanche; yes; 4/4; 4/4; 4/4; yes

1926   1593;   NEWSOME, Amy Bear; 1923[sic]-July-26; yes; F; Kiowa; yes; W; 1/2; 1/4; yes

1926   1335;   NEVACUAYA, Irene; 1925-July-25; yes; F; Comanche; yes; 4/4; 4/4; 4/4; yes

1926   455;   PAHDOCONY, Dorphus; 1926-May-6; yes; F; Comanche; yes; 4/4; 4/4; 4/4; yes

1926   372;   PARRIAECHIVIT, Audrey May; 1926-Jan-11; yes; F; Comanche; yes; 4/4; 4/4; 4/4; yes

1926   1777;   PAYABSAPE, Peggy Lois; 1925-Aug-15; yes; F; Kiowa; yes; 4/4; 4/4; 4/4; yes

1926   866;   PERKAQUANARD, May Susie; 1925-Dec-6; yes; F; Comanche; yes; 4/4; 4/4; 4/4; yes

State Oklahoma Reservation Kiowa Agency or Jurisdiction Kiowa

Office of Indian Affairs Births Occurring Between the Dates of July 1, 1925 and June 30, 1926 to Parents Enrolled at Jurisdiction

KEY: 1926 Census Roll Number; Surname and Given Name; Date of Birth; Live Birth (Yes or No); Sex; Tribe; Ward (yes or no); Degree of Father's blood; Degree of Mother's blood; Degree of Child's blood; At Jurisdiction Where Enrolled (yes or no); [If "no", where, if given]

1926   203;   PEWEWARDY, Geroge[sic]; 1925-Aug-22; yes; M; Comanche; yes; 4/4; 4/4; 4/4; yes

1926   1298;   PEWEWARDY, George Campbell; 1925-Aug-11; yes; M; Comanche; yes; 4/4; 4/4; 4/4; yes

1926   568;   PEWEWARDY, Junette Dora; 1926-Mar-29; yes; F; Comanche; yes; 4/4; 4/4; 4/4; yes

1926   988;   PEWEWARDY, Samuel, Jr; 1925-Sept-8; yes; M; Comanche; yes; 4/4; 4/4; 4/4; yes

1927   2388;   PINEZADDLELY, Horace; 1926-Jan-20; yes; M; Kiowa; yes; 4/4; 4/4; 4/4; yes

1926   740;   POHACSACUT, BettyLou; 1926-Apr-29; yes; F; Comanche; yes; 4/4; 4/4; 4/4; yes

1926   110;   POHAWPATCHOKE, Calvin C; 1925-Nov-27; yes; M; Comanche; yes; 4/4; 4/4; 4/4;yes

1926   672;   POOLAW, Flint Forest; 1926-Mar-10; yes; M; Kiowa; yes; 3/4; 1/2; 5/8; yes

1926   679;   POOLAW, Jerry Wayne; 1926-Apr-1; yes; M; Kiowa; yes; 3/4; yes; 4/4; 7/8; yes

1927   1896;   POOLAW, Rosalie; 1926-Jan-18; yes; F; Comanche; yes; 4/4; 4/4; 4/4; yes

1926   1079;   PORTILLO, Eva May; 1926-May-31; yes; F; Comanche; yes; Mex; 3/4; 3/8; yes

1926   1420;   POTIYO, Garnetta Ruth; 1926-Jan-4; yes; F; Kiowa; yes; 4/4; 4/4; 4/4; yes

1926   447;   QUETONE, Blossom White; 1926-Jan-19; yes; F; Kiowa; 1/2; 4/4; 3/4; yes

1926   441;   QUETONE, William Wayne; 1926-Feb-12; yes; M; Kiowa; 1/2; 1/2; 1/2; yes

21

State __Oklahoma__ Reservation __Kiowa__ Agency or Jurisdiction __Kiowa__
Office of Indian Affairs Births Occurring Between the Dates of July 1, 1925 and
June 30, 1926 to Parents Enrolled at Jurisdiction

KEY: 1926 Census Roll Number; Surname and Given Name; Date of Birth; Live Birth (Yes or No); Sex; Tribe; Ward (yes or no); Degree of Father's blood; Degree of Mother's blood; Degree of Child's blood; At Jurisdiction Where Enrolled (yes or no); [If "no", where, if given]

1926   1386;   RANDOLPH, Jacquelino Monita; 1926-Mar-26; yes; F; Kiowa; yes; 4/4; 4/4; 4/4; yes

1926   1025;   RIDDLE, June Mave; 1926-Feb-5; yes; F; Comanche; W; 4/4; 1/2; yes

1926   1244;   SAHMAUNT, Norman Lee; 1926-Apr-11; yes; M; Kiowa; yes; 4/4; 4/4; 4/4; yes

1926   1155;   SATEPAUHOODLE, Mildred Elsie; 1926-Feb-20; yes; F; Kiowa; yes; 4/4; 4/4; 4/4; yes

1926   874;   SAUPITTY, Bernice; 1926-May-6; yes; F; Comanche; yes; 4/4; 4/4; 4/4; yes

1926   1020;   SHORTNECK, Collene; 1926-Feb-3; yes; F; Kiowa; yes; 4/4; 4/4; 4/4; yes

1926   28;   SAHDENGKEI, Irwin; 1925-Dec-18; yes; M; Kiowa; yes; 4/4; 4/4; 4/4; yes

1926   649;   SAPCUT, Vincent Russell; 1925-Aug-8; yes; M; Comanche; yes; 4/4; 4/4; 4/4; yes

1926   1173;   SAUMTY, Bobbie Jean; 1925-Nov-30; yes; F; Kiowa; yes; 4/4; 4/4; 4/4; yes

1926   785;   SATOE, Virgil; 1925-Dec-6; yes; M; Kiowa; yes; 4/4; 4/4; 4/4; yes

1926   833;   SUNBEAR, Blossom; 1926-Apr-17; yes; F; Kiowa; yes; 4/4; 4/4; 4/4; yes

1926   845;   SUTTON, Allen Morrison; 1925-Nov-24; yes; M; Kiowa; yes; 4/4; 4/4; 4/4; yes

1926   36;   STAR, Clarence; 1925-Nov-14; yes; M; Apache; yes; 4/4; 4/4; 4/4; yes

1926   101;   TAH, Clifford Mitchell; 1926-May-24; yes; M; Apache; yes; 4/4; 4/4; 4/4; yes

1926   104;   TAH, Ralph; 1926-Mar-15; yes; M; Apache; yes; 4/4; 4/4; 4/4; yes

State Oklahoma Reservation Kiowa Agency or Jurisdiction Kiowa

Office of Indian Affairs Births Occurring Between the Dates of July 1, 1925 and June 30, 1926 to Parents Enrolled at Jurisdiction

KEY: 1926 Census Roll Number; Surname and Given Name; Date of Birth; Live Birth (Yes or No); Sex; Tribe; Ward (yes or no); Degree of Father's blood; Degree of Mother's blood; Degree of Child's blood; At Jurisdiction Where Enrolled (yes or no); [If "no", where, if given]

1926   766;   TAHAH, Vera; 1926-Mar-2; yes; F; Comanche; yes; 4/4; 4/4; 4/4; yes

1926   281;   TAHDOOAHNIPAH, Eldridge; 1926-May-11; yes; M; Comanche; yes; 4/4; 4/4; 4/4; yes

1926   717;   TAHCHAWICKAH, May Ellen; 1925-July-2; yes; F; Comanche; yes; 4/4; 4/4; 4/4; yes

1926   1044;   TAHPAY, Clarence; 1926-Feb-1116; yes; M; Comanche; yes; 4/4; 4/4; 4/4; yes

1926   45;   TAHMAHKEM, Houston; 1925-Dec-2; yes; M; Comanche; yes; 4/4; 4/4; 4/4; yes

1926   643;   TAKAWANA, Eleanor; 1925-July-25; yes; F; Comanche; yes; 4/4; 4/4; 4/4; yes

1926   1303;   TANA, Samuel Blair; 1925-Aug-4; yes; M; Comanche; yes; 4/4; 4/4; 4/4; yes

1926   1007;   TANEHIDDLE, Laura Claradinn; 1926-Apr-14; yes; F; Kiowa; yes; 4/4; 4/4; 4/4; yes

1926   1011;   TARKAH, Leta May; 1926-Jan-28; yes; F; Kiowa; yes; 4/4; 4/4; 4/4; yes

1926   14;   TARTSAH, Lincoln; 1925-Sept-5; yes; M; Kiowa; yes; 4/4; 4/4; 4/4; yes

1926   540;   TANEQUODLE, Aileen Marie; 1925-Dec-11; yes; F; Comanche; yes; 4/4; 4/4; 4/4; yes

1926   345;   TAUNAH, Leon; 1926-June-12; yes; M; Comanche; yes; 4/4; 4/4; 4/4; yes

1926   1628;   THOMPSON, Eula Bernadine; 1925-Nov-13; yes; F; Kiowa; yes; 4/4; 4/4; 4/4; yes

1926   313;   TOBAH, Ruth; 1925-Aug-20; yes; F; Comanche; yes; 4/4; 4/4; 4/4; yes

23

State __Oklahoma__ Reservation __Kiowa__ Agency or Jurisdiction __Kiowa__
Office of Indian Affairs Births Occurring Between the Dates of July 1, 1925 and
June 30, 1926 to Parents Enrolled at Jurisdiction

1926   1196;   TIDDARK, Lathram; 1925-Sept-18; yes; M; Comanche; yes; 4/4; 4/4; 4/4; yes

1926   861;   TOINTIGH, Eleanor; 1925-Aug-20; yes; F; Comanche; yes; 4/4; 4/4; 4/4; yes

1926   247;   TOFPI, Elsie Mae; 1925-Dec-15; yes; F; Comanche; yes; 4/4; 4/4; 4/4; yes

1926   1595;   TONIPA, J R; 1926-Mar-29; yes; M; Comanche; yes; 4/4; 4/4; 4/4; yes

1926   1522;   TOPPAH, Alice; 1926-May-7; yes; F; Kiowa; yes; 4/4; 4/4; 4/4; yes

1926   1148;   TOQUOTHTY, Gloria Marie; 1926-Mar-12; yes; F; Comanche; yes; 4/4; 4/4; 4/4; yes

1926   1030;   TOOANAPPE, Morris; 1926-Jan-21; yes; M; Comanche; yes; 4/4; 4/4; 4/4; yes

1927   688;   TRACY, Raymond Gene; 1926-Mar-16; yes; M; Comanche; yes; W; Mex; W & Mex; yes

1926   356;   TSALOTE, Lucile; 1926-Feb-6; yes; F; Kiowa; yes; 4/4; 4/4; 4/4; yes

1926   157;   TSOODLE, Brenan; 1925-Sept-26; yes; M; Kiowa; yes; 4/4; 4/4; 4/4; yes

1927   2144;   TWO HATCHET, Luke; 1926-Mar-3; yes; M; Kiowa; yes; 4/4; 4/4; 4/4; yes

1926   1107;   TWO HATCHET, Wallace; 1926-Mar-2; yes; M; Kiowa; yes; 4/4; 4/4; 4/4; yes

1926   1147;   VOLDER, Max; 1926-Mar-31; yes; M; Comanche; yes; Mex; 4/4; 1/2; yes

1926   258;   WERMY, John, Jr; 1925-Oct-31; yes; M; Comanche; yes; 4/4; 4/4; 4/4; yes

1926   253;   WERMY; 1926-May-18; yes; M; Comanche; yes; 4/4; 4/4; 4/4; yes

24

State __Oklahoma__ Reservation __Kiowa__ Agency or Jurisdiction __Kiowa__
Office of Indian Affairs Births Occurring Between the Dates of July 1, 1925 and
June 30, 1926 to Parents Enrolled at Jurisdiction

KEY: 1926 Census Roll Number; Surname and Given Name; Date of Birth; Live Birth (Yes or No); Sex; Tribe; Ward (yes or no); Degree of Father's blood; Degree of Mother's blood; Degree of Child's blood; At Jurisdiction Where Enrolled (yes or no); [If "no", where, if given]

1925   181;   WHITEFOX, Leonard; 1925-Sept-16; yes; M; Apache; yes; 4/4; 4/4; 4/4; yes

1926   1691;   WHITE HORSE, Anna Sue; 1925-Aug-8; yes; F; Kiowa; yes; 4/4; 4/4; 4/4; yes

1926   295;   WOLF, Lois Ruth; 1926-Feb-23; yes; F; Kiowa; yes; 4/4; 3/4; 7/8; yes

1926   1619;   YEAHOUO, Vivian; 1926-Apr-3; yes; F; Kiowa; yes; 4/4; 4/4; 4/4; yes

1926   1506;   YOUNICUT, Forest; 1926-May-7; yes; M; Comanche; yes; 4/4; 4/4; 4/4; yes

1925   52;   ZUREGA, Ben; 1925-Dec-10; yes; M; Apache; yes; Mex; 4/4; 1/2; yes

1926   542;   WOOMMOVOVAH, Genevia; 1926-Jan-1; yes; F; Comanche; yes; 4/4; 4/4; 4/4; yes

KIOWA INDIAN AGENCY
Kiowa Reservation
Oklahoma
1927

BIRTH ROLL
Kiowa, Comanche, Apache and
Fort Sill Apache Indians.

State __Oklahoma__ Reservation __Kiowa__ Agency or Jurisdiction __Kiowa__
Office of Indian Affairs Births Occurring Between the Dates of July 1, 1926 and
June 30, 1927 to Parents Enrolled at Jurisdiction

KEY: 1927 Census Roll Number; Surname and Given Name; Date of Birth; Live Birth (Yes or No); Sex; Tribe; Ward (yes or no); Degree of Father's blood; Degree of Mother's blood; Degree of Child's blood; At Jurisdiction Where Enrolled (yes or no); [If "no", where, if given]

1927   72;   AHKEAHBO, Maxine; 1926; yes; F; Kiowa; yes; 4/4; 4/4; 4/4; yes

1927   1815;   AHPEAHTO, Elmer; 1926-Oct-4; yes; M; Kiowa; yes; 4/4; 4/4; 4/4; yes

1927   99;   AHTONE, Vernon; 1926; yes; M; Kiowa; yes; 4/4; 4/4; 4/4; yes

1927   2767;   AKERS, Daniel; 1926-Nov-24; yes; M; Comanche; yes; W; 1/4; 1/8; yes

See #
1927   124;   AITSON, Etheline Mary; 1926-Dec-25; yes; F; Kiowa; yes; 3/4; 4/4; 7/8; yes

See #
1927   122;   AITSON, Leta May; 1927-Jan-17; yes; F; Kiowa; yes; 3/4; 3/4; 7/8[sic]; yes

See #
1927   106;   APAUTY, Lewis; 1926-Dec-10; yes; M; Kiowa; yes; 4/4; 4/4; 4/4; yes

1927   173;   APEKAUM, Marcus; 1927; yes; M; Kiowa; yes; 4/4; 4/4; 4/4; yes

1927   3796;   ARKEKETA, Johanna C; 1927-Mar-4; yes; F; Kiowa; yes; 1/2; W&Mex; 1/4; yes

1927   212;   ASEPERMY, Ruth; 1926-Nov-1; yes; F; Kio & Comanche; yes; 4/4; 4/4; 4/4; yes

See #
1927   265;   ATETEWATHTAKEUI; 1926-Aug-26; yes; F; Comanche; yes; 4/4; 4/4; 4/4; yes

1927   294;   AUCHCHIAH, Vernita Joyce; 1926-Aug-8; yes; F; Kiowa; yes; 4/4; 4/4; 4/4; yes

1927   2082;   AUNKO, Herwanna Dorothy; 1926-Nov-15; yes; F; Kiowa; yes; 4/4; 4/4; 4/4; yes

Office of Indian Affairs Births Occurring Between the Dates of July 1, 1926 and
June 30, 1927 to Parents Enrolled at Jurisdiction

KEY: 1927 Census Roll Number; Surname and Given Name; Date of Birth; Live Birth (Yes or No); Sex; Tribe; Ward (yes or no); Degree of Father's blood; Degree of Mother's blood; Degree of Child's blood; At Jurisdiction Where Enrolled (yes or no); [If "no", where, if given]

See #
1927   160;   APAUTY, Lewis; 1926-Dec-10; yes; M; Kiowa; yes; 4/4; 4/4; 4/4; yes

1927   184;   AUNQUOE, Verl; 1926; yes; F; Kiowa; yes; 4/4; 4/4; 4/4; yes

1927   1370;   AUNGKOTAYE, Lorina; 1926-Oct-17; yes; F; Kiowa; yes; 4/4; 4/4; 4/4; yes

See #
1927   339;   AUTAUBO, Lycester; 1927-May-25; yes; M; Kiowa; yes; 4/4; 4/4; 4/4; yes

1927   3038;   BEARTRACK, Lillian; 1927-May-7; yes; F; Kiowa; yes; 4/4; 4/4; 4/4; yes

1927   319;   BECK, Dale; 1927-Feb-21; yes; M; Kiowa; yes; 4/4; 4/4; 4/4; yes

1927   1929;   BECK, Mary Ann; 1926-July-14; yes; F; Comanche; W; 4/4; 1/2; yes

1927   436;   BOSIN, Darling Virginia; 1926-Oct-5; yes; F; Kio & Comanche; yes; 4/4; 4/4; 4/4; yes

1927   1717;   BOTONE, Leon; 1926-Oct-26; yes; M; Kiowa; yes; 3/4; 4/4; 7/8; yes

1927   147;   BOTONE, Vivian; 1926; yes; F; Kiowa; yes; 4/4; 4/4; 4/4; yes

1927   455;   BOTONE, Perry Lee; 1927-Feb-6; yes; M; Kiowa; yes; 4/4; 3/4; 7/8; yes

1927   474;   CANNON, Kenneth; 1926-July-13; yes; M; Kiowa; yes; 1/2; 4/4; 3/4; yes

1927   523;   CHAHTINNEGACKQUE, Dorothy; 1926-Oct-9; yes; F; Comanche; yes; 1/4; 4/4; 5/8; yes

1927   533;   CHALEPAH, Albert Clay; 1927-Mar-27; yes; M; Apache; yes; 4/4; 4/4; 4/4; yes

1931   1104;   CHANEY, Darnell Lewis; 1927-Jan-28; yes; M; Kiowa; yes; W; 4/4; 1/2; yes

State   Oklahoma   Reservation   Kiowa   Agency or Jurisdiction   Kiowa
Office of Indian Affairs Births Occurring Between the Dates of July 1, 1926 and
June 30, 1927 to Parents Enrolled at Jurisdiction

KEY: 1927 Census Roll Number; Surname and Given Name; Date of Birth; Live Birth (Yes or No); Sex; Tribe; Ward (yes or no); Degree of Father's blood; Degree of Mother's blood; Degree of Child's blood; At Jurisdiction Where Enrolled (yes or no); [If "no", where, if given]

1927   633;   CLARK, Teresa Louise; 1927-Apr-20; yes; F; Comanche; yes; 1/2; 1/2; 1/2; yes

1927   840;   CLEVELAND, Teddy Anderson; 1926-Oct-2; yes; M; Kiowa; yes; 4/4; 4/4; 4/4; yes

1927   3364;   COBAHTINE, Wade; 1927-Mar-19; yes; M; Comanche; yes; 4/4; 4/4; 4/4; yes

1927   648;   COBAHTINE, Wilbur; 1926-Nov-14; yes; M; Kiowa; yes; 4/4; 4/4; 4/4; yes

1927   658;   CODOOPONY, Virginia; 1926-Oct-23; yes; F; Comanche; yes; 4/4; 4/4; 4/4; yes

1927   672;   COFFEE, Pauline; 1926-Nov-2; yes; F; Comanche; yes; 4/4; 4/4; 4/4; yes

1927   677;   CONNAHVICHNAT, Joyce; 1927-Mar-22; yes; F; Comanche; yes; 4/4; 4/4; 4/4; yes

1927   2874;   CONNAHVICHNAT, Thelma; 1926; yes; F; Comanche; yes; 4/4; 4/4; 4/4; yes

1927   720;   COOSEWON, Rudolph; 1926-Nov-12; yes; M; Comanche; yes; 4/4; 4/4; 4/4; yes

1927   778;   DAUKEI, Horace; 1927-Feb-15; yes; M; Kiowa; yes; 4/4; 4/4; 4/4; yes

1927   789;   DAUTOBI, Marie; 1927-Feb-4; yes; F; Kiowa; yes; 4/4; 4/4; 4/4; yes

1928   841;   DOYEBI, Margie; 1927-May-10; yes; F; Kiowa; yes; 4/4; 4/4; 4/4; yes

1927   879;   ECKIWAUDAH, Agatha; 1926-July-14; yes; F; Comanche; yes; 3/4; 3/4; 3/4; yes

1927   224;   FANALLA, Lucy; 1926; yes; F; Comanche; yes; Mex; Mex; Mex; yes

1927   935;   FAWELL, Kit Carson, Jr; 1926-Aug-13; yes; M; Comanche; yes; W &M; W & M; W&Mex; yes

Office of Indian Affairs Births Occurring Between the Dates of July 1, 1926 and
June 30, 1927 to Parents Enrolled at Jurisdiction

KEY: 1927 Census Roll Number; Surname and Given Name; Date of Birth; Live Birth (Yes or No); Sex; Tribe; Ward (yes or no); Degree of Father's blood; Degree of Mother's blood; Degree of Child's blood; At Jurisdiction Where Enrolled (yes or no); [If "no", where, if given]

1927   3120;   FRANKLIN, Virgil R; 1927-Apr-10; yes; M; Kiowa; yes; 4/4; 1/2; 3/4; yes

1927   945;   FULLER, Lonnie Lee; 1926-Nov-8; yes; M; Comanche; yes; 4/4; 4/4; 4/4; yes

1927   943;   FULLER, Daniel Dee; 1926-Aug-15; yes; M; Comanche; yes; 1/8; 1/2; 5/16; yes

1927   963;   GEIMAUSADDLE, Bernice; 1926-Oct-9; yes; F; Kiowa; yes; 4/4; 4/4; 4/4; yes

1927   3273;   GEIONETY, Moses; 1927-Apr-12; yes; M; Kiowa; yes; 4/4; 4/4; 4/4; yes

1929   963;   GEIOGAMAH, Stanley; 1927-June-7; yes; M; Kiowa; yes; 4/4; 4/4; 4/4; yes

1928   898;   GONZALES, Rudolph; 1927-Apr-15; yes; M; Comanche; yes; Mex; W; M&W; yes

1927   1743;   GRAY, Wallace; 1926-Oct-1; yes; M; Comanche; yes; W; 3/4; 3/8; yes

1927   1010;   GWOLADDLE, Horace; 1926; yes; M; Kiowa; yes; 1/2; 3/4; 5/8; yes

1927   315;   HAUNPO, Mary Belle; 1926; yes; F; Kiowa; yes; 4/4; 4/4; 4/4; yes

1927   1064;   HAUNPY, Marcus; 1926-Oct-3; yes; M; Kiowa; yes; 4/4; 4/4; 4/4; yes

1927   1080;   HAWZIPTA, Flora Belle; 1927-Jan-12; yes; F; Kiowa; yes; 4/4; 4/4; 4/4; yes

1928   1093;   HEATH, Leo; 1927-Jan-8; yes; M; Comanche; yes; 4/4; 4/4; 4/4; yes

1927   1098;   HEMINOPEKY, Robert; 1926; yes; M; Com & Apache; yes; 4/4; 4/4; 4/4; yes

1929   1023;   HENRY, Lillie May; 1927-Apr-1; yes; F; Kiowa; W; 4/4; 1/2; yes

1930   30;   HOAG, Daniel; 1927-May-10; yes; M; Kiowa; yes; 4/4; 4/4; 4/4; yes

State __Oklahoma__ Reservation __Kiowa__ Agency or Jurisdiction __Kiowa__
Office of Indian Affairs Births Occurring Between the Dates of July 1, 1926 and
June 30, 1927 to Parents Enrolled at Jurisdiction

KEY: 1927 Census Roll Number; Surname and Given Name; Date of Birth; Live Birth (Yes or No); Sex; Tribe; Ward (yes or no); Degree of Father's blood; Degree of Mother's blood; Degree of Child's blood; At Jurisdiction Where Enrolled (yes or no); [If "no", where, if given]

See #

1927 1133; HOKEAH, Pauline; 1926-11-1; yes; F; Kiowa; yes; 4/4; 4/4; 4/4; yes

1927 1147; HORSE, Richard Buffington; 1926-Dec-27; yes; M; Kiowa; yes; 4/4; 4/4; 4/4; yes

1929 1174; HOVAKAH, Tyler; 1927-Feb-2; yes; M; Kiowa; yes; 4/4; 4/4; 4/4; yes

1927 872; HOWRY, Billy; 1926; yes; M; Comanche; W; 1/2; 1/4; yes

1927 871; HOWRY, Joyce; 1926; yes; F; Comanche; yes; W; 1/2; 1/4; yes

1928 1204; HUMMINGBIRD, Edward; 1927-June-27; yes; M; Kiowa; yes; 4/4; 4/4; 4/4; yes

1927 1198; HUMMINGBIRD, Rudolph; 1926-Dec-25; yes; M; Kiowa; yes; 4/4; 4/4; 4/4; yes

1927 1244; KADAYSO, Lincoln; 1926-Oct-30; yes; M; Kiowa; yes; 4/4; 7/8; 15/16; yes

1927 1265; KARTY, Billy; 1926-Sept-16; yes; M; Kiowa; yes; 4/4; 4/4; 4/4; yes

1927 3887; KASECHATA, Cleo Lester; 1927-Apr-7; yes; F; Comanche; yes; 4/4; 4/4; 4/4; yes

1927 1255; KASSANAVOID, Merrill; 1927-Apr-2; yes; M; Comanche; yes; 4/4; 4/4; 4/4; yes

1927 598; KAULAITY, Porter; 1927-May-7; yes; M; Kiowa; yes; 4/4; 4/4; 4/4; yes

1927 1296; KAUDLEKAULE, Naoma; 1927-May-7; yes; F; Apache; yes; 4/4; 4/4; 4/4; yes

1929 1314; KAULAITY, Vivian; 1927-Apr-11; yes; F; Kiowa; yes; 4/4; 4/4; 4/4; yes

1927 81; KAULAITY, Wm W; 1926; yes; M; Kiowa; yes; 4/4; 4/4; 4/4; yes

33

State <u>Oklahoma</u> Reservation <u>Kiowa</u> Agency or Jurisdiction <u>Kiowa</u>
Office of Indian Affairs Births Occurring Between the Dates of July 1, 1926 and
June 30, 1927 to Parents Enrolled at Jurisdiction

KEY: 1927 Census Roll Number; Surname and Given Name; Date of Birth; Live Birth (Yes or No); Sex; Tribe; Ward (yes or no); Degree of Father's blood; Degree of Mother's blood; Degree of Child's blood; At Jurisdiction Where Enrolled (yes or no); [If "no", where, if given]

1927   2163;   KAWAYKLA, Christian Natche; 1926-Dec-26; yes; F; Kiowa; yes; 4/4; 4/4; 4/4; yes

1927   1395;   KEAHTIGH, Paul; 1927-Apr-24; yes; M; Comanche; 1/2; 3/4; 5/8; yes

1927   3534;   KLINEKOLE, Estella; 1926-Oct-13; yes; F; Apache & Com; yes; 4/4; 4/4; 4/4; yes

See #
1927   1454;   KONAD, Estelline; 1926-July-27; yes; F; Kiowa; yes; 4/4; 4/4; 4/4; yes

1927   3886;   KOPADDY, Katherine; 1927-Apr-13; yes; F; Comanche; yes; 4/4; 4/4; 4/4; yes

1927   1478;   KOPEPASSAH7[sic], Delbert; 1926; yes; M; Kiowa; yes; 4/4; 4/4; 4/4; yes

1927   1767;   KOWENO, Louise; 1927-June-24; yes; F; Comanche; yes; 4/4; 4/4; 4/4; yes

1927   1541;   LeBARRE, Lydia F; 1927-May-1; yes; F; Comanche; yes; 1/2; 4/4; 3/4; yes

1928   1199;   LITTLE CHIEF, Garfield Pierce; 1927-June-20; yes; M; Kiowa; yes; 4/4; 4/4; 4/4; yes

See #
1928   1594;   LITTLE CHIEF, Lawrence Ralph; 1927-June-22; yes; M; Kiowa; yes; 4/4; 4/4; 4/4; yes

See #
1927   1568;   LITTLE CHIEF, Libbie; 1926-11-29; yes; F; Kiowa; yes; 4/4; 4/4; 4/4; yes

See #
1927   1561;   LITTLE CHIEF, Pearl; 1927-June-22; yes; F; Kiowa; yes; 4/4; 4/4; 4/4; yes

1928   1812;   LOOKINGGLASS, Lindy; 1927-June-26; yes; M; Comanche; yes; 4/4; 4/4; 4/4; yes

State __Oklahoma__ Reservation __Kiowa__ Agency or Jurisdiction __Kiowa__
Office of Indian Affairs Births Occurring Between the Dates of July 1, 1926 and
June 30, 1927 to Parents Enrolled at Jurisdiction

KEY: 1927 Census Roll Number; Surname and Given Name; Date of Birth; Live Birth (Yes or No); Sex; Tribe; Ward (yes or no); Degree of Father's blood; Degree of Mother's blood; Degree of Child's blood; At Jurisdiction Where Enrolled (yes or no); [If "no", where, if given]

1927   1634;   MAHSETKY, Ardis; 1927-Mar-31; yes; F; Comanche; yes; 4/4; 4/4; 4/4; yes

1928   1731;   MAUSOPE, Maude Wells; 1927-May-22; yes; F; Kiowa; yes; 4/4; 4/4; 4/4; yes

1927   1729;   McKENZIE, Estehr[sic] Evina; 1926-Dec-27; yes; F; Kiowa; yes; 1/4; 4/4; 5/8; yes

1927   1837;   MOPOPE, Alverdine; 1926-Oct-7; yes; F; Kiowa & Apache; yes; 4/4; 5/8; 15/16; yes

1927   2577;   MORRISON, Lena May; 1927-May-25; yes; F; Kiowa; yes; 4/4; 4/4; 4/4; yes

1927   1882;   MYERS, Norma Jean; 1926-Aug-26; yes; F; Comanche; yes; 1/4; W; 1/8; yes

1927   1880;   MYERS, Williardine; 1926-July-28; yes; F; Comanche; yes; 1/4; W; 1/8; yes

1927   3487;   NASHDELTE, Vincent George; 1927-Feb-17; yes; M; Apache; yes; 4/4; 4/4; 4/4; yes

1927   1981;   NESTELL, Vivian; 1926-Dec-9; yes; F; Kiowa & Apache; yes; 4/4; 4/4; 4/4; yes

1927   2021;   ODLEPOHQUOLE, John Wm; 1926-Sept-17; yes; M; Kiowa; yes; 4/4; 4/4; 4/4; yes

1928   2076;   OTIPPOBY, James Collins; 1927-May-18; yes; M; Comanche; yes; 4/4; W; 1/2; yes

1927   2108;   PAHCODDY, Rosalie; 1926; yes; F; Comanche; yes; 4/4; 4/4; 4/4; yes

         See #
1927   2150;   PAHDOPONY, Shell; 1926-Dec-5; yes; F; Comanche; yes; 4/4; 4/4; 4/4; yes

1927   1951;   PARKER, Leonard; 1926-Dec-29; yes; M; Comanche; yes; 3/4; 1/2; 5/8; yes

Office of Indian Affairs Births Occurring Between the Dates of July 1, 1926 and
June 30, 1927 to Parents Enrolled at Jurisdiction

KEY: 1927 Census Roll Number; Surname and Given Name; Date of Birth; Live Birth (Yes or No); Sex; Tribe; Ward (yes or no); Degree of Father's blood; Degree of Mother's blood; Degree of Child's blood; At Jurisdiction Where Enrolled (yes or no); [If "no", where, if given]

1928   3247;   PARKER, Lillian Margaret; 1927-Mar-3; yes; F; Comanche; yes; 1/2; 1/2; 1/2; yes

1929   175;   PARSONS, Jaunita May; 1927-Apr-14; yes; F; Comanche; yes; Mex; Mex; Mex; yes

1927   1040;   PAUDLETY, Bernice; 1926; yes; F; Kiowa; yes; 4/4; 4/4; 4/4; yes

1927   2253;   PEHEAHSY, Frank Rush; 1926-July-1; yes; M; Comanche; yes; 4/4; 4/4; 4/4; yes

1927   2289;   PEKAH, Eleanor; 1926-Oct-15; yes; F; Comanche; yes; 4/4; 4/4; 4/4; yes

       See #

1927   2324;   PERMAMSU, Juan; 1926-Aug-16; yes; M; Comanche; yes; 4/4; W; 1/2; yes

1927   2333;   PESUANY, Bonnie Louise; 1927-Apr-5; yes; F; Comanche; yes; W; 4/4; 1/2; yes

1927   2353;   PEWENOFKIT, Werta Jean; 1926-Oct-15; yes; F; Comanche & Apache; yes; 4/4; 4/4; 4/4; yes

1927   2383;   PEWO, Calvin Coolidge; 1927-Mar-13; yes; M; Comanche & Kio; yes; 4/4; 4/4; 4/4; yes

1927   2380;   PEWO, Samuel; 1927-Jan-11; yes; M; Comanche; yes; 4/4; 4/4; 4/4; yes

1927   2399;   POAHWAY, Bernadina; 1926-Sept-10; yes; F; Comanche & Apc; yes; 4/4; 4/4; 4/4; yes

1927   2406;   POAUTY, Chester; 1926-Nov-11; yes; M; Kiowa; yes; 4/4; 4/4; 4/4; yes

1927   705;   POLLOCK, Betty Ann; 1927-June-30; yes; F; Comanche; yes; W; White & Mex; W&M; yes

1927   2455;   POPETSARTKE, Cornelius; 1927-Feb-15; yes; M; Kiowa; yes; 4/4; 4/4; 4/4; yes

State __Oklahoma__ Reservation __Kiowa__ Agency or Jurisdiction __Kiowa__
Office of Indian Affairs Births Occurring Between the Dates of July 1, 1926 and
June 30, 1927 to Parents Enrolled at Jurisdiction

KEY: 1927 Census Roll Number; Surname and Given Name; Date of Birth; Live Birth (Yes or No); Sex; Tribe; Ward (yes or no); Degree of Father's blood; Degree of Mother's blood; Degree of Child's blood; At Jurisdiction Where Enrolled (yes or no); [If "no", where, if given]

1927 2466; PORTILLO, Ernestine Lorene; 1927-Feb-25; yes; F; Comanche; yes; Mex; 3/4; 3/8; yes

See #
1927 2507; PUEBLO, Burnell; 1926-Aug-26; yes; M; Comanche; yes; 4/4; 4/4; 4/4; yes

1927 2604; RIVAZ, Cicario; 1927; yes; M; Comanche; yes; Mex; Mex; Mex; yes

1927 2606; ROACHE, Harold L; 1927-Mar-13; yes; M; Comanche; yes; 1/4; W; 1/8; yes

1927 2304; ROENA, Marie; 1926-Dec-15; yes; F; Comanche; yes; 4/4; 4/4; 4/4; yes

1927 2686; SATEPEAHTAW, Freda Mary; 1926; yes; F; Kiowa; yes; 4/4; 4/4; 4/4; yes

1927 2703; SATOE, Mary Magdalena; 192-Mar-5; yes; F; Kiowa; yes; 4/4; 4/4; 4/4; yes

1927 2716; SAUMTY, Alice Ruth; 1926-Dec-30; yes; F; Kiowa; yes; 4/4; 4/4; 4/4; yes

1927 2723; SAUNKEAH, Elmer Thomas; 1927-June-3; yes; M; Kiowa; yes; 4/4; 4/4; 4/4; yes

1927 2734; SEAHMER, Marilyn; 1926-Dec-16; yes; F; Kiowa; yes; 4/4; 4/4; 4/4; yes

1927 694; SHIRLEY, Juanita Roe; 1927-May-4; yes; F; Comanche; yes; W; White & Mex; W&M; yes

1928 1961; SHORTNECK, Frances; 1927-Apr-30; yes; F; Kiowa; yes; 4/4; 4/4; 4/4; yes

1927 2667; SORGERWINNE, Elmer; 1926-Sept-4; yes; M; Comanche; yes; 4/4; 4/4; 4/4; yes

1928 2805; SOVO, Milton; 1927-Feb-26; yes; M; Comanche; yes; 4/4; 4/4; 4/4; yes

Office of Indian Affairs Births Occurring Between the Dates of July 1, 1926 and
June 30, 1927 to Parents Enrolled at Jurisdiction

KEY: 1927 Census Roll Number; Surname and Given Name; Date of Birth; Live Birth (Yes or No); Sex; Tribe; Ward (yes or no); Degree of Father's blood; Degree of Mother's blood; Degree of Child's blood; At Jurisdiction Where Enrolled (yes or no); [If "no", where, if given]

1928   2965;   SUTTON, Chas Lindberg; 1927-June-28; yes; M; Kiowa; yes; 4/4; 4/4; 4/4; yes

      See #
1928   3864;   TABBYTITE, John Lawrence; 1927-Mar-30; yes; M; Kiowa; yes; 1/2; 4/4; 3/4; yes

1927   2802;   TABBYTITE, Lester; 1926-July-21; yes; M; Comanche; yes; Mex; 1/2; 1/4; yes

1927   3834;   TABBYTITE, Susie; 1926-Nov-28; yes; F; Kiowa; yes; 4/4; 4/4; 4/4; yes

1927   2815;   TABBYTOSAVIT, Daisy; 1927-Jan-31; yes; F; Comanche; yes; 4/4; 4/4; 4/4; yes

1927   2856;   TAHCHAWWECKOLE, Velma; 1927-Apr-5; yes; F; Comanche; yes; 4/4; 4/4; 4/4; yes

1928   2922;   TAKKOPOODLE, Lavinia; 1927-Apr-29; yes; F; Kiowa; yes; 4/4; 1/2; 3/4; yes

1927   2908;   TAHLO, Elberta; 1926-Oct-31; yes; F; Kiowa; yes; 4/4; 4/4; 4/4; yes

1927   2724;   TAHMAHKERA, Carl Munroe; 1927-Mar-12; yes; M; Comanche; yes; 4/4; 4/4; 4/4; yes

1927   2991;   TAHSUDA, Thurman Ray; 1926-July-4; yes; M; Comanche; yes; 1/2; 7/8; 11/16; yes

1927   1087;   TAYLOR, Bessie; 1927-Feb-20; yes; F; Kiowa; yes; W; 4/4; 1/2; yes

1927   3164;   THOMAS, Dorothy Ann; 1926-Oct-20; yes; F; Kiowa; yes; 4/4; W; 1/2; yes

1927   3251;   TODOME, Velma Rose; 1927-Jan-23; yes; F; Kiowa; yes; 4/4; 4/4; 4/4; yes

1927   3270;   TOFPI, Ramona Belle; 1927-Mar-24; yes; F; Kiowa; yes; 4/4; 4/4; 4/4; yes

1927   7;   TOFPOIE, Katherine; 1926; yes; F; Kiowa; yes; 4/4; 4/4; 4/4; yes

State __Oklahoma__ Reservation __Kiowa__ Agency or Jurisdiction __Kiowa__
Office of Indian Affairs Births Occurring Between the Dates of July 1, 1926 and
June 30, 1927 to Parents Enrolled at Jurisdiction

KEY: 1927 Census Roll Number; Surname and Given Name; Date of Birth; Live Birth (Yes or No); Sex; Tribe; Ward (yes or no); Degree of Father's blood; Degree of Mother's blood; Degree of Child's blood; At Jurisdiction Where Enrolled (yes or no); [If "no", where, if given]

1927   3290;   TOINTIGH, Etta Sue; 1926-Dec-28; yes; F; Kiowa; yes; 4/4; 4/4; 4/4; yes

1927   3343;   TONEMAH, Juliette; 1926-July-29; yes; F; Kiowa; yes; 4/4; 4/4; 4/4; yes

1928   3448;   TOPETCHY, Bryan Vedol; 1927-June-30; yes; M; Comanche; yes; 4/4; 4/4; 4/4; yes

1928   3463;   TOPPIAH, Morris Edward; 1927-Jan-31; yes; M; Kiowa; yes; 4/4; 4/4; 4/4; yes

1927   3433;   TOQUOTHIB, Dennis Martin; 1927; yes; M; Comanche; yes; 4/4; 4/4; 4/4; yes

1927   3473;   TOSEE, Morris; 1927-Feb-28; yes; M; Comanche; yes; Mex; 1/2; 1/4; yes

1927   3446;   TOLITE, Thomas, Jr; 1926-Nov-24; yes; M; Comanche; yes; 4/4; 4/4; 4/4; yes

1927   1355;   TOYEBO, Carlos Wayne; 1926; yes; M; Kiowa; yes; 4/4; 4/4; 4/4; yes

1927   2584;   TREVINO, Irene; 1927-Jan-9; yes; F; Comanche; yes; Mex; Mex; Mex; yes

See #
1927   3488;   TSATAHSISKO, Mary; 1927-Apr-18; yes; F; Apache; yes; 4/4; 4/4; 4/4; yes

1927   3498;   TSATAKE, Jewel; 1926-Nov-15; yes; F; Kiowa; yes; 4/4; 4/4; 4/4; yes

1927   3514;   TSTAKE[sic], Aline; 1926-Aug-22; yes; F; Kiowa; yes; 4/4; 4/4; 4/4; yes

1927   1959;   TSELEE, Ruth; 1926-Sept-6; yes; F; Kiowa; yes; 4/4; 4/4; 4/4; yes

1927   3578;   TSOODLE, John Haws; 1927-Apr-18; yes; M; Kiowa; yes; 4/4; 4/4; 4/4; yes

State __Oklahoma__ Reservation __Kiowa__ Agency or Jurisdiction __Kiowa__
Office of Indian Affairs Births Occurring Between the Dates of July 1, 1926 and
June 30, 1927 to Parents Enrolled at Jurisdiction

KEY: 1927 Census Roll Number; Surname and Given Name; Date of Birth; Live Birth (Yes or No); Sex; Tribe; Ward (yes or no); Degree of Father's blood; Degree of Mother's blood; Degree of Child's blood; At Jurisdiction Where Enrolled (yes or no); [If "no", where, if given]

1927 3608; TUTSTSISAH, Harold; 1926-Nov-1; yes; M; Apache, yes; 4/4; 4/4; 4/4; yes

1927 3640; WAHHANNAH, Naoma Wanda; 1926; yes; F; Comanche; yes; 4/4; 4/4; 4/4; yes

1930 2304; WALKER, Lorene Maxine; 1926-July-30; yes; F; Delaware & Cad; yes; W; 4/4; 1/2; yes

1927 3651; WALLACE, Dorcas Dorothy; 1927-Mar-14; yes; F; Comanche; yes; 3/4; 4/4; 7/8; yes

        See #
1927 3655; WARE, Baby; 1927-Mar-27; yes; F; Kiowa; yes; 4/4; 4/4; 4/4; yes

1928 3721; WAYSEPAPPY, Ehoe; 1927-May-3; yes; M; Comanche; yes; 4/4; W; 1/2; yes

1927 3693; WERCHEVAHWAMY, Naomi; 1927-Apr-17; yes; F; Comanche; yes; 4/4; 4/4; 4/4; yes

1927 3144; WEBB, Lorene Mari; 1926-Sept-2; yes; F; Comanche; yes; W; 1/2; 1/4; yes

1927 3699; WERQUEGAH, Ella Alene; 1926-Sept-5; yes; F; Comanche; yes; 4/4; 4/4; 4/4; yes

1927 2341; WILLIAMS, Arnetta Mabel; 1927-May-12; yes; F; Comanche; yes; W; 4/4; 1/2; yes

        See #
1927 3768; WOOKSOOK, Edward Bill; 1927-June-9; yes; M; Comanche; yes; 4/4; 4/4; 4/4; yes

1927 3803; WYATT, Delia May; 1926-June-22; yes; F; Kiowa; yes; White & Mex; W&M; W&M; yes

1927 829; YELLOWHAIR, Asah; 1926-Nov-19; yes; F; Kiowa; yes; 4/4; 4/4; 4/4; yes

1927 1639; YELLOWHAIR, Darena; 1927-Jan-24; yes; F; Comanche; yes; 4/4; 4/4; 4/4; yes

KIOWA INDIAN AGENCY

Kiowa Reservation

Oklahoma

1928

BIRTH ROLL
Kiowa, Comanche, Apache and
Fort Sill Apache Indians.

State <u>Oklahoma</u> Reservation <u>Kiowa</u> Agency or Jurisdiction <u>Kiowa</u>
Office of Indian Affairs Births Occurring Between the Dates of July 1, 1927 and
June 30, 1928 to Parents Enrolled at Jurisdiction

1928   1861;   AHBOAH, Bill; 1927-Aug-23; yes; F; Kiowa; yes; 4/4; 4/4; 4/4; yes

1928   63;   AHHAITTY, Arville; 1927-Dec-27; yes; M; Kiowa; yes; 4/4; 4/4; 4/4; yes

1928   58;   AHHAITTY, Velma; 1928-Mar-3; yes; F; Kiowa; yes; 4/4; 4/4; 4/4; yes

1929   132;   AITSON, Amos; 1927-Oct-18; yes; M; Kiowa; yes; 3/4; 4/4; 7/8; yes

See #
1928   68;   AHKEAHBO, Alberto; 1928-May-1; yes; M; Kiowa; yes; 4/4; 4/4; 4/4; yes

See #
1928   108;   AHTONE, Flora; 1927-Aug-6; yes; F; Kiowa; yes; 4/4; 4/4; 4/4; yes

1928   141;   AKONETO, May Sheila; 1927-Sept-11; yes; F; Kiowa; yes; 4/4; 4/4; 4/4; yes

1929   168;   APAUTY, Cora Marie; 1927-Nov-27; yes; F; Kio & Comanche; yes; 4/4; 4/4; 4/4; yes

1928   195;   ASANEHIDDLE, Flora Bell; 1927-Sept-20; yes; F; Kiowa; yes; 4/4; 4/4; 4/4; yes

1928   215;   ASETAMY, Therma; 1927-July-10; yes; F; Comanche; yes; 4/4; 4/4; 4/4; yes

See #
1928   281;   AUCHCHIAH, James Allison; 1927-Sept-15; yes; M; Kiowa; yes; 4/4; 4/4; 4/4; yes

1928   183;   AUNCUOE, Marjorie; 1928-May-14; yes; F; Kiowa; yes; 4/4; 4/4; 4/4; yes

1928   342;   AUTAUBO, Julia; 1928-May-13; yes; F; Kiowa; yes; 4/4; 4/4; 4/4; yes

1929   329;   AUTAUBO, Sallie Anabell; 1928-Apr-24; yes; F; Kiowa; yes; 4/4; 4/4; 4/4; yes

State <u>Oklahoma</u> Reservation <u>Kiowa</u> Agency or Jurisdiction <u>Kiowa</u>
Office of Indian Affairs Births Occurring Between the Dates of July 1, 1927 and
June 30, 1928 to Parents Enrolled at Jurisdiction

1928   408;   BLACKSTAR, Onida; 1928-Mar-20; yes; F; Comanche; yes; 4/4; 4/4; 4/4; yes

1928   956;   BEARTRACK, Donald Roy; 1927-Sept-22; yes; M; Kiowa; yes; 4/4; 4/4; 4/4; yes

1929   389;   BITSEEDY, Thaymeus; 1928-Apr-17; yes; F; Apache; yes; 4/4; 4/4; 4/4; yes

1929   1805;   BOHAY, Phil Ragan; 1928-Apr-4; yes; M; Kiowa; yes; 4/4; 4/4; 4/4; yes

1928   423;   BOINTY, Charlotte Anne; 1927-Nov-20; yes; F; Kiowa; 1/2; 4/4; 3/4; yes

1929   935;   BROWN, Clarence Clifton; 1927-Nov-4; yes; M; Comanche; yes; W; 1/2; 1/4; yes

        See #
1928   2673;   BURNS, Hershel; 1928; yes; M; Kiowa; yes; 4/4; 4/4; 4/4; yes

1928   477;   CANNON; 1928-Mar-25; yes; M; Kiowa; yes; 1/2; 4/4; 3/4; yes

1929   3411;   CAMPBELL, Alfred Eugene; 1928-Mar-28; yes; M; Kiowa; yes; 1/2; 4/4; 3/4; yes

1928   513;   CHAHSENAH, Earl; 1927-Sept-11; yes; M; Comanche; yes; 4/4; 4/4; 4/4; yes

1928   156;   CHANATE, Colleen; 1927-Aug-17; yes; F; Kiowa; yes; 4/4; 4/4; 4/4; yes

1928   560;   CHAPPABITTY; 1927-Nov-17; yes; M; Comanche; yes; 4/4; 4/4; 4/4; yes

1928   585;   CHEBAHTAH, Mariam; 1927-Dec-21; yes; F; Comanche; yes; 4/4; 4/4; 4/4; yes

        See #
1931   629;   CHIBITTY, Letha May; 1928-June-14; yes; F; Comanche; yes; 4/4; 4/4; 4/4; yes

44

State___Oklahoma___ Reservation ___Kiowa___ Agency or Jurisdiction ___Kiowa___
Office of Indian Affairs Births Occurring Between the Dates of July 1, 1927 and
June 30, 1928 to Parents Enrolled at Jurisdiction

KEY: 1928 Census Roll Number; Surname and Given Name; Date of Birth; Live Birth (Yes or No); Sex; Tribe; Ward (yes or no); Degree of Father's blood; Degree of Mother's blood; Degree of Child's blood; At Jurisdiction Where Enrolled (yes or no); [If "no", where, if given]

1929   640;   COBAHTINE, Mary Louise; 1927-Nov-18; yes; F; Kiowa; yes; 4/4; 4/4; 4/4; yes

1928   665;   CODYNAH, Eloise Levena; 1927-Dec-17; yes; F; Comanche; yes; 4/4; 4/4; 4/4; yes

        See #
1928   666;   CODYNAH; 1927-Sept-3; yes; M; Comanche; yes; 4/4; 4/4; 4/4; yes

1928   683;   CONNYWERDY, Rena; 1927-Nov-16; yes; F; Comanche; yes; 4/4; 4/4; 4/4; yes

1928   737;   DAVIS, Eugene; 1927-Nov-30; yes; M; Comanche; yes; W; 1/2; 1/4; yes

1928   855;   DOYEBO, Daniel Herbert; 1928-Jan-13; yes; M; Kiowa; yes; 4/4; 4/4; 4/4; yes

1928   8;   DUPOINT, Hathaway; 1927-Oct-31; yes; M; Kiowa; yes; 4/4; 4/4; 4/4; yes

1928   898;   EMTADDLE, Clyde; 1927-Dec-2; yes; M; Kio & Apache; yes; 4/4; 4/4; 4/4; yes

1931   245;   FARRALLA, Gilbert; 1928-Feb-22; yes; M; Comanche; yes; Med[sic]; Mex; Mex; yes

1929   1069;   FAWBUSH, Ava; 1927-Nov-29; yes; F; Comanche; yes; W; 4/4; 1/2; yes

1929   932;   FULLER, Carmeleta; 1927-July-26; yes; F; Comanche; yes; 1/2; W; 1/4; yes

1929   955;   GEIOGAMIAH, Vernon Lee; 1928-June-10; yes; M; Kiowa; yes; 4/4; 4/4; 4/4; yes

1928   3577;   GIONETY; 1928-May-23; yes; M; Kiowa; yes; 4/4; 4/4; 4/4; yes

1928   243;   HAMILTON, Diana; 1927-Dec-30; yes; F; Kiowa; yes; 4/4; 4/4; 4/4; yes

1928   3924;   HAMZIPTA, Jacelyn; 1928-May-9; yes; F; Kiowa; yes; 4/4; Mex; 1/2; yes

45

State __Oklahoma__ Reservation __Kiowa__ Agency or Jurisdiction __Kiowa__
Office of Indian Affairs Births Occurring Between the Dates of July 1, 1927 and
June 30, 1928 to Parents Enrolled at Jurisdiction

KEY: 1928 Census Roll Number; Surname and Given Name; Date of Birth; Live Birth (Yes or No); Sex; Tribe; Ward (yes or no); Degree of Father's blood; Degree of Mother's blood; Degree of Child's blood; At Jurisdiction Where Enrolled (yes or no); [If "no", where, if given]

1928   1056;   HAUNGOOAH, Leonard; 1927-Nov-20; yes; M; Kiowa; yes; 4/4; 4/4; 4/4; yes

1928   1100;   HEMINOKEKY, Edmond; 1928-Jan-18; yes; M; Comanche & Apc; yes; 4/4; 4/4; 4/4; yes

1928   1115;   HERNASY, Ora Bell; 1928-Apr-21; yes; F; Comanche; yes; 4/4; 4/4; 4/4; yes

1928   1385;   HENRY, Carol; 1927-Oct-3; yes; F; Kiowa; yes; 4/4; 4/4; 4/4; yes

1929   2160;   HERMANDEZES, Robert; 1928-June-13; yes; M; Kiowa; yes; Mex; 4/4; 1/2; yes

1928   1138;   HOKEAH, Virgil Linn; 1928-Jan-24; yes; M; Kiowa; yes; 4/4; 4/4; 4/4; yes

1928   3629;   HOWRY, Johnny; 1928-Feb-3; yes; M; Kiowa; yes; 4/4; 4/4; 4/4; yes

1928   1174;   HOVAKAH, Jewell; 1927-Nov-5; yes; F; Kiowa; yes; 4/4; 4/4; 4/4; yes

1928   898;   HUMMINGBIRD, Clyde; 1927-Dec-2; yes; M; Kiowa & Apache; yes; 4/4; 4/4; 4/4; yes

1928   1218;   JONES, Emma Jean; 1928-Mar-21; yes; F; Kiowa; yes; 3/4; 3/4; 3/4; yes

1928   2627;   JOHNSON, Delores; 1927-Aug-13; yes; F; Kiowa; yes; W; 1/2; 1/4; yes

1929   1249;   KADAYSO, Fay; 1928-Apr-6; yes; F; Apache; yes; 4/4; 4/4; 4/4; yes

1928   2355;   KASSANAVOID; 1927-Nov-14; yes; F; Comanche; yes; 4/4; 4/4; 4/4; yes

1928   3184;   KASSANAVOID, Lillian; 1927-Sept-25; yes; F; Comanche; yes; 4/4; 4/4; 4/4; yes

1928   3184;   KOSECHEQUETAH; 1928-Apr-17; yes; M; Comanche; yes; 4/4; 4/4; 4/4; yes

46

State __Oklahoma__ Reservation __Kiowa__ Agency or Jurisdiction __Kiowa__
Office of Indian Affairs Births Occurring Between the Dates of July 1, 1927 and
June 30, 1928 to Parents Enrolled at Jurisdiction

KEY: 1928 Census Roll Number; Surname and Given Name; Date of Birth; Live Birth (Yes or No); Sex; Tribe; Ward (yes or no); Degree of Father's blood; Degree of Mother's blood; Degree of Child's blood; At Jurisdiction Where Enrolled (yes or no); [If "no", where, if given]

1928   1295;   KAUBIN, Pauline; 1927-Dec-29; yes; F; Kiowa; yes; 4/4; 4/4; 4/4; yes

1928   1323;   KAULAY, Arletta Joyce; 1928-Jan-3; yes; F; Kiowa; yes; 4/4; 4/4; 4/4; yes

1928   1334;   KAULAY, Lamont; 1927-Oct-14; yes; M; Kiowa; yes; 4/4; 1/2; 3/4; yes

1928   1329;   KAULAY, Patricia Joan; 1927-Dec-7; yes; F; Kiowa; yes; 4/4; 4/4; 4/4; yes

1929   1902;   KILLSFIRST, Floyd; 1928-May-9; yes; M; Apache; yes; 4/4; 4/4; 4/4; yes

         See #
1929   1900;   KILLSFIRST, Loyd; 1928-May-9; yes; M; Apache; yes; 4/4; 4/4; 4/4; yes

1928   1433;   KLATHCHALLAH, Raymond; 1927-Aug-30; yes; M; Kiowa; yes; 4/4; 4/4; 4/4; yes

1928   2059;   KEAHBONE, Mary Ruth; 1928-Jan-6; yes; F; Kiowa; yes; 4/4; 4/4; 4/4; yes

1928   1457;   KOMARDLEY, Doris Ann; 1928-June-12; yes; F; Apache; yes; 4/4; 4/4; 4/4; yes

1929   1466;   KONARD, Marland; 1928-Apr-16; yes; M; Kiowa; yes; 4/4; 4/4; 4/4; yes

1928   1528;   KATAY, Ralph; 1927-Sept-7; yes; M; Kiowa; yes; 4/4; 4/4; 4/4; yes

1928   1678;   LAURENZANA, Rudolph; 1927-Nov-25; yes; M; Comanche; yes; Mex; 3/4; 3/8; yes

         See #
1928   2246;   LEFTHAND; 1927-Nov-7; yes; F; Kiowa; yes; 4/4; 4/4; 4/4; yes

1929   1029;   LITTLECHIEF, Helena May; 1928-June-22; yes; F; Kiowa; yes; 4/4; 4/4; 4/4; yes

47

State __Oklahoma__ Reservation __Kiowa__ Agency or Jurisdiction __Kiowa__
Office of Indian Affairs Births Occurring Between the Dates of July 1, 1927 and
June 30, 1928 to Parents Enrolled at Jurisdiction

1929 1681; MARTINEZ, Vivian Travet; 1927-Sept-16; yes; F; Comanche; yes; 1/4; W; 1/8; yes

See #
1928 1732; MAUSOPE, Paul; 1927-Sept-29; yes; M; Kiowa; yes; 4/4; 4/4; 4/4; yes

1928 1748; MAYNAHMAH, Austin; 1927-Nov-25; yes; M; Apache; yes; 4/4; 4/4; 4/4; yes

1929 1751; McKENZIE, Robert Allen, Jr; 1928-June-30; yes; M; Kiowa; yes; 1/4; W; 1/8; yes

1928 1755; McKENZIE, Robert Allen; 1928-Mar-1; yes; M; Kiowa; yes; 1/4; 4/4; 5/8; yes

1929 1781; MIHECOBY, Virgil; 1927-July-21; yes; M; Comanche; yes; 4/4; 4/4; 4/4; yes

1928 1857; MIHECOBY; 1928-May-3; yes; M; Comanche; yes; 4/4; 4/4; 4/4; yes

1928 1857; MOPOPE, Alfred; 1927-Nov-26; yes; M; Kiowa; yes; 4/4; 4/4; 4/4; yes

1928 1864; MOPOPE, Vanette; 1928-June-10; yes; F; Kiowa & Comanche; yes; 4/4; 7/8; 15/16; yes

1929 1891; MOWWAT, Spencer; 1928-June-12; yes; M; Comanche; yes; 4/4; 4/4; 4/4; yes

1928 2590; MORRISON, Marie Belle; 1928-Feb-24; yes; F; Kiowa; yes; 4/4; 4/4; 4/4; yes

1928 3765; MOUNTAIN, Wallace; 1927-Aug-12; yes; M; Kiowa; yes; 4/4; 4/4; 4/4; yes

1928 1930; NAHMO, Walter, Jr; 1928-Jan-22; yes; M; Comanche; yes; 4/4; 4/4; 4/4; yes

1929 3567; NASHDELTE, Marjorie Alice; 1928-Mar-14; yes; F; Apache; yes; 4/4; 4/4; 4/4; yes

State __Oklahoma__ Reservation __Kiowa__ Agency or Jurisdiction __Kiowa__
Office of Indian Affairs Births Occurring Between the Dates of July 1, 1927 and
June 30, 1928 to Parents Enrolled at Jurisdiction

KEY: 1928 Census Roll Number; Surname and Given Name; Date of Birth; Live Birth (Yes or No); Sex; Tribe; Ward (yes or no); Degree of Father's blood; Degree of Mother's blood; Degree of Child's blood; At Jurisdiction Where Enrolled (yes or no); [If "no", where, if given]

1928 372; NEWSOME, Horace Meredith; 1928-Jan-9; yes; M; Kiowa; yes; W; 1/2; 1/4; yes

1938[sic] 2009; NEWOOKAHKER, Gerald D; 1928-Jan-19; yes; M; Comanche & Ap; yes; 4/4; 4/4; 4/4; yes

See #
1928 2024; NIYAH; 1928-Feb-1; yes; F; Comanche; yes; 4/4; 4/4; 4/4; yes

1928 200; PAHDOCONY, Billie Allen; 1928-Apr-3; yes; M; Comanche; yes; 4/4; 4/4; 4/4; yes

See #
1928 2167; PAHDOPONY; 1927-Dec-27; yes; M; Comanche; yes; 4/4; 4/4; 4/4; yes

1928 2179 PAHKOTOQUODLE, Rupert Hughes; 1928- May-24; yes; M; Kiowa; yes; 4/4; 4/4; 4/4; yes

1928 1849; PALMER, Ruth; 1927-Nov-8; yes; F; Kiowa; yes; 1/2; 4/4; 5/18[sic]; yes

1928 2272; PEBEAHSY; 1927-Dec-20; yes; M; Comanche; yes; 4/4; 4/4; 4/4; yes

1928 2337; PERMAMSU, Hubert; 1927-Sept-21; yes; M; Comanche; yes; 4/4; 4/4; 4/4; yes

1928 2346; PERMAMSU, Winifred Loraine; 1928; yes; F; Comanche; yes; 4/4; 4/4; 4/4; yes

1929 2405; PEWO, Marie; 1928-July-20; yes; F; Comanche; yes; 4/4; 4/4; 4/4; yes

1929 2435; POAUTY, Neoma Ruth; 1928-Apr-20; yes; F; Kiowa; yes; 4/4; 4/4; 4/4; yes

1929 2438; POAUTY, Silas Wayne; 1928-May-27; yes; M; Kiowa; yes; 4/4; 4/4; 4/4; yes

See #
1928 2441; POHACSUCUT, Jack Permamsu; 1928-June-22; yes; M; Comanche; yes; 4/4; 4/4; 4/4; yes

State __Oklahoma__ Reservation __Kiowa__ Agency or Jurisdiction __Kiowa__
Office of Indian Affairs Births Occurring Between the Dates of July 1, 1927 and
June 30, 1928 to Parents Enrolled at Jurisdiction

KEY: 1928 Census Roll Number; Surname and Given Name; Date of Birth; Live Birth (Yes or No); Sex; Tribe; Ward (yes or no); Degree of Father's blood; Degree of Mother's blood; Degree of Child's blood; At Jurisdiction Where Enrolled (yes or no); [If "no", where, if given]

1928   2452;   POOLAW, Wanada; 1927-Dec-8; yes; F; Kiowa; yes; 4/4; 4/4; 4/4; yes

1928   2490;   PORTILLO, Isabel; 1928-May-6; yes; F; Comanche; yes; Mex; 3/4; 3/8; yes

1928   1014;   PRENTISS, Beatrice; 1927-July-27; yes; F; Kiowa; yes; 4/4; 4/4; 4/4; yes

1928   70;   PESO; 1928-Apr-21; yes; F; Apache & Wich; yes; 4/4; 4/4; 4/4; yes

1929   3859;   QUETONE, Carol Louise; 1928-May-17; yes; F; Kiowa; yes; 1/2; 4/4; 3/4; yes

1931   449;   QUETONE, Majel[sic] Irene; 1927-Nov-9; yes; F; Kiowa; yes; 1/2; 1/2; 1/2; yes

1930   3524;   REDBIRD, Vincent; 1928-June-12; yes; M; Comanche; yes; 4/4; 4/4; 4/4; yes

1928   1880;   RIDDLE, Ella Fay; 1927-Aug-17; yes; F; Comanche; yes; W; 4/4; 1/2; yes

1928   2650;   SAHMAUNT, Mildred Virginia; 1927-Sept-10; yes; F; Kiowa; yes; 4/4; 4/4; 4/4; yes

1929   2728;   SATEPEEAHTAW, Marion; 1928-June-21; yes; M; Kiowa; yes; 4/4; 4/4; 4/4; yes

1928   21;   SEELTOE, Viola; 1927-Sept-12; yes; F; Kiowa; yes; 4/4; 4/4; 4/4; yes

1929   2825;   SOONTAY, Bernice Mary; 1928-Mar-9; yes; F; Kiowa & Apache; yes; 4/4; 4/4; 4/4; yes

1929   2839;   STARR, Rudolph; 1928-May-6; yes; M; Apache; yes; 4/4; 4/4; 4/4; yes

1928   2253;   STUMBLING BEAR, Richard Glen; 1927-Sept-13; yes; M; Kiowa; yes; 4/4; 4/4; 4/4; yes

1928   2827;   TABBYTITE, Joe Beryle; 1927-Sept-3; yes; M; Kiowa & Com; yes; 1/4; 4/4; 5/8; yes

State ___Oklahoma___ Reservation ___Kiowa___ Agency or Jurisdiction ___Kiowa___
Office of Indian Affairs Births Occurring Between the Dates of July 1, 1927 and
June 30, 1928 to Parents Enrolled at Jurisdiction

KEY: 1928 Census Roll Number; Surname and Given Name; Date of Birth; Live Birth (Yes or No); Sex; Tribe; Ward (yes or no); Degree of Father's blood; Degree of Mother's blood; Degree of Child's blood; At Jurisdiction Where Enrolled (yes or no); [If "no", where, if given]

1928   2852;   TAH, Harry; 1928-Apr-1; yes; M; Apache; yes; 4/4; 4/4; 4/4; yes

1929   2896;   TAHBONE, Horace; 1927-Sept-4; yes; M; Kiowa; yes; 4/4; 4/4; 4/4; yes

1928   2872;   TAHBONEMAH; 1927-Sept-11; yes; M; Kiowa; yes; 4/4; 4/4; 4/4; yes

        See #
1928   2881;   TAHDOOAHNIPOT; 1928-Jan-11; yes; F; Comanche; yes; 4/4; 4/4; 4/4; yes

1928   3009;   TAHSEQUAW; 1928-Apr-11; yes; M; Comanche; yes; 4/4; 4/4; 4/4; yes

        See #
1928   3043;   TAINPEAH, Ray; 1928-June-2; yes; M; Kiowa; yes; 4/4; 4/4; 4/4; yes

        See #
1928   3043;   TAINPEAH, Roy; 1928-June-2; yes; M; Kiowa; yes; 4/4; 4/4; 4/4; yes

        See #
1928   3048;   TAKEWAHPOOR, May Frances; 1928-May-31; yes; F; Comanche; yes; 4/4; 4/4; 4/4; yes

1928   3068;   TANEDOOAH, Katherine; 1927-Sept-14; yes; F; Kiowa; yes; 4/4; 4/4; 4/4; yes

1928   3075;   TANEQUODLE, Peggy Lou; 1927-Oct-5; yes; F; Kiowa; yes; 4/4; 4/4; 4/4; yes

1928   3080;   TANEQUODLE, Wm Charles; 1928-May-6; yes; M; Kiowa; yes; 4/4; 4/4; 4/4; yes

1928   3925;   TARTSAH, Emaline Virginia; 1928-May-14; yes; F; Kiowa & Apache; yes; 4/4; 4/4; 4/4; yes

1928   3131;   TANA, Alona; 1927-Sept-16; yes; F; Kiowa; yes; 4/4; 4/4; 4/4; yes

1928   3353;   TIDDARK, Edward; 1928-May-10; yes; M; Comanche; yes; 4/4; 4/4; 4/4; yes

State __Oklahoma__ Reservation __Kiowa__ Agency or Jurisdiction __Kiowa__
Office of Indian Affairs Births Occurring Between the Dates of July 1, 1927 and
June 30, 1928 to Parents Enrolled at Jurisdiction

KEY: 1928 Census Roll Number; Surname and Given Name; Date of Birth; Live Birth (Yes or No); Sex; Tribe; Ward (yes or no); Degree of Father's blood; Degree of Mother's blood; Degree of Child's blood; At Jurisdiction Where Enrolled (yes or no); [If "no", where, if given]

1928   3195;   TIDDARD, Napoleon; 1927-Oct-10; yes; M; Comanche; yes; 4/4; 4/4; 4/4; yes

        2204;   TICEAHKIE, Chas Lindberg; 1927-July-29; yes; M; Comanche; yes; 4/4; 4/4; 4/4; yes

1928   3427;   TOPAUM, Margaret; 1928-Apr-13; yes; F; Kiowa; yes; 4/4; 4/4; 4/4; yes

1928   3460;   TOPPAH; 1927-Sept-27; yes; M; Kiowa; yes; 4/4; 4/4; 4/4; yes

1929   3507;   TOPPAH, Velma May; 1928-Apr-8-; yes; F; Kiowa; yes; 4/4; 4/4; 4/4; yes

        See #
1928   3518;   TSATAHSISKO, Flo; 1928-Mar-18; yes; F; Apache; yes; 4/4; 4/4; 4/4; yes

1928   3921;   TSATAKE, Madge Ella; 1928-Apr-7; yes; F; Kiowa; yes; 4/4; 4/4; 4/4; yes

1928   3626;   TSOTIGH, Sadie Lue; 1928-Feb-6; yes; F; Kiowa; yes; 4/4; 4/4; 4/4; yes

1929   3880;   TOOHEMPA, Peggy Joy; 1928-May-13; yes; F; Comanche; yes; 4/4; 4/4; 4/4; yes

1929   3686;   TSOTIGH, Hubert; 1928-Mar-26; yes; M; Kiowa; yes; 4/4; 4/4; 4/4; yes

1929   683;   TRACY, Ramona Fay; May-17-1928; yes; F; Comanche; W; White & Mex; W & M; yes

1929   2167;   TWO HATCHET; Laverne Grace; 1928-May-1; yes; F; Kiowa; yes; 4/4; 4/4; 4/4; yes

1928   3669;   WAHAHKINNEY, Collins; 1928-Apr-22; yes; F; Comanche; yes; 4/4; 4/4; 4/4; yes

1928   3708;   WANAHDOOAH; 1927-Dec-26; yes; F; Comanche; yes; 4/4; 4/4; 4/4; yes

State __Oklahoma__ Reservation __Kiowa__ Agency or Jurisdiction __Kiowa__
Office of Indian Affairs Births Occurring Between the Dates of July 1, 1927 and
June 30, 1928 to Parents Enrolled at Jurisdiction

KEY: 1928 Census Roll Number; Surname and Given Name; Date of Birth; Live Birth (Yes or No); Sex; Tribe; Ward (yes or no); Degree of Father's blood; Degree of Mother's blood; Degree of Child's blood; At Jurisdiction Where Enrolled (yes or no); [If "no", where, if given]

1928   3753;   WARE, Gerald Claudine; 1927-Aug-31; yes; M; Kiowa; yes; 4/4; 4/4; 4/4; yes

1928   3719;   WAYSEPAPPY; 1927-July-2; yes; F; Comanche; yes; 4/4; 4/4; 4/4; yes

1928   3923;   WEBB, Eyote; 1928-Apr-18; yes; F; Comanche; yes; W; 1/2; 1/4; yes

1928   3740;   WERMY; 1928-Mar-3; yes; M; Comanche; yes; 4/4; 4/4; 4/4; yes

1928   3744;   WERQUEYAH, Lena May; 1928-Apr-17; yes; F; Comanche; yes; 4/4; 4/4; 4/4; yes

1928   3790;   WINNERCHY, Rose Mary; 1927-Nov-30; yes; F; Comanche; yes; 4/4; 4/4; 4/4; yes

1929   478;   WHITE BUFFALO, Raymond; 1928-June-16; yes; M; Kiowa; yes; 4/4; 4/4; 4/4; yes

1928   3782;   WHITEWOLF; 1928-May-27; yes; F; Comanche; yes; 4/4; 4/4; 4/4; yes

1928   2366;   WILLIAMS; 1928-July-10; yes; F; Comanche; yes; 4/4; 4/4; 4/4; yes

1928   3905;   WILLIS, Robt Oscar; 1928-Apr-17; yes; M; Kiowa; yes; Mex; mex[sic]; Mex; yes

1928   3214;   WOLF, John Wilkin; 1928-Apr-12; yes; M; Kiowa; yes; 4/4; 3/4; 7/8; yes

1928   3380;   WOLF CHIEF, Aleta; 1927-Oct-3; yes; F; Kiowa; yes; 4/4; 4/4; 4/4; yes

1928   3381;   WOLF CHIEF, Vineta; 1927-Oct-3; yes; F; Kiowa; yes; 4/4; 4/4; 4/4; yes

1928   3850;   YACKESCHI; 1928-Jan-7; yes; M; Comanche; yes; 4/4; 4/4; 4/4; yes

1928   3208;   YEAHQUO, Irene Margie; 1927-Oct-9; yes; F; Kiowa; yes; 4/4; 4/4; 4/4; yes

1928   3525;   YEAHQUO, Rudolph; 1928-Mar-25; yes; M; Kiowa; yes; 4/4; 4/4; 4/4; yes

State __Oklahoma__ Reservation __Kiowa__ Agency or Jurisdiction __Kiowa__
Office of Indian Affairs Births Occurring Between the Dates of July 1, 1927 and
June 30, 1928 to Parents Enrolled at Jurisdiction

1929   1659;   YELLOWFISH, Simon; 1928-Apr-4; yes; M; Comanche; yes; 4/4; 4/4; 4/4; yes

1929   83;   ZUREGA, Mary; 1928-Mar-4; yes; F; Apache & Wich; yes; Mex; 4/4; 1/2; yes

KIOWA INDIAN AGENCY
Kiowa Reservation
Oklahoma
1929

BIRTH ROLL
Kiowa, Comanche, Apache and Fort Sill Apache Indians.

State __Oklahoma__ Reservation __Kiowa__ Agency or Jurisdiction __Kiowa__
Office of Indian Affairs Births Occurring Between the Dates of July 1, 1928 and
June 30, 1929 to Parents Enrolled at Jurisdiction

KEY: 1929 Census Roll Number; Surname and Given Name; Date of Birth; Live Birth (Yes or No); Sex; Tribe; Ward (yes or no); Degree of Father's blood; Degree of Mother's blood; Degree of Child's blood; At Jurisdiction Where Enrolled (yes or no); [If "no", where, if given]

1929　　10;　　AGOPETAH, George Edward; 1929-Feb-20; yes; M; Kiowa; yes; 4/4; 4/4; 4/4; yes

　　　　See #
1929　　38;　　AHDOKOBO, Lamar; 1929-Feb-9; yes; M; Kiowa; yes; 4/4; 4/4; 4/4; yes

1929　　36;　　AHDOKOBO, Perry; 1928-Dec-1; yes; M; Kiowa; yes; 4/4; 4/4; 4/4; yes

1929　　48;　　AHGOOM, James Herman; 1928-July-8; yes; M; Kiowa; yes; 4/4; 4/4; 4/4; yes

1929　　126;　　AITSON, Laverne; 1928-Sept-4; yes; M; Kiowa; yes; 3/4; 4/4; 7/8; yes

1930　　137;　　AITSON, William; 1929-May-26; yes; M; Kiowa; yes; 3/4; 4/4; 7/8; yes

1929　　163;　　AMAUTY, Dorine Jane; 1929-Jan-18; yes; F; Kiowa; yes; 4/4; 4/4; 4/4; yes

1929　　535;　　ANDERSON, Charles Donald; 1929-Feb-28; yes; M; Comanche; yes; W; Mex & W; Mex & W; yes

1929　　1923;　　ASENAP, Eugene; 1929-May-25; yes; M; Comanche; yes; 4/4; 4/4; 4/4; yes

1929　　206;　　ASEPERMY, Curtis Clayton; 1928-Nov-17; yes; M; Comanche; yes; 4/4; 4/4; 4/4; yes

1930　　2975;　　AUNKO, Perry; 1929-Mar-31; yes; M; Kiowa; yes; 4/4; 4/4; 4/4; yes

1929　　394;　　BLACKBEAR, Birdie Mae; 1929-Jan-9; yes; F; Kiowa; yes; 4/4; 4/4; 4/4; yes

1930　　368;　　BECK, Adeline Gladys; 1929-Mar-16; yes; F; Kiowa; yes; W; 4/4; 1/2; yes

1929　　408;　　BOINTY, Marylyne Mae; 1929-Jan-18; yes; F; Kiowa; 1/2; 3/4; 5/8; yes

State __Oklahoma__ Reservation __Kiowa__ Agency or Jurisdiction __Kiowa__
Office of Indian Affairs Births Occurring Between the Dates of July 1, 1928 and
June 30, 1929 to Parents Enrolled at Jurisdiction

KEY: 1929 Census Roll Number; Surname and Given Name; Date of Birth; Live Birth (Yes or No); Sex; Tribe; Ward (yes or no); Degree of Father's blood; Degree of Mother's blood; Degree of Child's blood; At Jurisdiction Where Enrolled (yes or no); [If "no", where, if given]

1930   4488;   BOINTY, Phillip Adolphus; 1929-June-16; yes; M; Comanche; 1/2; 3/4; 5/8; yes

1929   423;   BOONE, Bruce; 1928-Sept-18; yes; M; Kiowa; yes; 4/4; 3/4; 7/8; yes

1929   441;   BOSIN, Marline Ann; 1928-Oct-3; yes; F; Kiowa; yes; 4/4; 4/4; 4/4; yes

1929   459;   BOYIDDLE, Juan; 1928-Sept-10; yes; M; Kiowa; yes; 4/4; 4/4; 4/4; yes

1929   1899;   BULL, Angeline; 1929-Jan-3; yes; F; Comanche; yes; 4/4; 4/4; 4/4; yes

1929   549;   BULLBEAR, Julia Ann; 1928-Nov-4; yes; F; Comanche; yes; 4/4; 4/4; 4/4; yes

See #
1929   2696;   BURNS, Herschel; 1928-July-2; yes; M; Kiowa; yes; 4/4; 4/4; 4/4; yes

1929   3126;   CABLE, Butty[sic] Ruth; 1928-Dec-5; yes; F; Comanche; yes; 3/4; 4/4; 7/8; yes

1929   545;   CADDO, Jean Elgin; 1928-Dec-9; yes; M; Comanche; yes; 1/4; 1/2; 3/8; yes

See #
1929   2092;   CAT, Dorian Nita; 1929-June-7; yes; F; Kiowa; yes; 4/4; 4/4; 4/4; yes

1929   985;   CHANCY; Gene Cecil; 1929-Feb-3; yes; M; Kiowa; yes; W; 4/4; 1/2; yes

1931   545;   CHAHSENAH, Denton Martin; 1929-Mar-27; yes; M; Comanche; yes; 4/4; 4/4; 4/4; yes

1931   563;   CHAHTINNEYACKQUE, Pauline; 1928; yes; F; Comanche; yes; 1/2; 4/4; 3/4; yes

See #
1930   697;   CHANATE, Dollie Vivian; 1929-Feb-20; yes; F; Kiowa; yes; 4/4; 4/4; 4/4; yes

58

State __Oklahoma__ Reservation __Kiowa__ Agency or Jurisdiction __Kiowa__
Office of Indian Affairs Births Occurring Between the Dates of July 1, 1928 and
June 30, 1929 to Parents Enrolled at Jurisdiction

KEY: 1929 Census Roll Number; Surname and Given Name; Date of Birth; Live Birth (Yes or No); Sex; Tribe; Ward (yes or no); Degree of Father's blood; Degree of Mother's blood; Degree of Child's blood; At Jurisdiction Where Enrolled (yes or no); [If "no", where, if given]

1929   603;   CHOCKPOYAH, James; 1928-Dec-11; yes; M; Comanche; yes; 4/4; 4/4; 4/4; yes

1929   625;   CLARK, Albert, Jr; 1928-Sept-26; yes; M; Comanche; yes; 1/2; W; 1/4; yes

1929   628;   CLARK, Bobbie Joe; 1929-Feb-23; yes; M; Comanche; yes; 1/2; W; 1/4; yes

1929   640;   COBAHTINE, Mary Louise; 1929-Jan-27; yes; F; Kiowa; yes; 4/4; 4/4; 4/4; yes

1929   641;   COBAHTINE, Margaret Lucile; 1929-Jan-27; yes; F; Kiowa; yes; 4/4; 4/4; 4/4; yes

1929   650;   CODAPONY, Voris; 1928-Sept-17; yes; F; Comanche; yes; 4/4; 4/4; 4/4; yes

1929   665;   COFFEE, Mabel Ann; 1929-Jan-16; yes; F; Comanche; yes; 4/4; 4/4; 4/4; yes

1929   709;   CONOWOOP, Bud; 1928-Nov-12; yes; M; Comanche; yes; 4/4; 4/4; 4/4; yes

1929   824;   CLEVELAND, Pauline; 1928-Sept-5; yes; F; Kiowa; yes; 4/4; 4/4; 4/4; yes

        See #
1929   3083;   COMANCHE, Thelma Mae; 1929-July-16; yes; F; Apache; yes; 4/4; 4/4; 4/4; yes

        See #
1929   724;   DAVIS, Joe Allen; 1928-Nov-8; yes; M; Comanche; W; 1/2; 1/4; yes

1929   759;   DOUGOMAH, Juanita May; 1928-July-7; yes; F; Kiowa; yes; 4/4; 4/4; 4/4; yes

        See #
1929   761;   DOUKEI, Eva Lula; 1928-Oct-19; yes; F; Kiowa; yes; 4/4; 4/4; 4/4; yes

1930   1028;   FIVE, Elizabeth Ellen; 1929-June-28; yes; F; Comanche; yes; W; W & Mex; W & Mex; yes

59

State __Oklahoma__ Reservation __Kiowa__ Agency or Jurisdiction __Kiowa__
Office of Indian Affairs Births Occurring Between the Dates of July 1, 1928 and
June 30, 1929 to Parents Enrolled at Jurisdiction

KEY: 1929 Census Roll Number; Surname and Given Name; Date of Birth; Live Birth (Yes or No); Sex; Tribe; Ward (yes or no); Degree of Father's blood; Degree of Mother's blood; Degree of Child's blood; At Jurisdiction Where Enrolled (yes or no); [If "no", where, if given]

1929   4330;   FRANKLIN, Edith Marie; 1929-June-19; yes; F; Kiowa; yes; 4/4; 3/4; 7/8; yes

1930   1242;   FRYEAR, Eddie Lee; 1929-Mar-16; yes; M; Comanche; yes; W; Mex; W & Mex; yes

1929   930;   FULLER, Billie D; 1928-Oct-18; yes; M; Comanche; yes; 1/8; 1/2; 3/8; yes

1929   926;   FULLER, Iris Dawn; 1929-Mar-12; yes; F; Comanche; yes; 1/2; W; 1/4; yes

1929   958;   GEIOGAMAH, Chas Curtis; 1928-July-3; yes; M; Kiowa; yes; 4/4; 4/4; 4/4; yes

See #
1929   964;   GEIONETY, Phoebe; 1928-July-7; yes; F; Kiowa; yes; 4/4; 4/4; 4/4; yes

See #
1929   945;   GEIMAUSADDLE, Catherine Belle; 1928-Nov-18; yes; F; Kiowa; yes; 4/4; 4/4; 4/4; yes

1929   2538;   GOODAY, Flora; 1928-Oct-16; yes; F; Comanche; yes; 4/4; 1/2; 3/4; yes

1929   1772;   GRAY, Harold Merrick; 1929-Feb-1; yes; M; Comanche & Cad; yes; 1/4; 1/2; 3/8; yes

1929   3351;   GUTHRIE, Rita Joyce; 1928-Aug-8; yes; F; Kiowa; yes; 4/4; 4/4; 4/4; yes

1929   1004;   GWOLADDLE, Lola Cora; 1928-Oct-3; yes; F; Kiowa; yes; 3/4; 3/4; 3/4; yes

1931   1139;   GWOLADDLE, Thelma Joyce; 1929-Jan-6; yes; F; Kiowa; yes; 1/2; 4/4; 3/4; yes

1929   85;   HAAG, Bradford Bancroft; 1928-Oct-24; yes; M; Kiowa; yes; 4/4; 4/4; 4/4; yes

1929   1065;   HAUNPY, Farina Joyce; 1928-Oct-28; yes; F; Kiowa; yes; 4/4; 4/4; 4/4; yes

State __Oklahoma__ Reservation __Kiowa__ Agency or Jurisdiction __Kiowa__
Office of Indian Affairs Births Occurring Between the Dates of July 1, 1928 and
June 30, 1929 to Parents Enrolled at Jurisdiction

KEY: 1929 Census Roll Number; Surname and Given Name; Date of Birth; Live Birth (Yes or No); Sex; Tribe; Ward (yes or no); Degree of Father's blood; Degree of Mother's blood; Degree of Child's blood; At Jurisdiction Where Enrolled (yes or no); [If "no", where, if given]

1929   1530;   HAWZIOTA, Roland Lee; 1929-May-9; yes; M; Kiowa; yes; 4/4; Mex; 1/2; yes

1929   1094;   HEATH, Perry Lonseome[sic]; 1928-Sept-6; yes; M; Comanche; yes; 4/4; 4/4; 4/4; yes

1930   1390;   HENRY, Armand Berwyn; 1929-Aug-4; yes; M; Kiowa; yes; W; 4/4; 1/2; yes

1929   1135;   HOAHWAH, Carlton Howard; 1928-Sept-16; f[sic]; Comanche; yes; 4/4; 4/4; 4/4; yes

1929   1139;   HOKEAH, Eugene; 1929-Apr-9; yes; M; Kiowa; yes; 4/4; 4/4; 4/4; yes

1930   238;   HOPKINS, Amos Abe; 1929-Jan-5; yes; M; Kiowa; yes; W; 4/4; 1/2; yes[sic]; Lordsburg, N.Mex.

1929   1153;   HORSE, Myers; 1928-Sept-22; yes; M; Kiowa; yes; 4/4; 4/4; 4/4; yes

1929   1163;   HORSE, Virginia Mae; 1928-July-20; yes; F; Kiowa; yes; 4/4; 4/4; 4/4; yes

1929   1209;   HUMMINGBIRD, Jackson Floyd; 1928-Aug-27; yes; M; Kiowa; yes; 4/4; 4/4; 4/4; yes

1929   1707;   HUMMINGBIRD, Jerome; 1928-June-27; yes; M; Kiowa; yes; 4/4; 4/4; 4/4; yes

1929   1243;   JONES, John Calvin; 1928-Aug-5; yes; M; Kiowa; yes; 1/4; W; 1/8; yes

1929   2647;   JOHNSON, Jocelyn Ruth; 1928-Sept-6; yes; F; Kiowa; yes; W; 1/2; 1/4; yes

1929   1256;   KADAYSO, Raymond Wayne; 1928-Oct-21; yes; M; Apache & Kiowa; yes; 4/4; 4/4; 4/4; yes

1929   1276;   KARTY, Kenneth Kay; 1929-Feb-18; yes; M; Comanche & Kio; yes; 4/4; 3/4; 7/8; yes

1930   1873;   KAWAHQUO, Jobyna; 1928-Nov-14; yes; F; Kiowa; yes; 4/4; 4/4; 4/4; yes

State __Oklahoma__ Reservation __Kiowa__ Agency or Jurisdiction __Kiowa__
Office of Indian Affairs Births Occurring Between the Dates of July 1, 1928 and
June 30, 1929 to Parents Enrolled at Jurisdiction

KEY: 1929 Census Roll Number; Surname and Given Name; Date of Birth; Live Birth (Yes or No); Sex; Tribe; Ward (yes or no); Degree of Father's blood; Degree of Mother's blood; Degree of Child's blood; At Jurisdiction Where Enrolled (yes or no); [If "no", where, if given]

1930   1891;   KAUDLEKAULE, Rita; 1929-Nov-14; yes; F; Apache; yes; 4/4; 4/4; 4/4; yes

1929   1315;   KAULAITY, Mary Lee; 1929-Feb-19; yes; F; Kiowa; yes; 4/4; 4/4; 4/4; yes

1930   1956;   KAUYEDAUTY, Rosalie Grace; 1929; yes; F; Kiowa; yes; 4/4; 4/4; 4/4; yes

1930   2012;   KEITHTAHROCO, Mark; 1928-June-3; yes; M; Kiowa; yes; 4/4; 4/4; 4/4; yes

1929   3081;   KLINEKOLE, Gladys; 1928-Aug-24; yes; F; Apache; yes; 4/4; 4/4; 4/4; yes

1929   1434;   KOASSECHENY, Timothy Reuben; 1928-Dec-24; yes; M; Comanche; yes; 4/4; 4/4; 4/4; yes

See #
1929   881;   KODASEET, Ruth; 1928-Sept-11; yes; F; Kiowa; yes; Mex; Mex; Mex; yes

1930   2093;   KOMAHTY, Hartley; 1929-June-21; yes; M; Kiowa; yes; 4/4; 4/4; 4/4; yes

See #
1929   1762;   KOWENO, Robert John; 1928-Dec-9; yes; M; Comanche; yes; 4/4; 4/4; 4/4; yes

1929   3788;   LUNA, Hilburn; 1929-June-25; yes; M; Comanche; yes; Mex; Mex; Mex; yes

1930   2369;   MAHSETKY, Mansey; 1929-May-7; yes; M; Comanche; yes; 4/4; 4/4; 4/4; yes

See #
1929   1705;   MANNAKEI, Curtis; 1928-Nov-8; yes; M; Kiowa; yes; 4/4; 4/4; 4/4; yes

1929   1661;   MERRICK, Ramona Malcolm; 1928-July-3; yes; F; Comanche; yes; 3/4; W; 3/8; yes

State __Oklahoma__ Reservation __Kiowa__ Agency or Jurisdiction __Kiowa__
Office of Indian Affairs Births Occurring Between the Dates of July 1, 1928 and
June 30, 1929 to Parents Enrolled at Jurisdiction

KEY: 1929 Census Roll Number; Surname and Given Name; Date of Birth; Live Birth (Yes or No); Sex; Tribe; Ward (yes or no); Degree of Father's blood; Degree of Mother's blood; Degree of Child's blood; At Jurisdiction Where Enrolled (yes or no); [If "no", where, if given]

1929   1782;   MIHECOBY, Joyce; 1928-Feb-3; yes; F; Comanche; yes; 4/4; 4/4; 4/4; yes

See #
1929   1859;   MOPOPE, Poman Tresa; 1929-June-22; yes; F; Kiowa; yes; 4/4; 4/4; 4/4; yes

1929   2609;   MORRISON, Anna Lou; 1929-June-26; yes; F; Kiowa; yes; 4/4; 4/4; 4/4; yes

1929   1911;   MYERS, Lena May; 1928-Dec-7; yes; F; Comanche; yes; 1/4; W; 1/8; yes

1930   1045;   NECONIE, Georgie; 1929-Feb-22; yes; F; Kiowa; yes; 4/4; 4/4; 4/4; yes

1929   2006;   NESTELL, Chas Curtis; 1929-Mar-2; yes; M; Apache & Kiowa; yes; 4/4; 4/4; 4/4; yes

1929   2010;   NEVAQUAYA, Felix Thompson; 1928-Oct-16; yes; M; yes; Comanche; yes; 4/4; 4/4; 4/4; yes

1929   2015;   NEIDO, Wywena May; 1928-Dec-9; yes; F; Comanche; yes; 4/4; 4/4; 4/4; yes

1929   612;   OTIPPOBY, Robert Louis; 1929-Jan-4; yes; M; Comanche; yes; 4/4; 4/4; 4/4; yes

1929   997;   PADDLETY, Cloie Ruth; 1928-July-10; yes; F; Kiowa; yes; 4/4; 4/4; 4/4; yes

1929   999;   PADDLETY, Freda; 1928; yes; F; Kiowa; yes; 4/4; 4/4; 4/4; yes

1929   2131;   PAHCODDY, Irene; 1929-Feb-2; yes; F; Comanche; yes; 4/4; 4/4; 4/4; yes

1929   2135;   PAHCODDY, Juanita; 1928-Aug-14; yes; F; Comanche; yes; 4/4; 4/4; 4/4; yes

See #
1929   2132;   PAHCODDY, Mary Ann; 1929-Jan-1; yes; F; Comanche; yes; 4/4; 4/4; 4/4; yes

State __Oklahoma__ Reservation __Kiowa__ Agency or Jurisdiction __Kiowa__
Office of Indian Affairs Births Occurring Between the Dates of July 1, 1928 and
June 30, 1929 to Parents Enrolled at Jurisdiction

KEY: 1929 Census Roll Number; Surname and Given Name; Date of Birth; Live Birth (Yes or No); Sex; Tribe; Ward (yes or no); Degree of Father's blood; Degree of Mother's blood; Degree of Child's blood; At Jurisdiction Where Enrolled (yes or no); [If "no", where, if given]

1929   2158;   PAHDINGKEI, Myrtle May; 1928-Aug-1; yes; F; Kiowa; yes; 4/4; 4/4; 4/4; yes

1929   2227;   PARRIAECKIVIT, Benton June; 1928-July-1; yes; M; Comanche; yes; 4/4; 4/4; 4/4; yes

See #
1929   2271;   PEBEAHSY, Malcolm Melvin; 1927-June-1; yes; M; Comanche; yes; 4/4; 4/4; 4/4; yes

1929   2314;   PEKAH, Mada Louise; 1929-May-29; yes; F; Comanche; yes; 4/4; 4/4; 4/4; yes

1929   2347;   PERMAMSU, Esther Mae; 1929-Feb-23; yes; F; Comanche; yes; 4/4; 4/4; 4/4; yes

1929   2378;   PEWENAFKIT, Blossom; 1929-Mar-27; yes; F; Comanche & Apa; yes; 4/4; 4/4; 4/4; yes

1930   3288;   PEWEWARDY, Leatrice Joyce; 1929-June-28; yes; F; Kiowa; yes; 4/4; 4/4; 4/4; yes

1929   2405;   PEWO, Marie; 1928-July-20; yes; F; Comanche; yes; 4/4; 4/4; 4/4; yes

1929   2409;   PEWO, Revina; 1928-Oct-28; yes; F; Comanche & Kio; yes; 4/4; 4/4; 4/4; yes

1929   2415;   PINEZADDLETY, Wm Bissell; 1928-Oct-27; yes; M; Kiowa; yes; 4/4; 4/4; 4/4; yes

1929   1443;   PALMER, Clayton Edwards; 1928-Aug-18; yes; M; Kiowa; yes; 1/2; 4/4; 5/8; yes

1930   2427;   POAHWAY, Pay Balindo; 1928-Sept-19; yes; M; Comanche & Kio; yes; 4/4; 4/4; 4/4; yes

1930   3359;   POEMOCEAH, Apaletta; 1929-June-26; yes; F; Comanche; yes; 4/4; 4/4; 4/4; yes

1929   2443;   POEMOCEAH, Velma; 1928-Aug-16; yes; F; Comanche; yes; 4/4; 4/4; 4/4; yes

State Oklahoma   Reservation Kiowa   Agency or Jurisdiction Kiowa

Office of Indian Affairs Births Occurring Between the Dates of July 1, 1928 and June 30, 1929 to Parents Enrolled at Jurisdiction

KEY: 1929 Census Roll Number; Surname and Given Name; Date of Birth; Live Birth (Yes or No); Sex; Tribe; Ward (yes or no); Degree of Father's blood; Degree of Mother's blood; Degree of Child's blood; At Jurisdiction Where Enrolled (yes or no); [If "no", where, if given]

1930   3355;   POEMOCEAH, Kelly Waddell; 1929-Aug-19; yes; M; Comanche; yes; 4/4; 4/4; 4/4; yes

1929   2472;   POOLAW, Catherine; 1928-Nov-6; yes; F; Kiowa; yes 4/4; 4/4; 4/4; yes

1929   2494;   POPETSAITK, Agnes; 1928-Sept-8; yes; F; Kiowa; yes; 4/4; 4/4; 4/4; yes

1929   2489;   POPETSAITK, Florence; 1929-Apr-7; yes; F; Kiowa; yes; 4/4; 4/4; 4/4; yes

1929   2521;   POTIYE, Iris May; 1928-Nov-9; yes; F; Kiowa; yes; 4/4; 4/4; 4/4; yes

1929   1010;   PRENTISS, Flora Mina; 1929-Mar-29; yes; F; Kiowa; yes; 4/4; 4/4; 4/4; yes

1929   2548;   PUEBLO, Billie Malcolm; 1928-Aug-4; yes; M; Comanche; yes; 4/4; 4/4; 4/4; yes

1929   1881;   RIDDLE, Stanley; 1929-Feb-5; yes; M; Comanche; yes; W; 4/4; 1/2; yes

1929   2637;   RIVAZ, Benita; 1929-Mar-21; yes; F; Comanche; yes; Mex; Mex; Mex; yes

1929   2651;   RHOADES, Dorothy Lyzette; 1928-Oct-9; yes; F; Kiowa; yes; W; 1/2; 1/4; yes

1929   2611;   ROACHE, Marcus; 1929-Jan-21; yes; M; Comanche; yes; Mex; Mex; Mex; yes

1929   1706;   SAHDINGKEI, Daniel Roger; 1928-Aug-7; yes; M; Kiowa; yes; 4/4; 3/4; 7/8; yes

1929   2672;   SAHMAUNT, Geraldine Clare; 1929-Feb-28; yes; F; Kiowa; yes; 4/4; 4/4; 4/4; yes

1929   2695;   SANKADOTA, Patsy Ruth; 1929-Feb-23; yes; F; Kiowa; yes; 4/4; 4/4; 4/4; yes

Office of Indian Affairs Births Occurring Between the Dates of July 1, 1928 and
June 30, 1929 to Parents Enrolled at Jurisdiction

KEY: 1929 Census Roll Number; Surname and Given Name; Date of Birth; Live Birth (Yes or No); Sex; Tribe; Ward (yes or no); Degree of Father's blood; Degree of Mother's blood; Degree of Child's blood; At Jurisdiction Where Enrolled (yes or no); [If "no", where, if given]

See #

1929 2700; SAPCUT, Leland Virgil; [blank]; yes; M; Comanche; yes; 4/4; 4/4; 4/4; yes

1929 2712; SATEPAUHOODLE, Marland; 1929-Dec-30; yes; F; Kiowa; yes; 4/4; 4/4; 4/4; yes

1929 2739; SATOE, Alice; 1928-July-7; yes; F; Kiowa; yes; 4/4; 4/4; 4/4; yes

1929 2749; SATOE, Joseph Spurgeon; 1929-Mar-25; yes; M; Kiowa; yes; 4/4; 4/4; 4/4; yes

1929 2771; SAUPITTY, Louis Julian; 1928-Dec-31; yes; M; Comanche; yes; 4/4; 4/4; 4/4; yes

1929 2775; SAUPITTY, Leo; 1929-Apr-22; yes; M; Comanche; yes; 4/4; 4/4; 4/4; yes

1929 2812; SMOKEY, Yvonne; 1929-Mar-11; yes; F; Kiowa; yes; 4/4; 3/4; 7/8; yes

1929 2835; SOVO, Ida; 1929-Jan-7; yes; F; Comanche; yes; 4/4; 4/4; 4/4; yes

1929 1043; STARR, Rosana; 1928-July-3; yes; F; Kiowa; yes; 4/4; 4/4; 4/4; yes

1929 3942; TABBYTITE, Bert Hoover; 1928-July-15; yes; M; Kiowa; yes; 1/2; 4/4; 3/4; yes

1929 2868; TABBYTOSAVIT, Floy Juanita; 1929-Apr-21; yes; F; Comanche; yes; 4/4; 4/4; 4/4; yes

1929 2891; TAHAH, Rowena Mae; 1929-May-3; yes; F; Comanche; yes; 4/4; 4/4; 4/4; yes

1929 2912; TAHCHAWUICKAH, Rose Edith; 1929-Mar-3; yes; F; Comanche; yes; 4/4; 4/4; 4/4; yes

1929 2926; TAHDOOAHNYPAH, Gertrude; 1929-Mar-10; yes; F; Comanche; yes; 4/4; 4/4; 4/4; yes

1929 4096; TAHKOPOODLE, Mary Ruth; 1929-June-22; yes; F; Kiowa; yes; 4/4; 1/2; 3/4; yes

State ___Oklahoma___ Reservation ___Kiowa___ Agency or Jurisdiction ___Kiowa___
Office of Indian Affairs Births Occurring Between the Dates of July 1, 1928 and
June 30, 1929 to Parents Enrolled at Jurisdiction

KEY: 1929 Census Roll Number; Surname and Given Name; Date of Birth; Live Birth (Yes or No); Sex; Tribe; Ward (yes or no); Degree of Father's blood; Degree of Mother's blood; Degree of Child's blood; At Jurisdiction Where Enrolled (yes or no); [If "no", where, if given]

1929   2975;   TAHLO, Ralston; 1928-July-8; yes; M; Kiowa; yes; 4/4; 4/4; 4/4; yes

1921   2235;   TAHSEQUAW, Corwin; 1929-May-4; yes; M; Comanche; yes; 4/4; 4/4; 4/4; yes

1929   4178;   TAHQUECHI, Gordon Coleman; 1929-Mar-29; yes; M; Comanche; yes; 4/4; 4/4; 4/4; yes

1930   4242;   TAKEWAHPOOR, Maser; 1929-June-10; yes; M; Comanche; yes; 4/4; 4/4; 4/4; yes

1929   2049   TANEDOOAH, Vivian Joy; 1928-July-25; yes; F; Kiowa; yes; 4/4; 4/4; 4/4; yes

1929   3106;   TANEQUODLE, Velma; 1929-July-3; yes; F; Kiowa; yes; 4/4; 4/4; 4/4; yes

See #
1929   3020;   TOPPAH, Madalene; 1929-Apr-15; yes; F; Kiowa; yes; 4/4; 4/4; 4/4; yes

1930   4272;   TANEQUOOT, Patsy Ruth; 1928-Aug-25; yes; F; Kiowa; yes; 4/4; 4/4; 4/4; yes

1929   3153;   TARTSAH, Rudolph; 1928-Oct-31; yes; M; Apache; yes; 4/4; 4/4; 4/4; yes

1930   4365;   TEE, Lindy; 1929-June-2; yes; M; Apache; yes; 4/4; 4/4; 4/4; yes

1929   3227;   THOMPSON; 1928-Sept-28; yes; F; Kiowa; yes; 4/4; 4/4; 4/4; yes

1930   4525;   TODOME, Thelma; 1929-May-3; yes; F; Kiowa; yes; 4/4; 4/4; 4/4; yes

1929   3320;   TOEHAY, Thelma; 1928-Aug-6; yes; F; Kiowa; yes; 4/4; 4/4; 4/4; yes

1929   3324;   TOFPI, Harry Lee; 1928-Aug-10; yes; M; Kiowa; yes; 4/4; 4/4; 4/4; yes

1930   4546;   TOFPI, Ilona Yvonne; 1929-May-28; yes; F; Kiowa; yes; 4/4; 4/4; 4/4; yes

State __Oklahoma__ Reservation __Kiowa__ Agency or Jurisdiction __Kiowa__
Office of Indian Affairs Births Occurring Between the Dates of July 1, 1928 and
June 30, 1929 to Parents Enrolled at Jurisdiction

KEY: 1929 Census Roll Number; Surname and Given Name; Date of Birth; Live Birth (Yes or No); Sex; Tribe; Ward (yes or no); Degree of Father's blood; Degree of Mother's blood; Degree of Child's blood; At Jurisdiction Where Enrolled (yes or no); [If "no", where, if given]

1930   4578;   TOINTIGH, Thomas; 1929-June-20; yes; M; Kiowa; yes; 4/4; 4/4; 4/4; yes

1929   3373;   TOMAH, Kent Aurl; 1928-Dec-19; yes; M; Comanche; yes; 1/2; 4/4; 3/4; yes

1929   3407;   TONEMAH, Francis Chester; 1928-Nov-8; yes; M; Kiowa; yes; 4/4; 4/4; 4/4; yes

1929   3432;   TONGKEAMBA, Corrine Mae; 1929-Mar-9; yes; F; Kiowa; yes; 4/4; 4/4; 4/4; yes

1929   3436;   TONIPS, Juanita; 1929-Feb-13; yes; F; Kiowa & Com; yes; 4/4; 4/4; 4/4; yes

1929   3449;   TOOAHIMPAH, Alma; 1928-Sept-2; yes; F; Comanche; yes; 4/4; 4/4; 4/4; yes

1929   3466;   TOOENAPPER, Verl Lee; 1929-Feb-27; yes; M; Comanche; yes; 4/4; 4/4; 4/4; yes

1929   3511;   TOQUOTHLY, LaVerne; 1928-Sept-20; yes; M; Comanche; yes; 4/4; 4/4; 4/4; yes

       See #
1929   3525;   TOTITE, Clyde; 1928-Aug-29; yes; M; Comanche; yes; 4/4; 4/4; 4/4; yes

1929   4837;   TSATAKE, Lee Mennett; 1929-Mar-21; yes; M; Kiowa; yes; 4/4; 4/4; 4/4; yes

1929   3596;   TSATAKE, Vivian; 1928-July-1; yes; F; Kiowa; yes; 4/4; 4/4; 4/4; yes

1930   4911;   TOYEBO, Delores; 1929-May-4; yes; F; Kiowa; yes; 4/4; 4/4; 4/4; yes

1929   1365;   TOYEBO, Fern; 1929-Feb-24; yes; F; Kiowa; yes; 4/4; 4/4; 4/4; yes

1930   4350;   TAWKOYTY, Boulder; 1929-June-13; yes; M; Kiowa; yes; 4/4; 4/4; 4/4; yes

State __Oklahoma__ Reservation __Kiowa__ Agency or Jurisdiction __Kiowa__
Office of Indian Affairs Births Occurring Between the Dates of July 1, 1928 and
June 30, 1929 to Parents Enrolled at Jurisdiction

KEY: 1929 Census Roll Number; Surname and Given Name; Date of Birth; Live Birth (Yes or No); Sex; Tribe; Ward (yes or no); Degree of Father's blood; Degree of Mother's blood; Degree of Child's blood; At Jurisdiction Where Enrolled (yes or no); [If "no", where, if given]

1930   3567;   TREVINO, Christa Belle; 1929-Mar-15; yes; F; Comanche; yes;
               Mex; Mex; Mex; yes

1930   4902;   TSOODLE, Cleo Jean; 1929-June-9; yes; F; Kiowa; yes; 4/4; 4/4;
               4/4; yes

1929   3657;   TSOODLE, Glorietta; 1929-Apr-8; yes; F; Kiowa; yes; 4/4; 4/4; 4/4;
               yes

1929   2336;   VALDES, Wilberton; 1928-Aug-26; yes; M; Comanche; Mex; 4/4;
               1/2; yes

1929   3730;   WAHAHROCKAH, Billie Rose; 1929-Mar-24; yes; F; Comanche;
               yes; 4/4; 4/4; 4/4; yes

       See #
1929   3746;   WALLACE, Powhoneat; 1929-Aug-13; yes; M; Comanche; yes; 3/4;
               1/2; 5/8; yes

1929   3955;   WARE, Gerald; 1928-Oct-3; yes; M; Kiowa; yes; 4/4; 4/4; 4/4; yes

1929   3754;   WARE, Wesley Andrew; 1928-Oct-20; yes; M; Kiowa; yes; 4/4; 4/4;
               4/4; [blank]

1930   5069;   WERHEVAHWERMY, Naoma; 1929-Mar-22; yes; F; Comanche;
               yes; 4/4; 4/4; 4/4; yes

1931   3598;   WHITEFOX, Virgil; 1929-Feb-1; yes; M; Kiowa; yes; 4/4; 4/4; 4/4;
               yes

1929   2371;   WILLIAMS, Betty Jean; 1928-July-10; yes; F; Comanche; yes; W;
               4/4; 1/2; yes

1929   2675;   WILLIAMS, Frances Harriet; 1928-Oct-22; yes; F; Kiowa; yes; 4/4;
               4/4; 4/4; yes

1929   3946;   YEAHOUO, Stanley; 1929-Apr-11; yes; M; Kiowa; yes; 4/4; 4/4;
               4/4; yes

1930   760;   YOKESUITE, Gloria Marie; 1928-May-11; yes; F; Comanche; yes;
               4/4; 4/4; 4/4; yes

State___Oklahoma___ Reservation ___Kiowa___ Agency or Jurisdiction ___Kiowa___
Office of Indian Affairs Births Occurring Between the Dates of July 1, 1928 and
June 30, 1929 to Parents Enrolled at Jurisdiction

KEY: 1929 Census Roll Number; Surname and Given Name; Date of Birth; Live Birth (Yes or No); Sex; Tribe; Ward (yes or no); Degree of Father's blood; Degree of Mother's blood; Degree of Child's blood; At Jurisdiction Where Enrolled (yes or no); [If "no", where, if given]

1930   5409;   YOUNICUT, Grace Marie; 1929-June-2; yes; F; Comanche; yes; 4/4; 4/4; 4/4; yes

1929   3995;   ZOTIGH, Wm Baggett; 1929-Apr-24; yes; M; Kiowa; yes; 4/4; 4/4; 4/4; yes

KIOWA INDIAN AGENCY

Kiowa Reservation

Oklahoma

1930

BIRTH ROLL
Kiowa, Comanche, Apache and
Fort Sill Apache Indians.

State __OKLAHOMA__ Reservation __Kiowa__ Agency or Jurisdiction __Kiowa__
Office of Indian Affairs Births Occurring Between the Dates of July 1, 1929 and
June 30, 1930 to Parents Enrolled at Jurisdiction

KEY: 1930 Census Roll Number; Surname and Given Name; Date of Birth; Live Birth (Yes or No); Sex; Tribe; Ward (yes or no); Degree of Father's blood; Degree of Mother's blood; Degree of Child's blood; At Jurisdiction Where Enrolled (yes or no); [If "no", where, if given]

1930   68;   AHHAITTY, Anna Mary; 1930-Jan-18; yes; F; Kiowa; yes; 4/4; 4/4; 4/4; yes

1930   75;   AHKEAHBO, Betty Lou; 1929-Oct-7; yes; F; Kiowa; yes; 4/4; 4/4; 4/4; yes

1930   131;   AITSON, Forest; 1930-Feb-24; yes; M; Kiowa; yes; 3/4; 4/4; 7/8; yes

1930   158;   AKONETO, Lansing; 1930-Jan-16; yes; M; Kiowa; yes; 4/4; 4/4; 4/4; yes

1930   168;   AKONETO, Leona Rose; 1929-July-18; yes; F; Kiowa; yes; 4/4; 4/4; 4/4; yes

1930   3865;   AKERS, Jesse; 1930-Jan-15; yes; M; Comanche; yes; W; 1/2; 1/4; yes

1930   193;   APAUTY, Velma; 1929-Nov-23; yes; F; Kiowa; yes; 4/4; 4/4; 4/4; yes

See #
1930   241;   ASANEHIDDLE, Mary Bell; 1930-Jan-20; yes; F; Kiowa; yes; 4/4; 4/4; 4/4; yes

1930   259;   ASETAMMY, Mary Olivia; 1930-Feb-28; yes; F; Kiowa; yes; 4/4; 4/4; 4/4; yes

1930   1612;   ATCHHAVIT, Rebecca Jean; 1929-July-9; yes; F; Comanche; yes; 4/4; 4/4; 4/4; yes

1930   320;   ATETEWUTHTAKEWA, Zona; 1930-Feb-28; yes; F; Kiowa; yes; 4/4; 4/4; 4/4; yes

1931   300;   ATTOCKNIE, Kay; 1930-Apr-29; yes; F; Kiowa; yes; 4/4; 4/4; 4/4; yes

1930   345;   AUCHCHIAH, Titus; 1929-July-29; yes; F; Comanche; yes; 4/4; 4/4; 4/4; yes

1930   381;   AUNGUOE, Cormele; 1930-Mar-4; yes; M; Kiowa; yes; 4/4; 4/4; 4/4; yes

State __OKLAHOMA__ Reservation __Kiowa__ Agency or Jurisdiction __Kiowa__
Office of Indian Affairs Births Occurring Between the Dates of July 1, 1929 and
June 30, 1930 to Parents Enrolled at Jurisdiction

KEY: 1930 Census Roll Number; Surname and Given Name; Date of Birth; Live Birth (Yes or No); Sex; Tribe; Ward (yes or no); Degree of Father's blood; Degree of Mother's blood; Degree of Child's blood; At Jurisdiction Where Enrolled (yes or no); [If "no", where, if given]

1930   231;   AUGUOE, Anita Joyce; 1930-Mar-1; yes; F; Kiowa; yes; 4/4; 4/4; 4/4; yes

1931   3312;   BEARTRACK, Edmond Raymond; 1930-May-1; yes; M; Kiowa; yes; 4/4; 4/4; 4/4; yes

1931   2393;   BIG WHIP, Paul; 1930-June-17; yes; M; Kiowa; yes; Mex; 4/4; 1/2; yes

1931   1972;   BOHAY, Lena Jean; 1930-Mar-29; yes; F; Kiowa; yes; 4/4; 4/4; 4/4; yes

1930   504;   BOINTY, Ronald Jack; 1929-Dec-17; yes; M; Kiowa; yes; 1/2; 4/4; 3/4; yes

1931   163;   BOTONE, Genus Franklin; 1930-May-11; yes; M; Kiowa; yes; 3/4; 3/4; 3/4; yes

1930   1277;   BROWN, John Richard; 1929-Sept-12; yes; M; Comanche; yes; Mex; Mex; Mex; yes

1931   2035;   BURGESS, Betty Lou; 1930-Jan-8; yes; F; Comanche; yes; 4/4; 4/4; 4/4; yes

1931   587;   CADDO, Rudolph; 1930-Mar-16; yes; M; Comanche; yes; 4/4; 4/4; 4/4; yes

1930   619;   CANNON, Budda Gean; 1930-Feb-3; yes; M; Kiowa; yes; 1/2; 4/4; 3/4; yes

1930   784;   CHOCKPOYAH, Marie Joyce; 1930-Feb-26; yes; F; Comanche; yes; 4/4; 4/4; 4/4; yes

1930   802;   CLARK, Alfred Alan; 1930-Feb-26; yes; M; Comanche; yes; 1/2; [?]; 1/4; yes

1931   636;   CHIBITTY, Stephen; 1930-Apr-25; yes; M; Kiowa; yes; 4/4; 4/4; 4/4; yes

1931   733;   CONNAHVICHNAH, Jeanette; 1930-May-24; yes; F; Comanche; yes; 4/4; 4/4; 4/4; yes

State __OKLAHOMA__ Reservation __Kiowa__ Agency or Jurisdiction __Kiowa__
Office of Indian Affairs Births Occurring Between the Dates of July 1, 1929 and
June 30, 1930 to Parents Enrolled at Jurisdiction

KEY: 1930 Census Roll Number; Surname and Given Name; Date of Birth; Live Birth (Yes or No); Sex; Tribe; Ward (yes or no); Degree of Father's blood; Degree of Mother's blood; Degree of Child's blood; At Jurisdiction Where Enrolled (yes or no); [If "no", where, if given]

1930   875;   CONNYWERDY, Tyler; 1930-Feb-9; yes; M; Comanche; yes; 4/4; 4/4; 4/4; yes

1930   920;   COOSEWON, Kenneth Guy; 1929-Sept-29; yes; M; Comanche; yes; 4/4; 4/4; 4/4; yes

1930   924;   COOSEWON, Patsy Ruth; 1929-Sept-22; yes; F; Comanche; yes; 4/4; 4/4; 4/4; yes

1930   789;   COOSEWON, Mabel Jean; 1930-June-5; yes; F; Comanche; yes; 4/4; 4/4; 4/4; yes

         See #
1930   4230;   COMANCHE, Alice; 1929-Sept-29; yes; F; Apache; yes; 4/4; 4/4; 4/4; yes

1930   987;   DAUKEI, Margeline; 1930-Feb-24; yes; F; Kiowa; yes; 4/4; 4/4; 4/4; yes

1930   3798;   ELMA, Neoma Jean; 1929-Oct-12; yes; F; Comanche; yes; W; Mex; & Mex; yes

1930   1176;   EMHOOLAH, John, Jr; 1929-Oct-12; yes; M; Kiowa; yes; 4/4; 4/4; 4/4; yes

1930   1186;   EMTADDLE, Eugene; 1929-Aug-25; yes; M; Kiowa; yes; 4/4; 4/4; 4/4; yes

1930   4367;   EVANS, Arvol, Jr; 1930-Jan-31; yes; M; Comanche; yes; [?]; 1/4; 1/8; yes

1931   246;   FARRALLA, William; 1929-Dec-14; yes; M; Comanche; yes; Mex; Mex; Mex; yes

1931   1014;   FULLER, Shirley Ann; 1930-June-6; yes; F; Comanche; yes; 1/2; [?]; 1/4; yes

1930   1337;   GUYDILKON, Medford Anthony; 1929-Oct-3; yes; M; Fort Sill Apache; yes; 4/4; 4/4; 4/4; yes

1931   1097;   GOINKEEN, David Lee; 1930-Jan-5; yes; M; Kiowa; yes; 4/4; 4/4; 4/4; yes

State __OKLAHOMA__ Reservation __Kiowa__ Agency or Jurisdiction __Kiowa__
Office of Indian Affairs Births Occurring Between the Dates of July 1, 1929 and
June 30, 1930 to Parents Enrolled at Jurisdiction

KEY: 1930 Census Roll Number; Surname and Given Name; Date of Birth; Live Birth (Yes or No); Sex; Tribe; Ward (yes or no); Degree of Father's blood; Degree of Mother's blood; Degree of Child's blood; At Jurisdiction Where Enrolled (yes or no); [If "no", where, if given]

1930   1371;   GOOMBI, Lillian Marie; 1929-Aug-4; yes; F; Kiowa; yes; 3/4; 3/4; 3/4; yes

1931   1121;   GUOLADDLE, Wm Newton; 1930-June-25; yes; M; Kiowa; yes; 3/4; 1/2; 5/8; yes

1930   3165;   GUOLADDLE, Lindbergh; 1930-Feb-14; yes; M; Kiowa; yes; 4/4; 4/4; 4/4; yes

        See #
1930   1460;   HAINTA; 1930-Apr-16; yes; F; Kiowa; yes; 4/4; 4/4; 4/4; yes

1930   1512;   HAUGOOAH, Bessie; 1930-Jan-19; yes; F; Kiowa; yes; 4/4; 4/4; 4/4; yes

1930   1550;   HEATH, Rosa Ann; 1929-Oct-22; yes; F; Comanche; yes; 4/4; 4/4; 4/4; yes

1930   1554;   HEMINOKOKY, Reba Jo; 1930-Feb-20; yes; F; Comanche; yes; 4/4; 4/4; 4/4; yes

1930   1638;   HOAHWAH, Joebyna; 1930-Feb-24; yes; F; Comanche; yes; 4/4; 4/4; 4/4; yes

        See #
1930   1647;   HOKEAH, Perry Jack; 1930-May-2; f[sic]; Kiowa; yes; 4/4; 4/4; 4/4; yes

1931   2912;   HOAUN, Adrian Richard; 1930-Jan-26; yes; M; Kiowa; yes; 4/4; 4/4; 4/4; yes

1931   1303;   HOVAKAH, Waidy Overtin; 1930-Jan-25; yes; F; yes; Kiowa; yes; 4/4; 4/4; 4/4; yes

1930   1721;   HUMMINGBIRD, Carroll; 1930-Mar-9; yes; F; Kiowa; yes; 4/4; 4/4; 4/4; yes

1931   1321;   HUMMINGBIRD, Doris; 1930-Apr-26; yes; F; Kiowa; yes; 4/4; 4/4; 4/4; yes

1930   3610;   JOHNSON, Onida Mae; 1930-Mar-31; yes; F; Kiowa; yes; [?]; 1/2; 1/4; yes

Office of Indian Affairs Births Occurring Between the Dates of July 1, 1929 and
June 30, 1930 to Parents Enrolled at Jurisdiction

KEY: 1930 Census Roll Number; Surname and Given Name; Date of Birth; Live Birth (Yes or No); Sex; Tribe; Ward (yes or no); Degree of Father's blood; Degree of Mother's blood; Degree of Child's blood; At Jurisdiction Where Enrolled (yes or no); [If "no", where, if given]

1930   1801;   JONES, Lewis Cozad; 1930-Mar-29; yes; M; Kiowa; yes; 3/4; 3/4; 3/4; yes

1930   2124;   KASECHATA, Nada; 1930-Mar-7; yes; F; Comanche; yes; 4/4; 4/4; 4/4; yes

1931   1428;   KAUBIN, Elaine Belle; 1930-May-1; yes; F; Kiowa; yes; 4/4; 4/4; 4/4; yes

1931   1474;   KAULAY, Ronald C; 1930-Apr-8; yes; M; Kiowa; yes; 4/4; 4/4; 4/4; yes

1931   1468;   KAULAY, Wanada Leona; 1930-Feb-18; yes; F; Kiowa; yes; 4/4; 4/4; 4/4; yes

1930   89;   KAULAITY, Thelma Jean; 1929-Sept-4; yes; F; Kiowa; yes; 4/4; 4/4; 4/4; yes

1931   2260;   KEAHBONE, Donald D; 1930-Apr-11; yes; M; Kiowa; yes; 4/4; 4/4; 4/4; yes

1930   1977;   KEAHBONE, Refred Aaron; 1929-Aug-17; yes; M; Kiowa; yes; 4/4; 4/4; 4/4; yes

See #
1930   4224;   KLINEKOLE, Mary; 1930-June-2; yes; F; Apache; yes; 4/4; 4/4; 4/4; yes

1930   2057;   KOASSECHONY, Lila Jo; 1930-Jan-21; yes; F; Comanche; yes; 4/4; 4/4; 4/4; yes

1930   1194;   KODASEET, Cleo; 1930-Jan-31; yes; F; Kiowa; yes; 3/4; 4/4; 7/8; yes

1930   2128;   KOSECHEQUETAH, Billy; 1930-Apr-2; yes; M; Comanche; yes; 4/4; 4/4; 4/4; yes

1931   1828;   LAMENZANA, Ivaine Joy; 1930-Apr-17; yes; F; Comanche; yes; Mex; 3/4; 3/8; yes

1931   2435;   LEFTHAND, Irene; 1930-June-30; yes; F; Kiowa; yes; 4/4; 4/4; 4/4; yes

State __OKLAHOMA__ Reservation __Kiowa__ Agency or Jurisdiction __Kiowa__
Office of Indian Affairs Births Occurring Between the Dates of July 1, 1929 and
June 30, 1930 to Parents Enrolled at Jurisdiction

KEY: 1930 Census Roll Number; Surname and Given Name; Date of Birth; Live Birth (Yes or No); Sex; Tribe; Ward (yes or no); Degree of Father's blood; Degree of Mother's blood; Degree of Child's blood; At Jurisdiction Where Enrolled (yes or no); [If "no", where, if given]

1930   2468;   MAYNAHONAH, Ruth; 1930-Feb-20; yes; F; Apache; yes; 4/4; 4/4; 4/4; yes

1930   2590;   MOBEADLEMAH, Caroline Mae; 1929-Dec-12; yes; F; Kiowa; yes; 4/4; 4/4; 4/4; yes

1930   3255;   MOORE, Carl; 1930-Feb-5; yes; M; Comanche; yes; 4/4; 4/4; 4/4; yes

        See #
1930   2747;   NAHNO; 1930-June-13; yes; F; Comanche; yes; 4/4; 4/4; 4/4; yes

1930   2803;   NECONIE, Adaline; 1930-Jan-29; yes; F; Kiowa; yes; 4/4; 4/4; 4/4; yes

1930   2806;   NECONIE, Charles; 1929-July-22; yes; M; Kiowa; yes; 4/4; 4/4; 4/4; yes

1930   425;   NEWSOME, Wm Riley; 1929-Dec-19; yes; M; Kiowa; yes; W; 1/2; 1/4; yes

1930   3024;   PAHDOPONY, Linda Joy; 1930-Mar-11; yes; F; Comanche; yes; 4/4; 4/4; 4/4; yes

1931   3507;   PARKER, Henry Lem; 1930-Mar-29; yes; M; Comanche; yes; 1/2; 1/2; 1/2; yes

1930   70;   PAUKUNE, Ralph; 1930-Mar-9; yes; M; Kiowa; yes; 1/2; 4/4; 3/4; yes

1930   3299;   PEWO, Gloria Etta; 1929-Oct-29; yes; F; Comanche; yes; 4/4; 4/4; 4/4; yes

1931   2600;   PEWO, Wilbur, Jr; 1930-June-13; yes; M; yes; Comanche; yes; 4/4; 4/4; 4/4; yes

1930   3331;   POAFOYBITTY, Wm Reynolds; 1930-Mar-3; yes; M; Comanche; yes; 4/4; 4/4; 4/4; yes

1930   903;   POLLOCK, Clyde Franklin; 1929-Oct-13; yes; M; M; Comanche; yes; W; Mex; W & Mex; yes

State __OKLAHOMA__ Reservation __Kiowa__ Agency or Jurisdiction __Kiowa__
Office of Indian Affairs Births Occurring Between the Dates of July 1, 1929 and
June 30, 1930 to Parents Enrolled at Jurisdiction

KEY: 1930 Census Roll Number; Surname and Given Name; Date of Birth; Live Birth (Yes or No); Sex; Tribe; Ward (yes or no); Degree of Father's blood; Degree of Mother's blood; Degree of Child's blood; At Jurisdiction Where Enrolled (yes or no); [If "no", where, if given]

1930   3476;   QUANNANEMY WERMY, Jerry; 1930-Jan-9; yes; M; Comanche; yes; 4/4; 4/4; 4/4; yes

1930   3498;   QUERDIBITTY, Jed; 1929-Oct-4; yes; M; Comanche; yes; 4/4; 4/4; 4/4; yes

1931   450;   QUETONE, Frances Lucile; 1929-Aug-23; yes; F; Kiowa; yes; 1/2; 1/2; 1/2; yes

1931   1230;   ROBBLES, Ralph; 1930-Apr-12; yes; M; Comanche; yes; Mex; Mex; Mex; yes

1930   3674;   SAPCUT, Loraine; 1929-Sept-27; yes; F; Comanche; yes; 4/4; 4/4; 4/4; yes

1930   3680;   SARYERVINNE, Houston; 1929-Sept-17; yes; M; Comanche; yes; 4/4; 4/4; 4/4; yes

1930   4187;   SAOUPITTY, Vivian Verda; 1930-Jan-6; yes; F; Comanche; yes; 4/4; 4/4; 4/4; yes

1930   125;   SHERIDAN, Thomas; 1929-Nov-18; yes; M; Kiowa; yes; 4/4; 4/4; 4/4; yes

1931   2149;   SHORTNECK, Roscoe; 1930-May-31; yes; M; Kiowa; yes; 4/4; 4/4; 4/4; yes

       See #
1930   3149;   STUMBLING BEAR, Lavinia; 1930-June-29; yes; F; Kiowa; yes; 4/4; 4/4; 4/4; yes

1930   4153;   SUTTON, Catherine Pauline; 1929-Oct-22; yes; F; Kiowa; yes; 4/4; 4/4; 4/4; yes

1931   3059;   TABBYTITE, Rose Marie; 1930-June-10; yes; F; Comanche; yes; Mex; 1/2; 1/4; yes

1931   3090;   TAH, Frances Owen; 1930-June-28; yes; M; Apache; yes; 4/4; 4/4; 4/4; yes

1931   3112;   TAHBONEMAH, Marland; 1930-Apr-27; yes; M; Kiowa; yes; 4/4; 4/4; 4/4; yes

State __OKLAHOMA__ Reservation __Kiowa__ Agency or Jurisdiction __Kiowa__
Office of Indian Affairs Births Occurring Between the Dates of July 1, 1929 and
June 30, 1930 to Parents Enrolled at Jurisdiction

KEY: 1930 Census Roll Number; Surname and Given Name; Date of Birth; Live Birth (Yes or No); Sex; Tribe; Ward (yes or no); Degree of Father's blood; Degree of Mother's blood; Degree of Child's blood; At Jurisdiction Where Enrolled (yes or no); [If "no", where, if given]

1931   3150;   TAHDOOAHNYPAH, Blanche Elizabeth; 1930-June-18; yes; F; Comanche; yes; 4/4; 4/4; 4/4; yes

1931   3198;   TAHMAHKERA, Leatrice Joy; 1931-May-10; yes; F; Comanche; yes; 4/4; 4/4; 4/4; yes

1931   2370;   THOMPSON, Mathew; 1930-May-8; yes; M; Kiowa; yes; 4/4; 4/4; 4/4; yes

1931   3532;   TODEESSY, Nicholas; 1929-Oct-23; yes; M; Comanche; yes; 4/4; 4/4; 4/4; yes

1930   4605;   TOMAH, Jaunita Eleanor; 1930-Feb-7; yes; F; Comanche; yes; 1/2; 4/4; 3/4; yes

1930   4604;   TOMAH, Verneta Ruth; 1930-Feb-7; yes; F; Comanche; yes; 1/2; 4/4; 3/4; yes

1930   4615;   TOMAHSAH, John Alden; 1939-July-5; yes; M; Comanche; yes; 4/4; 4/4; 4/4; yes

1930   4623;   TONAHCAT, Thela May; 1929-Sept-29; yes; F; Kiowa; yes; 4/4; 4/4; 4/4; yes

1930   4640;   TONEMAH, John Orin; 1930-Jan-18; yes; M; Kiowa; yes; 4/4; 4/4; 4/4; yes

1930   4687;   TOOAHIMPAN, Veokra; 1929-Dec-1; yes; F; Comanche; yes; 4/4; 4/4; 4/4; yes

1930   3219;   TYPECONNIC, Verne Debrio; 1929-Oct-29; yes; M; Comanche; yes; 4/4; 4/4; 4/4; yes

1930   4730;   TOPETCHY, Gary Mihesuah; 1929-Nov-17; f[sic]; Comanche; yes; 4/4; 4/4; 4/4; yes

1931   3750;   TOPPAH, Ruth Wamsey; 1930-Mar-11; yes; F; Kiowa; yes; 4/4; 4/4; 4/4; yes

1930   4783;   TOYEBO, Patricia; 1929-Sept-23; yes; F; Kiowa; yes; 4/4; 4/4; 4/4; yes

State __OKLAHOMA__ Reservation __Kiowa__ Agency or Jurisdiction __Kiowa__
Office of Indian Affairs Births Occurring Between the Dates of July 1, 1929 and
June 30, 1930 to Parents Enrolled at Jurisdiction

KEY: 1930 Census Roll Number; Surname and Given Name; Date of Birth; Live Birth (Yes or No); Sex; Tribe; Ward (yes or no); Degree of Father's blood; Degree of Mother's blood; Degree of Child's blood; At Jurisdiction Where Enrolled (yes or no); [If "no", where, if given]

1931   3813;   TSALATE, Imogene; 1929-July-13; yes; F; Kiowa; yes; 4/4; 4/4; 4/4; yes

1931   3827;   TSATIGH, Mary Ruth; 1920-June-24; yes; F; Kiowa; yes; 4/4; 4/4; 4/4; yes

1931   3838;   TSATAKE, Stella May; 1930-Apr-4; yes; F; Kiowa; yes; 4/4; 4/4; 4/4; yes

1930   4851;   TSOTIGH, Lorene; 1930-Feb-2; yes; F; Kiowa; yes; 4/4; 4/4; 4/4; yes

1930   5284;   WACKMETOOAH, Arlene; 1929-Dec-29; yes; F; Comanche; yes; 4/4; 4/4; 4/4; yes

1930   5011;   WAVE, Cornelia Jean; 1929-Oct-4; yes; F; Kiowa; yes; 3/4; 1/2; 5/8; yes

See #
1930   5071;   WERMY, Billy Murphy; 1930-May-20; yes; M; Comanche; yes; 4/4; 4/4; 4/4; yes

1931   946;   WHITE, Samuel; 1930-Apr-5; yes; M; Kiowa; yes; W; 4/4; 1/2; yes

1931   3046;   WHITESHIELD, Sophia Lee; 1930-Apr-20; yes; F; Apache; yes; 4/4; 4/4; 4/4; yes

1930   453;   WILKINSON, Donna Ann; 1939-July-8; yes; F; Comanche; yes; W; 1/4; 1/8; yes

1930   5327;   WOOEHTAKEWAHBITTY, Neta June; 1930-Jan-17; yes; F; Comanche; yes; 4/4; 4/4; 4/4; yes

1931   4220;   YERNIPCUT, Ramona Marie; 1930-Apr-2; yes; F; Comanche; yes; 4/4; 4/4; 4/4; yes

1930   1632;   YOUNGMAN, Rosella Adella; 1929-July-26; yes; F; Comanche; yes; 4/4; 4/4; 4/4; yes

See #
1930   4255;   TANEDOOAH, Ruby; 1929-Oct-9; yes; F; Kiowa; yes; 4/4; 4/4; 4/4; yes

KIOWA INDIAN AGENCY

Kiowa Reservation

Oklahoma

1931

BIRTH ROLL
Kiowa, Comanche, Apache and
Fort Sill Apache Indians

State __Oklahoma__ Reservation __Kiowa__ Agency or Jurisdiction __Kiowa__
Office of Indian Affairs Births Occurring Between the Dates of April 1, 1930 and
March 31, 1931 to Parents Enrolled at Jurisdiction

KEY: 1931 Census Roll Number; Surname and Given Name; Date of Birth; Live Birth (Yes or No); Sex; Tribe; Ward (yes or no); Degree of Father's blood; Degree of Mother's blood; Degree of Child's blood; At Jurisdiction Where Enrolled (yes or no); [If "no", where, if given]

1931   44;   AHGOOM, Ruby Ruth; 1930-July-18; yes; F; Kiowa; yes; 4/4; 4/4; 4/4; yes

1931   56;   AHHAITY, Merlin; 1930-Dec-23; yes; M; Kiowa; yes; 4/4; 4/4; 4/4; yes

1931   101;   AHTONE, Nellie; 1930-Dec-19; yes; F; Kiowa; yes; 1/2; 1/4; 3/4; yes

1931   134;   AITSON, Lucius Weeks; 1930-Dec-8; yes; M; Kiowa; yes; 3/4; 3/4; 3/4; yes

1931   173;   AMAUTY, Billie Gene; 1930-July-19; yes; F; Kiowa; yes; 4/4; 4/4; 4/4; yes

1931   218;   ASENAP, Winifred; 1930-Aug-15; yes; F; Comanche; yes; 3/4; 3/4; 3/4; yes

1931   261;   ASEWAYNAH, Henry Rudolph; 1930-July-4; yes; M; Comanche; yes; 1/2; 1/2; 1/2; yes

1931   300;   ATTOCKNIE, Kay; 1930-Apr-29; yes; F; Comanche; yes; 4/4; 4/4; 4/4; yes

1931   347;   AUNCUOE, Charlene Fay; 1930-Aug-8; yes; F; Apache; yes; 4/4; 4/4; 4/4; yes

1931   359;   AUTAUBO, Laveda Jean; 1930-June-18; yes; F; Kiowa; yes; 4/4; 4/4; 4/4; yes

1931   362;   AUTAUBO, Geo Clay; 1931-Feb-23; yes; M; Kiowa; yes; 4/4; 4/4; 4/4; yes

1931   2855;   BANTISTA, Rudolph; 1930-Sept-24; yes; M; Kiowa; yes; 4/4; W; 1/2; yes

1931   3312;   BEARTRACK, Edmond Raymond; 1930-May-1; yes; M; Kiowa; yes; 4/4; 4/4; 4/4; yes

1931   2393;   BIGWHIP, Paul; 1930-June-17; yes; M; Kiowa; yes; [?]; 5/8; 5/16; yes

1931   425;   BLACKSTAR, Carnela; 1930-Aug-22; yes; F; Comanche; yes; 4/4; 4/4; 4/4; yes

85

State __Oklahoma__ Reservation __Kiowa__ Agency or Jurisdiction __Kiowa__
Office of Indian Affairs Births Occurring Between the Dates of April 1, 1930 and
March 31, 1931 to Parents Enrolled at Jurisdiction

KEY: 1931 Census Roll Number; Surname and Given Name; Date of Birth; Live Birth (Yes or No); Sex; Tribe; Ward (yes or no); Degree of Father's blood; Degree of Mother's blood; Degree of Child's blood; At Jurisdiction Where Enrolled (yes or no); [If "no", where, if given]

See #
193   466;   BOSIN, Corrine Ann; 1930-Sept-7; yes; F; Comanche; yes; 4/4; 4/4; 4/4; yes

1931   163;   BOTONE, Genus Franklin; 1930-May-11; Kiowa; yes; 4/4; 4/4; 4/4; yes

See #
1931   596;   BULLBEAR, Cornelius; 1930-Oct-8; yes; M; Kiowa; yes; 4/4; 4/4; 4/4; yes

1931   3346; CABLE, Bert, Jr; 1930-Nov-9; yes; M; Comanche; yes; 3/4; 4/4; 7/8; yes

1931   501;   CADDO, Rose Mae; 1930-Nov-25; yes; F; Comanche; yes; 4/4; W; 1/2; yes

1931   1105; CHANEY, Ralph; 1930-Aug-6; yes; M; Kiowa; yes; [?]; 4/4; 1/2; yes

1930   604;   CHAPPABITTY, Betty Lou; 1930-Dec-29; yes; F; Comanche; yes; 4/4; 4/4; 4/4; yes

1931   622;   CHEMAH, Clyde Lee; 1930-Nov-18; yes; M; Comanche; yes; 4/4; [?]; 1/2; yes

1931   636;   CHIBITTY, Stephen; 1930-Apr-25; yes; M; Comanche; yes; 4/4; 4/4; 4/4; yes

1931   679;   CLARK, Nina Alice; 1930-Nov-25; yes; F; Comanche; yes; 1/2; 1/2; 1/2; yes

1931   889;   CLEVELAND, Tessie May; 1931-Jan-25; yes; F; Kiowa; yes; 4/4; 4/4; 4/4; yes

1931   733;   CONNAHVICHNAH, Jeanette; 1930-May-24; yes; F; Comanche; yes; 4/4; 4/4; 4/4; yes

1931   756;   CONOVER, Freddie Joe; 1930-Dec-15; yes; M; Comanche; yes; Mex & W; Mex & W; Mex & W; yes

1931   776;   CONOWOOP, Delores; 1931-Feb-1; yes; F; Comanche; yes; 4/4; 4/4; 4/4; yes

86

State __Oklahoma__ Reservation __Kiowa__ Agency or Jurisdiction __Kiowa__
Office of Indian Affairs Births Occurring Between the Dates of April 1, 1930 and
March 31, 1931 to Parents Enrolled at Jurisdiction

KEY: 1931 Census Roll Number; Surname and Given Name; Date of Birth; Live Birth (Yes or No); Sex; Tribe; Ward (yes or no); Degree of Father's blood; Degree of Mother's blood; Degree of Child's blood; At Jurisdiction Where Enrolled (yes or no); [If "no", where, if given]

1931   789;   COOSEWON, Mabel Jean; 1930-June-5; yes; F; Comanche; yes; 4/4; 4/4; 4/4; yes

1931   3066;   CRAWFORD, LaDenna Vita; 1931-Feb-15; yes; F; Comanche; yes; W; 1/4; 1/8; yes

1931   825;   DAUGOMAH, Mamie; 1931-Jan-7; yes; F; Kiowa; yes; 4/4; 4/4; 4/4; yes

1931   909;   DAYETO, Juanita; 1930-Aug-1; yes; F; Kiowa; yes; 4/4; 4/4; 4/4; yes

1931   894;   DOYEBI, Abbie; 1930-Nov-13; yes; F; Kiowa; yes; 4/4; 4/4; 4/4; yes

1931   936;   EMHE, Mary Ruth; 1930-Dec-18; yes; F; Kiowa; yes; 4/4; 4/4; 4/4; yes

1931   1184;   FAWBUSH, Jeriyah Dedodge; 1930-Sept-9; yes; M; Comanche; yes; [?]; 4/4; 1/2; yes

1931   3396;   FRANKLIN, Colonel Mone; 1931-Jan-21; yes; M; Kiowa; yes; [?]; 1/2; 1/4; yes

1931   1011;   FULLER, Ronald Walker; 1930-Nov-18; yes; M; Comanche; yes; [?]; 1/8; 3/8; yes

1931   1014;   FULLER, Shirley Ann; 1930-June-6; yes; F; Comanche; yes; 1/2; W; 1/4; yes

1931   1020;   GALLAHER, Willard Andrez; 1931-Feb-9; yes; M; Kiowa; yes; 1/2; 1/2; 1/2; yes

1931   721;   GOVER, Pauline Zella; 1930-Aug-8; yes; F; Comanche; yes; 4/4; 4/4; 4/4; yes

1931   1121;   GWOLADDLE, Wm Newton; 1930-June-23; yes; M; Kiowa; yes; 3/4; 1/2; 5/8; yes

1931   1058;   HADLEY, Madaline; 1930-Aug-9; yes; F; Kiowa; yes; 4/4; 4/4; 4/4; yes

        See #
1931   1148;   HAINTA; 1930-Apr-16; yes; F; Kiowa; yes; 4/4; 4/4; 4/4; yes

87

Office of Indian Affairs Births Occurring Between the Dates of April 1, 1930 and
March 31, 1931 to Parents Enrolled at Jurisdiction

KEY: 1931 Census Roll Number; Surname and Given Name; Date of Birth; Live Birth (Yes or No); Sex; Tribe; Ward (yes or no); Degree of Father's blood; Degree of Mother's blood; Degree of Child's blood; At Jurisdiction Where Enrolled (yes or no); [If "no", where, if given]

1931   1188;   HAWZIPTA, Albert, Jr; 1931-Jan-28; yes; M; Kiowa; yes; 4/4; [?];
1/2; yes

1931   1193;   HAWZIPTA; 1931-Mar-4; yes; F; Kiowa; yes; 4/4; 4/4; 4/4; yes

1931   1178;   HAUNPY, Johnnie; 1931-Mar-6; yes; M; Kiowa; yes; 4/4; 4/4; 4/4;
yes

See #
1931   1203;   HEMINOKOKY, Givens Rain; 1931-Jan-20; yes; F; Comanche &
Apa; yes; 4/4; 4/4; 4/4; yes

See #
1931   1241;   HIGH, Dorita; 1930-Nov-6; yes; F; Apache; yes; 4/4; 4/4; 4/4; yes

See
1931 #1259;   HOKEAH, Perry Jack; 1930-May-2; yes; M; Kiowa; yes; 4/4; 4/4;
4/4; yes

1931   1282;   HORSE, Chester Wallace; 1930-Nov-1; yes; M; Kiowa; yes; 4/4; 4/4;
4/4; yes

1931   1286;   HORSE, Vivian Ramona; 1930-Oct-2; yes; F; Kiowa; yes; 4/4; 4/4;
4/4; yes

1931   420;   HORSECHIEF, Rose Marie; 1930-Sept-5; yes; F; Kiowa; yes; 4/4;
4/4; 4/4; yes

1931   1321;   HUMMINGBIRD, Doris; 1930-Apr-26; yes; F; Kiowa; yes; 4/4; 4/4;
4/4; yes

1931   1328;   HUMMINGBIRD, Edmond; 1930-Apr-12; yes; M; Kiowa; yes; 4/4;
4/4; 4/4; yes

1931   1040;   KASSANAVOID, Geneva Terchey; 1930-Sept-1; yes; F; Comanche;
yes; 4/4; 4/4; 4/4; yes

1931   1428;   KAUBIN, Elaine Belle; 1930-May-1; yes; F; Kiowa; yes; 4/4; 4/4;
4/4; yes

1931   1474;   KAULAY, Ronald C; 1930-Apr-8; yes; M; Kiowa; yes; 4/4; 1/4; 3/4;
yes

State __Oklahoma__ Reservation __Kiowa__ Agency or Jurisdiction __Kiowa__
Office of Indian Affairs Births Occurring Between the Dates of April 1, 1930 and
March 31, 1931 to Parents Enrolled at Jurisdiction

KEY: 1931 Census Roll Number; Surname and Given Name; Date of Birth; Live Birth (Yes or No); Sex; Tribe; Ward (yes or no); Degree of Father's blood; Degree of Mother's blood; Degree of Child's blood; At Jurisdiction Where Enrolled (yes or no); [If "no", where, if given]

1931   1511;   KAWAYKLE, Jewel L; 1930-Dec-11; yes; F; Kiowa & Fort Sill Apache; yes; 4/4; 4/4; 4/4; yes

1931   2260;   KEAHBONE, Donald D; 1930-Apr-11; yes; M; Kiowa; yes; 4/4; 4/4; 4/4; yes

See #
1931   3292;   KLINEKALE, Mary; 1930-June-21; yes; F; Apache; yes; 4/4; 4/4; 4/4; yes

1931   3871;   KLINEKALE, Wyala; 1930-Nov-30; yes; F; Apache; yes; 4/4; 4/4; 4/4; yes

1931   1601;   KOMARDLEY, Alva Dean; 1930-July-27; yes; F; Apache; yes; 4/4; 4/4; 4/4; yes

1931   1605;   KOMESTATADDLE, Lois Linette; 1930-July-24; yes; F; Kiowa; yes; 4/4; 4/4; 4/4; yes

See #
1931   1611;   KOPADDY, Thelma; 1931-Jan-26; yes; F; Comanche; yes; 4/4; 4/4; 4/4; yes

1931   1636;   KOSECHEQUETAH, Billy; 1930-Apr-2; yes; M; Comanche; yes; 4/4; 4/4; 4/4; yes

1931   1923;   KOWENO, Henry; 1931-Jan-28; yes; M; Comanche; yes; 4/4; 4/4; 4/4; yes

1931   1292;   LARGE, Vivian Lee; 1930-Nov-11; yes; F; Comanche; yes; [?]; 4/4; 1/2; yes

1931   1828;   LAURENZANA, Ivarine Joy; 1931-Apr-17; yes; F; Comanche; yes; [?]; 3/4; 3/8; yes

1931   1623;   LeBARRE, Vivian Lee; 1931-Mar-28; yes; F; Kiowa; yes; [?]; 4/4; 1/4; yes

1931   2437;   LEFTHAND, Irene; 1930-June-30; yes; F; Kiowa; yes; 4/4; 4/4; 4/4; yes

89

Office of Indian Affairs Births Occurring Between the Dates of April 1, 1930 and
March 31, 1931 to Parents Enrolled at Jurisdiction

KEY: 1931 Census Roll Number; Surname and Given Name; Date of Birth; Live Birth (Yes or No); Sex; Tribe; Ward (yes or no); Degree of Father's blood; Degree of Mother's blood; Degree of Child's blood; At Jurisdiction Where Enrolled (yes or no); [If "no", where, if given]

See #
1931 1309; McARTHUR, Doris Jean; 1930-Sept-30; yes; F; Comanche; yes; [?]; 1/2; 1/4; yes

1931 593; MITCHELL, Billy Lee; 1931-Mar-16; yes; M; Comanche; yes; [?]; Mex; [?]; yes

1931 2024; MOPOPE, Denna Jean; 1930-July-5; yes; F; Kiowa; yes; 4/4; 1/4; 3/4; yes

1931 2028; MOPE, Laquenta Joy; 1930-Aug-10; yes; F; Kiowa; yes; 4/4; 7/8; 7/8; yes

1931 2173; MORA, Raymond; 1930-Oct-18; yes; M; Comanche; yes; [?]; 4/4; 1/2; yes

1931 4163; MOSES, Billy Edena; 1930-Nov-25; yes; M; Kiowa; yes; Mex; 4/4; 1/2; yes

1931 2078; MYERS, Barbara Ann; 1930-Dec-17; yes; F; Comanche; yes; 1/4; 1/4; 1/4; yes

1931 2127; NAHWOOKSY, Reaves; 1930-Oct-7; yes; M; Comanche; yes; 4/4; 4/4; 4/4; yes

See #
1931 3662; OTIPPOBY, Wm Henry; 1930-Oct-25; yes; M; Comanche; yes; 3/4; 4/4; 7/8; yes

1931 2317; PAHCHEKA, Elton, Jr; 1931-Jan-19; yes; M; Comanche; yes; 4/4; 4/4; 4/4; yes

1931 2328; PAHCODDY, Spencer Lee; 1931-Jan-14; yes; M; Comanche; yes; 4/4; 4/4; 4/4; yes

1931 2016; PALMER, Dorothy Ann; 1931-Aug-9; yes; F; Kiowa; yes; [?]; 4/4; 5/8; yes

See #
1931 2456; PEBEAKSY, Runnell; 1930-Oct-17; yes; M; Comanche; yes; 4/4; 4/4; 4/4; yes

State Oklahoma Reservation Kiowa Agency or Jurisdiction Kiowa
Office of Indian Affairs Births Occurring Between the Dates of April 1, 1930 and
March 31, 1931 to Parents Enrolled at Jurisdiction

KEY: 1931 Census Roll Number; Surname and Given Name; Date of Birth; Live Birth (Yes or No); Sex; Tribe; Ward (yes or no); Degree of Father's blood; Degree of Mother's blood; Degree of Child's blood; At Jurisdiction Where Enrolled (yes or no); [If "no", where, if given]

1931   2511;   PERDASOPPY, Billy Edward; 1931-Feb-14; yes; M; Comanche; yes; 4/4; 4/4; 4/4; yes

1931   2524;   PERKAQUANARD, Edw Lehman; 1930-Nov-18; yes; M; Comanche; yes; 4/4; 4/4; 4/4; yes

1931   2587;   PEWARDY, Wanda; 1930-Oct-19; yes; F; Comanche; yes; 4/4; 4/4; 4/4; yes

1931   2600;   PEWO, Wilbur, Jr; 1930-June-13; yes; M; Comanche; yes; 4/4; 4/4; 4/4; yes

1931   2640;   POEMOCEAH, Alfred Malcolm; 1930-Aug-10; yes; M; Kiowa; yes; 4/4; 4/4; 4/4; yes

1931   3994;   POEMOCEAH, Oma Jean; 1930-Dec-17; yes; F; Comanche; yes; 4/4; 4/4; 4/4; yes

1931   2693;   POPETSAITKE, Oleta; 1930-Aug-3; yes; F; Kiowa; yes; 4/4; 4/4; 4/4; yes

1931   2620;   POOHWAY; 1931-Mar-28; yes; M; Com & Apache; yes; 4/4; 4/4; 4/4; yes

1931   2670;   POOLAW, Helen Marie; 1930-Nov-17; yes; F; Kiowa; yes; 4/4; 4/4; 4/4; yes

1931   1133   PRENTISS, Reuben; 1930-Sept-1; yes; M; Kiowa; yes; 4/4; 4/4; 4/4; yes

1931   2741;   PUEBLO, Rita Mae; 1930-July-31; yes; F; Comanche; yes; 4/4; 4/4; 4/4; yes

1931   2814;   ROACHE, Audrea; 1930-Nov-10; yes; F; Comanche; yes; Mex; Mex; Mex; yes

1931   34;   ROACHE, Rudolph; 1930-Oct-1; yes; M; Comanche; yes; 4/4; Mex; 1/2; yes

1931   2846;   ROWELL, Geo Frederick; 1931-Jan-19; yes; M; Kiowa; yes; 1/2; [?]; 1/4; yes

State __Oklahoma__ Reservation __Kiowa__ Agency or Jurisdiction __Kiowa__
Office of Indian Affairs Births Occurring Between the Dates of April 1, 1930 and
March 31, 1931 to Parents Enrolled at Jurisdiction

KEY: 1931 Census Roll Number; Surname and Given Name; Date of Birth; Live Birth (Yes or No); Sex; Tribe; Ward (yes or no); Degree of Father's blood; Degree of Mother's blood; Degree of Child's blood; At Jurisdiction Where Enrolled (yes or no); [If "no", where, if given]

1931 2894;   SANKADOTA, Esther Fay; 1931-Mar-4; yes; F; Kiowa; yes; 4/4;
4/4; 4/4; yes

1931 3018;   SATEPAUHOOLDE, Royce Edwin; 1930-Sept-19; yes; M; Kiowa;
yes; 4/4; 3/4; 7/8; yes

1931 2949;   SATOE, Joseph James; 1930-Oct-26; yes; M; Kiowa; yes; 4/4; 4/4;
4/4; yes

1931 2980;   SEELTOE, Melvin; 1930-Dec-5; yes; M; Kiowa FSA; yes; 4/4; 4/4;
4/4; yes

1931 3035;   SOVO, Eunice; 1930-Sept-3; yes; F; Comanche; yes; 4/4; 4/4; 4/4;
yes

1931 3043;   STARR, Geo David; 1931-Jan-24; yes; M; Apache; yes; 4/4; 4/4; 4/4;
yes

       See #
1931 2438;   STUMBLING BEAR, Lavinia; 1930-June-29; yes; F; Kiowa; yes;
4/4; 4/4; 4/4; yes

1931 3063;   TABBYTITE, Lilly Jean; 1930-July-19; yes; F; Kiowa; yes; 1/4; 4/4;
5/8; yes

1931 3082;   TABBYYETCHY, Richard; 1930-Sept-27; yes; M; Comanche; yes;
4/4; 4/4; 4/4; yes

1931 3059;   TABBYTITE, Rose Marie; 1930-June-10; yes; F; Comanche; yes;
4/4; 4/4; 4/4; yes

1931 3090;   TAH, Frances Owen; 1930-June-28; yes; M; Apache; yes; 4/4; 4/4;
4/4; yes

1931 3112;   TAHBONEMAH, Marland; 1930-Apr-27; yes; M; Kiowa; yes; 4/4;
4/4; 4/4; yes

1931 3125;   TAHCHAWWICKAH, John A; 1930-Oct-23; yes; M; Comanche;
yes; 4/4; 4/4; 4/4; yes

1931 3150;   TAHDOOAHMPOAH, Blanch Elizabeth; 1930-June-18; yes; F;
Comanche; yes; 4/4; 4/4; 4/4; yes

92

State __Oklahoma__ Reservation __Kiowa__ Agency or Jurisdiction __Kiowa__
Office of Indian Affairs Births Occurring Between the Dates of April 1, 1930 and
March 31, 1931 to Parents Enrolled at Jurisdiction

KEY: 1931 Census Roll Number; Surname and Given Name; Date of Birth; Live Birth (Yes or No); Sex; Tribe; Ward (yes or no); Degree of Father's blood; Degree of Mother's blood; Degree of Child's blood; At Jurisdiction Where Enrolled (yes or no); [If "no", where, if given]

1931 3186; TAHLO, Hattie Jean; 1930-Nov-2; yes; F; Kiowa; yes; 4/4; 4/4; 4/4; yes

1931 3198; TAHMAHKERA, Leatrice Joy; 1930-May-10; yes; F; Comanche; yes; 4/4; 4/4; 4/4; yes

1931 3210; TAHMAHKERA; 1931-Mar-9; yes; F; Comanche; yes; 4/4; 4/4; 4/4; yes

See #
1931 3234; TAHSEQUAW, Rudolph Alvin; 1930-July-21; yes; M; Comanche; yes; 4/4; 4/4; 4/4; yes

1931 3385; TANA, Allen, Jr; 1930-Sept-19; yes; M; Kiowa; yes; 4/4; 4/4; 4/4; yes

1931 2246; TANEDOOAH, Betty Lou; 1931-Jan-24; yes; F; Kiowa; yes; 4/4; 4/4; 4/4; yes

1931 3327; TANEQUODLE, Paul; 1930-Sept-23; yes; M; Kiowa; yes; 4/4; 4/4; 4/4; yes

See #
1931 3373; TARTSAH, Vernon; 1930-July-28; yes; M; Apache; yes; 4/4; 4/4; 4/4; yes

See #
1931 3401; TAUNAH, Eilena Floy; 1930-May-8; yes; F; Comanche; yes; 4/4; 4/4; 4/4; yes

1931 2378; TANEQUER, Wm Bob; 1931-Jan-1; yes; M; Comanche; yes; 4/4; 4/4; 4/4; yes

1931 3456; THOMPSON, Delores Jean; 1930-Oct-9; yes; F; Kiowa; yes; 4/4; 4/4; 4/4; yes

1931 2370; THOMPSON, Mathew; 1930-May-8; yes; M; Kiowa; yes; 4/4; 4/4; 4/4; yes

1931 4065; TINEYUYAH, Betty Joyce; 1930-Aug-1; yes; F; Comanche; yes; 4/4; 4/4; 4/4; yes

State __Oklahoma__ Reservation __Kiowa__ Agency or Jurisdiction __Kiowa__
Office of Indian Affairs Births Occurring Between the Dates of April 1, 1930 and
March 31, 1931 to Parents Enrolled at Jurisdiction

KEY: 1931 Census Roll Number; Surname and Given Name; Date of Birth; Live Birth (Yes or No); Sex; Tribe; Ward (yes or no); Degree of Father's blood; Degree of Mother's blood; Degree of Child's blood; At Jurisdiction Where Enrolled (yes or no); [If "no", where, if given]

1931 3652; TONEMAH, Laverne; 1930-July-25; yes; F; Kiowa; yes; 4/4; 4/4; 4/4; yes

       See #
1931 3660; TONEPAHTOTE, Wm Beemen; 1930-July-15; Kiowa; yes; 4/4; 4/4; 4/4; yes

1931 3677; TONGKEAMHA, Wallace; 1930-Nov-5; yes; M; Kiowa; yes; 4/4; 4/4; 4/4; yes

       See #
1931 3678; TONIPS, Kenneth Leon; 1930-Dec-29; yes; M; Kio & Com; yes; 4/4; 4/4; 4/4; yes

1931 3703; TOOAHNIPAH, Kenneth Devere; 1931-Mar-4; yes; M; Comanche; yes; 4/4; 4/4; 4/4; yes

       See
1931 #3693; TOOAHIMPAH, Feokra; 1930-May-6; yes; F; Comanche; yes; 4/4; 4/4; 4/4; yes

       See #
1931 3713; TOPAUM, Rudolph; 1930-Aug-19; yes; M; Kiowa; yes; 4/4; 4/4; 4/4; yes

1931 3735; TOPETCHY, Billie June; 1930-July-3; yes; F; Comanche; yes; 4/4; 4/4; 4/4; yes

1931 3759; TOQUOTHTY, Lee Daniel; 1930-Sept-7; yes; M; Comanche; yes; 4/4; 4/4; 4/4; yes

1931 3814; TSALATE, Lillian; 1931-Jan-8; yes; F; Kiowa; yes; 4/4; 4/4; 4/4; yes

1931 3821; TSATAHSISKO, Basil Devere; 1930-Aug-3; yes; M; Apache; yes; 4/4; 4/4; 4/4; yes

1931 3827; TSATIGH, Mary Ruth; 1930-June-24; yes; F; Kiowa; yes; 4/4; 4/4; 4/4; yes

1931 3838; TSATOKE, Stella May; 1930-Apr-4; yes; F; Kiowa; yes; 4/4; 4/4; 4/4; yes

94

State Oklahoma   Reservation Kiowa   Agency or Jurisdiction Kiowa
Office of Indian Affairs Births Occurring Between the Dates of April 1, 1930 and
March 31, 1931 to Parents Enrolled at Jurisdiction

KEY: 1931 Census Roll Number; Surname and Given Name; Date of Birth; Live Birth (Yes or No); Sex; Tribe; Ward (yes or no); Degree of Father's blood; Degree of Mother's blood; Degree of Child's blood; At Jurisdiction Where Enrolled (yes or no); [If "no", where, if given]

See #
1931   350;   TSOODLE, Vena Joyce; 1930-Aug-29; yes; F; Kiowa; yes; 4/4; 4/4; 4/4; yes

1931   256;   VILLIVANA, Genevieve; 1930-Aug-16; yes; F; Comanche; yes; Mex; Mex; Mex; yes

1931   3992;   WALLACE, Vincente Wilfred; 1930-July-11; yes; M; Comanche; yes; 3/4; 4/4; 7/8; yes

1931   4004;   WARE, Eugene Perry; 1930-Nov-21; yes; M; Kiowa; yes; 4/4; [?]; 1/2; yes

1931   4007;   WARE, Georgia Ann Alice; 1930-Sept-22; yes; F; Kiowa; yes; 3/4; 4/4; 7/8; yes

1931   4030;   WAUQUA, Eleanor; 1930-Oct-6; yes; F; Comanche; yes; 4/4; 4/4; 4/4; yes

See #
1931   4022;   WAUQUA, Rena Mae; 1931-Mar-29; yes; F; Comanche; yes; 4/4; 4/4; 4/4; yes

See #
1931   4051;   WERMY, Billy Murphy; 1930-May-20; yes; M; Comanche; yes; 4/4; 4/4; 4/4; yes

1931   4078;   WETSELLINE, Arnold; 1930-Sept-9; yes; M; Apache; yes; 4/4; 4/4; 4/4; yes

1931   946;   WHITE, Samuel; 1930-Apr-5; yes; M; Kiowa; yes; W; 4/4; 1/2; yes

1931   3598;   WHITEFOX, Virgil; 1931-Feb-13; yes; M; Kiowa; yes; 4/4; 4/4; 4/4; yes

1931   3046;   WHITESHIELD, Sophia Lee; 1930-Apr-30; yes; F; Apache; yes; 4/4; 4/4; 4/4; yes

1931   2558;   WILLIAMS; 1930-July-23; yes; F; Kiowa; yes; W; 4/4; 1/2; yes

1931   2558;   WILLIAMS, Waltsie Ruth; 1930-Nov-24; yes; F; Kiowa; yes; 4/4; 4/4; 4/4; yes

State __Oklahoma__ Reservation __Kiowa__ Agency or Jurisdiction __Kiowa__
Office of Indian Affairs Births Occurring Between the Dates of April 1, 1930 and
March 31, 1931 to Parents Enrolled at Jurisdiction

1931   1812;   YELLOWFISH, Clifton; 1931-Jan-7; yes; M; Comanche; yes; 4/4; 4/4; 4/4; yes

1931   4255;   ZOTIGH, Kirby Perry; 1931-Jan-7; yes; M; Kiowa; yes; 4/4; 4/4; 4/4; yes

KIOWA INDIAN AGENCY
Kiowa Reservation
Oklahoma
1932

BIRTH ROLL
Kiowa, Comanche, Apache and Fort Sill Apache Indians

Office of Indian Affairs Births Occurring Between the Dates of April 1, 1931 and
March 31, 1932 to Parents Enrolled at Jurisdiction

KEY: 1932 Census Roll Number; Surname and Given Name; Date of Birth; Live Birth (Yes or No); Sex; Tribe; Ward (yes or no); Degree of Father's blood; Degree of Mother's blood; Degree of Child's blood; At Jurisdiction Where Enrolled (yes or no); [If "no", where, if given]

1932   5;   AGOPETAH, Jules Ernest; 1931-July-16; yes; M; Kiowa; yes; 3/4; 3/4; 3/4; yes

1932   32;   AHDOKOBO, Christine; 1931-May-21; yes; F; Kiowa; yes; 4/4; 4/4; 4/4; yes

1932   71;   AHKEAHBO, Frank; 1931-Sept-15; yes; M; Kiowa; yes; 4/4; 4/4; 4/4; yes

      See #
1932   126;   AITSON, Mary; 1932-Jan-3; yes; F; Kiowa; yes; 3/4; 4/4; 7/8; yes

      See #
1932   133;   AKO, David; 1931-June-19; yes; M; Kiowa; yes; 3/4; 4/4; 7/8; yes

1932   145;   AKONETO, Everett Gene; 1932-Jan-3; yes; M; Kiowa; yes; 4/4; 4/4; 4/4; yes

1932   180;   APAUTY, Rhoda May; 1932-Aug-8; yes; F; Kiowa; yes; 4/4; 4/4; 4/4; yes

1932   225;   ASENAP, Lavena; 1932-Jan-14; yes; F; Comanche; yes; 3/4; 7/8; 7/8; yes

1932   2529;   ASENAP, William; 1932-Jan-5; yes; M; Comanche; yes; 4/4; 4/4; 4/4; yes

1932   1250;   ATCHAVIT, Robert, Jr; 1931-Aug-6; yes; M; Comanche; yes; 4/4; 4/4; 4/4; yes

1932   292;   ATEWOOPTAKEWA, Bonnie Jean; 1932-Oct-10; yes; F; Comanche; yes; 4/4; 4/4; 4/4; yes

1932   1047;   AUNGUO, Leasy Marie; 1932-Mar-14; yes; F; Kiowa; yes; 4/4; 4/4; 4/4; yes

1932   199;   AUNGUOE, Mary Anne; 1931-Oct-28; yes; F; Kiowa; yes; 4/4; 4/4; 4/4; yes

1932   412;   BITSEEDY, Hope; 1931-Oct-8; yes; F; Apache; yes; 4/4; 4/4; 4/4; yes

State __Oklahoma__ Reservation __Kiowa__ Agency or Jurisdiction __Kiowa__
Office of Indian Affairs Births Occurring Between the Dates of April 1, 1931 and
March 31, 1932 to Parents Enrolled at Jurisdiction

KEY: 1932 Census Roll Number; Surname and Given Name; Date of Birth; Live Birth (Yes or No); Sex; Tribe; Ward (yes or no); Degree of Father's blood; Degree of Mother's blood; Degree of Child's blood; At Jurisdiction Where Enrolled (yes or no); [If "no", where, if given]

1932   416;   BLACKBEAR, Jacquelin; 1931-Oct-22; yes; F; Apache; yes; 4/4; 4/4; 4/4; yes

1932   3124;   BURGESS, Bobbie Ronald; 1932-Feb-3; yes; M; Comanche; yes; 4/4; 4/4; 4/4; yes

1932   2745;   CERDY, Neoma Louise; 1931-Dec-24; yes; F; Comanche; yes; Mex; Mex; Mex; yes

1932   519;   CHAHKEAH, Justin M; 1931-July-20; yes; M; Kiowa; yes; 3/4; 3/4; 3/4; yes

1932   569;   CHALEPAH, Mary Ella; 1932-Jan-16; yes; F; Apache; yes; 4/4; 4/4; 4/4; yes

1932   575;   CHANATE, LaVerda; 1931-May-10; yes; F; Kiowa; yes; 4/4; 4/4; 4/4; yes

1932   533;   CHASENAH, Betsy Lois; 1931-June-28; yes; F; Comanche; yes; 4/4; 4/4; 4/4; yes

1932   658;   CHOCKPOYAH, Lavera Faye; 1932-Mar-7; yes; F; Comanche; yes; 4/4; W; 1/2; yes

1932   655;   CHOCKPOYAH, Vernon; 1931-Apr-30; yes; M; Comanche; yes; 4/4; 4/4; 4/4; yes

1932   670;   CLARK, Patsy Pauline; 1931-July-5; yes; F; Comanche; yes; 1/2; 1/4; yes

1932   701;   COBAHTINE, Ruby Mae; 1931-Nov-17; yes; F; Kiowa; yes; 4/4; 4/4; 4/4; yes

1932   711;   CODOPONY, Barbara; 1931-June-17; yes; F; Comanche; yes; 4/4; 4/4; 4/4; yes

1932   729;   COFFEE, Lauvoice; 1931-July-21; yes; F; Comanche; yes; 4/4; 4/4; 4/4; yes

1932   744;   CONNYWERDY, Aline; 1931-Nov-30; yes; F; Comanche; yes; 4/4; 4/4; 4/4; yes

State __Oklahoma__ Reservation __Kiowa__ Agency or Jurisdiction __Kiowa__
Office of Indian Affairs Births Occurring Between the Dates of April 1, 1931 and
March 31, 1932 to Parents Enrolled at Jurisdiction

KEY: 1932 Census Roll Number; Surname and Given Name; Date of Birth; Live Birth (Yes or No); Sex; Tribe; Ward (yes or no); Degree of Father's blood; Degree of Mother's blood; Degree of Child's blood; At Jurisdiction Where Enrolled (yes or no); [If "no", where, if given]

1932   774;   CONOVER, Una Josephine; 1931-Apr-6; yes; F; Comanche; yes; Mex; 1/4; 1/8; yes

1932   792;   COOSEWON, Ralphie; 1932-Jan-20; yes; M; Comanche; yes; 4/4; 4/4; 4/4; yes

1932   797;   COX, Quannah Eda; 1931-May-28; yes; M; Comanche; yes; 1/2; W; 1/4; yes

1932   941;   EMHE, Reuben; 1931-Apr-23; yes; M; Kiowa; yes; 4/4; 4/4; 4/4; yes

1932   946;   EMHOOLAH, Parker; 1931-Nov-23; yes; M; Kiowa; yes; 4/4; 4/4; 4/4; yes

1932   3477;   EVANS, Eva Lois; 1931-Sept-21; yes; F; Comanche; yes; 1/4; 1/4; 1/4; yes

1932   249;   FARRALLA, Balinda Mary; 1931-Aug-24; yes; F; Comanche; yes; Mex; Mex; Mex; yes

1932   3269;   FRANKLIN, Belford; 1932-Feb-28; yes; M; Kiowa; yes; 4/4; 4/4; 4/4; yes

1932   1009;   FULLER, Gerald Howard; 1931-Oct-24; yes; M; Comanche; yes; 1/8; W; 1/4; yes

1932   1042;   GEIMAUSADDLE, Robert; 1931-Nov-2; yes; M; Kiowa; yes; 4/4; 4/4; 4/4; yes

1932   1094;   GOODAY, Georgia Aileen; 1931-Apr-19; yes; F; Comanche; yes; 4/4; 1/2; 3/4; yes

1932   723;   GOVER, Phyllis Ann; 1932-Jan-27; yes; F; Kiowa; yes; 4/4; 4/4; 4/4; yes

1932   1956;   GRAY, Patricia Ann; 1931-Oct-19; yes; F; Comanche; yes; 1/2; 3/4; 3/8; yes

1932   1156;   HAINTA, Joseph Taft; 1931-July-17; yes; M; Kiowa; yes; 4/4; 4/4; 4/4; yes

1832   1228;   HERNASSY, Ida; 1931-Apr-12; yes; F; Comanche; yes; 4/4; 4/4; 4/4; yes

State __Oklahoma__ Reservation __Kiowa__ Agency or Jurisdiction __Kiowa__
Office of Indian Affairs Births Occurring Between the Dates of April 1, 1931 and
March 31, 1932 to Parents Enrolled at Jurisdiction

KEY: 1932 Census Roll Number; Surname and Given Name; Date of Birth; Live Birth (Yes or No); Sex; Tribe; Ward (yes or no); Degree of Father's blood; Degree of Mother's blood; Degree of Child's blood; At Jurisdiction Where Enrolled (yes or no); [If "no", where, if given]

See #

1932 1259; HOAHWAH, Harvey; 1931-Dec-2; yes; M; Comanche; yes; 4/4; 4/4; 4/4; yes

1932 1274; HOKEAH, Paul Bradley; 1931-June-14; yes; M; Comanche; yes; 4/4; 4/4; 4/4; yes

1932 1315; HOOAKAH, Virgil Lee; 1931-Dec-29; yes; M; Kiowa; yes; 4/4; 4/4; 4/4; yes

1932   207; HOPKINS, Tribly Dan; 1931-June-15; yes; M; Kiowa; yes; W; 3/4; 3/8; yes

1932 1235; HOSETOSAVIT, Cleta Ruth; 1931-Aug-13; yes; F; Comanche; yes; 4/4; 4/4; 4/4; yes

1932 1342; HUMMINGBIRD, Alfred; 1931-Apr-11; yes; M; Kiowa; yes; 4/4; 4/4; 4/4; yes

1932 2873; JOHNSON, Beverly Sue; 1931-Sept-24; yes; F; Kiowa; yes; W; 1/2; 1/4; yes

1932 1361; JONES, Billy Saumty; 1931-Sept-15; yes; M; Kiowa; yes; 3/4; 3/4; 3/4; yes

1932 1720; JORDAN, Albert Austin, Jr; 1931-Apr-19; yes; M; Comanche; yes; 1/2; W; 1/4; yes

1932 1395; KADAYSO, Ruby May; 1931-Aug-5; yes; F; Apache; yes; 4/4; 4/4; 4/4; yes

1932 1416; KARTY, Dennis King; 1931-Oct-8; yes; M; Comanche; yes; 4/4; 7/8; 15/16; yes

1932 1445; KAUBIN, Dorothy; 1932-Feb-18; yes; F; Kiowa; yes; 4/4; 4/4; 4/4; yes

1932   85; KAULAITY, Donald; 1931-July-4; yes; M; Kiowa; yes; 4/4; 4/4; 4/4; yes

1932 1473; KAULAY, Harry; 1932-Jan-28; yes; M; Kiowa; yes; 4/4; 4/4; 4/4; yes

State __Oklahoma__ Reservation __Kiowa__ Agency or Jurisdiction __Kiowa__
Office of Indian Affairs Births Occurring Between the Dates of April 1, 1931 and
March 31, 1932 to Parents Enrolled at Jurisdiction

KEY: 1932 Census Roll Number; Surname and Given Name; Date of Birth; Live Birth (Yes or No); Sex; Tribe; Ward (yes or no); Degree of Father's blood; Degree of Mother's blood; Degree of Child's blood; At Jurisdiction Where Enrolled (yes or no); [If "no", where, if given]

1932   625;   KAULAITY, Juanita Marie; 1931-July-29; yes; F; Kiowa; yes; 7/8/ 7/8; 7/8; yes

1932   1521;   KAUYEDAUTY, Roland Eugene; 1931-Nov-21; yes; M; Kiowa; yes; 4/4; 4/4; 4/4; yes

1932   1557;   KEAHTIGH, Francella Ann; 1932-Feb-20; yes; F; Kiowa; yes; 1/2; 3/4; 5/8; yes

1932   1565;   KEAHTIGH, Knute Kenneth; 1932-Feb-14; yes; M; Kiowa; yes; 1/2; 3/4; 3/4; yes

1932   1574;   KEITHTAHCOCO, Gloria; 1931-June-4; yes; F; Comanche; yes; 4/4; 4/4; 4/4; yes

1932   3337;   KLINEKOLE, Austine; 1931-Aug-19; yes; M; Apache; yes; 4/4; 4/4; 4/4; yes

1932   1593;   KOOSEECHONY, Lanora Bell; 1931-May-22; yes; F; Comanche; yes; 4/4; 4/4; 4/4; yes

1932   1634;   KOMESATADDLE, Nannie Belle; 1931-Dec-26; yes; F; Kiowa; yes; 4/4; 4/4; 4/4; yes

1932   1619;   KOMAHTY, Ruth Marie; 1931-Nov-6; yes; F; Kiowa; yes; 4/4; 3/4; 7/8; yes

1932   1770;   LOCOL, Woodrow Warren; 1931-Apr-28; yes; M; Fort Sill Apa; yes; 4/4; 4/4; 4/4; yes

1932   3027;   LUNA, Mary Lucy; 1931-Oct-8; yes; F; Comanche; yes; Mex; Mex; Mex; yes

1932   1829;   MAHSETKY, Larry; 1931-Nov-7; yes; M; Comanche; yes; 4/4; 4/4; 4/4; yes

1932   1921;   MAYNAHONAH, Oliver, Jr; 1932-Feb-10; yes; M; Apache; yes; 4/4; 4/4; 4/4; yes

1932   2091;   MIHECOBY, Kelton; 1932-Feb-5; yes; M; Comanche; yes; 4/4; 4/4; 4/4; yes

1932   1996;   MOBEADEMAH, Buster Roy; 1931-Oct-19; yes; M; Kiowa; yes; 4/4; 4/4; 4/4; yes

State __Oklahoma__ Reservation __Kiowa__ Agency or Jurisdiction __Kiowa__
Office of Indian Affairs Births Occurring Between the Dates of April 1, 1931 and
March 31, 1932 to Parents Enrolled at Jurisdiction

KEY: 1932 Census Roll Number; Surname and Given Name; Date of Birth; Live Birth (Yes or No); Sex; Tribe; Ward (yes or no); Degree of Father's blood; Degree of Mother's blood; Degree of Child's blood; At Jurisdiction Where Enrolled (yes or no); [If "no", where, if given]

1932   2171;   NASON, Barbara Ellen; 1931-Apr-19; yes; F; Comanche; yes; 1/4; W; 1/8; yes

1932   2188;   NECONIE, Orval; 1931-Nov-11; yes; M; Kiowa; yes; 4/4; 4/4; 4/4; yes

1932   2223;   NESTELL, Paul; 1931-Sept-9; yes; M; Apache; yes; 4/4; 4/4; 4/4; yes

1932   384;   NEWSOME, Garland; 1932-Jan-17; yes; M; Kiowa; yes; 1/2; 1/2; 1/2; yes

1932   2240;   NIEDO, Marjorie Marie; 1931-May-13; yes; F; Comanche; yes; 4/4; 4/4; 4/4; yes

1932   2545;   PADDYAKER, Edward; 1931-Aug-1; yes; M; Comanche; yes; 1/2; 4/4; 3/4; yes

1932   2373;   PADDINGKEI, Anna Belle; 1932-Feb-28; yes; F; Kiowa; yes; 4/4; 4/4; 4/4; yes

1932   2443;   PARKER, Esther Jean; 1931-Apr-3; yes; F; Comanche; yes; 3/4; 3/4; 3/4; yes

1932   2451;   PARRIAECKIVIT, Victor; 1931-June-2; yes; M; Comanche; yes; 1/2; 4/4; 3/4; yes

1932   2500;   PEBEABSY, Gokey; 1931-Dec-15; yes; M; Comanche; yes; 4/4; 4/4; 4/4; yes

       See #
1932   2562;   PERMAMSU, Willa Dean; 1931-Sept-13; yes; F; Comanche; yes; 4/4; 4/4; 4/4; yes

1932   2624;   PEWO, Vernon Lee; 1931-Sept-15; yes; M; Comanche; yes; 4/4; 4/4; 4/4; yes

1932   2659;   POAUTY, Lucille; 1931-Oct-27; yes; F; Kiowa; yes; 4/4; 4/4; 4/4; yes

1932   2677;   POEMOCEAH, Imogene; 1932-Mar-6; yes; F; Comanche; yes; 4/4; 4/4; 4/4;

State __Oklahoma__ Reservation __Kiowa__ Agency or Jurisdiction __Kiowa__
Office of Indian Affairs Births Occurring Between the Dates of April 1, 1931 and
March 31, 1932 to Parents Enrolled at Jurisdiction

KEY: 1932 Census Roll Number; Surname and Given Name; Date of Birth; Live Birth (Yes or No); Sex; Tribe; Ward (yes or no); Degree of Father's blood; Degree of Mother's blood; Degree of Child's blood; At Jurisdiction Where Enrolled (yes or no); [If "no", where, if given]

1932 2668; POCOWATCHIT, Harold Jerome; 1931-Sept-28; yes; M; Comanche; yes; 4/4; 4/4; 4/4; yes

1932 2357; PONCEY, Fred Gene; 1932-Jan-3; yes; M; Comanche; yes; 4/4; 4/4; 4/4; yes

1932 445; QUETONE, Jimmie Donald; 1931-June-10; yes; M; Kiowa; yes; 1/2; 1/2; 1/2; yes

1932 2878; RHODES, Everet Ronald; 1931-Oct-24; yes; M; Kiowa; yes; W; 1/2; 1/4; yes

1932 2848; SAHDONGKEI, Eulis Edmond; 1931-Dec-13; yes; M; Kiowa; yes; 4/4; 3/4; 7/8; yes

1932 24900[sic] SAHMAUNT, Sarah Jane; 1931-Sept-8; yes; F; Kiowa; yes; 4/4; 4/4; 4/4; yes

1932 2951; SATEPAUHOODLE, Evans Roy; 1931-Aug-2; yes; M; Kiowa; yes; 4/4; 4/4; 4/4; yes

1932 2967; SATEPAUHOODLE, Frostinn[sic] Ruth; 1931-Jan-1; yes; F; Kiowa; yes; 4/4; 1/2; 3/4; yes

1932 2958; SATEPAUHOODLE, Jaunema[sic]; 1931-June-17; yes; F; Kiowa; yes; 4/4; 4/4; 4/4; yes

See #
1932 2974; SATOE, Ensey; 1931-Sept-6; yes; M; Kiowa; yes; 4/4; 4/4; 4/4; yes

1932 3504; SHOEMATE, Jimmie, Jr; 1931-Oct-19; yes; M; Comanche; yes; W; 4/4; 1/2; yes

1932 2180; SHORTNECK, Virgil Lee; 1931-Oct-12; yes; M; Kiowa; yes; 4/4; 4/4; 4/4; yes

1932 3063; SOONTAY, Bertha Alice; 1932-Feb-10; yes; F; Apache; yes; 4/4; 4/4; 4/4; yes

1932 2420; SPOTTED CROW, Geneva; 1931-Sept-30; yes; F; Apache; yes; 4/4; 4/4; 4/4; yes

State   Oklahoma   Reservation   Kiowa   Agency or Jurisdiction   Kiowa
Office of Indian Affairs Births Occurring Between the Dates of April 1, 1931 and
March 31, 1932 to Parents Enrolled at Jurisdiction

KEY: 1932 Census Roll Number; Surname and Given Name; Date of Birth; Live Birth (Yes or No); Sex; Tribe; Ward (yes or no); Degree of Father's blood; Degree of Mother's blood; Degree of Child's blood; At Jurisdiction Where Enrolled (yes or no); [If "no", where, if given]

1932   3080;   STARR, Geo David; 1931-Jan-24; yes; M; Apache; yes; 4/4; 4/4; 4/4; yes

1932   2483;   STUMBLING BEAR, Leatrice Joy; 1931-Dec-27; yes; F; Kiowa; yes; 4/4; 4/4; 4/4; yes

1932   3113;   TABBYTOSAVIT, Ida Lee; 1931-Apr-8; yes; F; Comanche; yes; 4/4; 4/4; 4/4; yes

1932   1403;   TAH, Sharon Louise; 1931-Dec-9; yes; F; Apache; yes; 4/4; 4/4; 4/4; yes

1932   3210;   TAHKOFPER, Ailene; 1931-Apr-14; yes; F; Comanche; yes; 4/4; 1/2; 3/4; yes

1932   3220;   TAKKOPOODLE, John Frank; 1932-Jan-17; yes; M; Kiowa; yes; 4/4; 1/2; 3/4; yes

1932   3368;   TANEQUODLE, Audria; 1931-Dec-9; yes; F; Kiowa; yes; 4/4; 4/4; 4/4; yes

1932   3363;   TANEDOOAH, Silas; 1931-May-4; yes; M; Kiowa; yes; 4/4; 4/4; 4/4; yes

1932   3374;   TANEQUOADLE, Preston; 1931-June-20; yes; M; Kiowa; yes; 4/4; 4/4; 4/4; yes

1932   3398;   TAPTTO, Mary Patricia; 1931-Oct-5; yes; F; Kiowa; yes; 4/4; 3/4; 7/8; yes

1932   3416;   TARTSAH, Barbara Marie; 1931-Aug-24; yes; F; Apache; yes; 4/4; 4/4; 4/4; yes

1932   3556;   TITCHWY, Delores; 1931-May-11; yes; F; Comanche; yes; 4/4; 4/4; 4/4; yes

1932   3619;   TOFPI, Curtis; 1931-Sept-4; yes; M; Kiowa; yes; 4/4; 4/4; 4/4; yes

1932   3607;   TOFPI, Etheline May; 1931-June-21; yes; F; Kiowa; yes; 4/4; 4/4; 4/4; yes

1932   3636;   TOINTIGH, Bettie; 1931-Aug-3; yes; F; Kiowa; yes; 4/4; 4/4; 4/4; yes

State   Oklahoma   Reservation   Kiowa   Agency or Jurisdiction   Kiowa
Office of Indian Affairs Births Occurring Between the Dates of April 1, 1931 and
March 31, 1932 to Parents Enrolled at Jurisdiction

KEY: 1932 Census Roll Number; Surname and Given Name; Date of Birth; Live Birth (Yes or No); Sex; Tribe; Ward (yes or no); Degree of Father's blood; Degree of Mother's blood; Degree of Child's blood; At Jurisdiction Where Enrolled (yes or no); [If "no", where, if given]

1932   3633;   TOINTIGH, Billie Jean; 1931-July-29; yes; F; Kiowa; yes; 4/4; 4/4; 4/4; yes

1932   3663;   TOMAH, Bobby Wayne; 1932-Jan-30; yes; M; Comanche; yes; 1/2; 4/4; 3/4; yes

See #
1932   3677;   TONAHCUT, Evangeline; 1931-Nov-3; yes; F; Kiowa; yes; 4/4; 4/4; 4/4; yes

1932   3733;   TOOAHIMPAH, Vincent; 1931-Oct-19; yes; M; Comanche; yes; 4/4; 4/4; 4/4; yes

1932   3449;   TOOAHIMPAH, Larry; 1932-Jan-4; yes; M; Comanche; yes; 4/4; 4/4; 4/4; yes

See #
1932   3811;   TOSWEE, Benneta; June-23-1931; yes; F; Comanche; yes; 1/2; 1/2; 1/2; yes

1932   3867;   TSATAHSISKO, Eugene; 1931-Dec-12; yes; M; Apache; yes; 4/4; 4/4; 4/4; yes

1932   3956;   TSONETOKAY, Patsy Ruth; 1931-Aug-10; yes; F; Kiowa; yes; 4/4; 7/8; 7/8; yes

1932   3960;   TSOODLE, Altie Dorene; 1931-Dec-14; yes; F; Kiowa; yes; 4/4; 4/4; 4/4; yes

1932   3989;   TSOTADDLE, Lonnie Bert; 1931-May-14; yes; M; Apache; yes; 4/4; 4/4; 4/4; yes

1932   1037;   TURTLE, Murry; 1931-Oct-30; yes; M; Apache; yes; 4/4; 4/4; 4/4; yes

1932   4012;   TUTSTISAH, Marylene; 1931-Apr-14; yes; F; Apache; yes; 4/4; 4/4; 4/4; yes

1932   4031;   WAHAHKINNEY, Boy Haymie; 1932-Jan-2; yes; M; Comanche; yes; 4/4; 7/8; 15/16; yes

1932   4045;   WAHKAHCUAH, David Lee; 1931-Nov-16; yes; M; Comanche; yes; yes; F; 4/4; 4/4; yes

State __Oklahoma__ Reservation __Kiowa__ Agency or Jurisdiction __Kiowa__
Office of Indian Affairs Births Occurring Between the Dates of April 1, 1931 and
March 31, 1932 to Parents Enrolled at Jurisdiction

KEY: 1932 Census Roll Number; Surname and Given Name; Date of Birth; Live Birth (Yes or No); Sex; Tribe; Ward (yes or no); Degree of Father's blood; Degree of Mother's blood; Degree of Child's blood; At Jurisdiction Where Enrolled (yes or no); [If "no", where, if given]

1932   4040;   WAHAHROCKAH, Glen Courtney; 1931-May-24; yes; M; Comanche; yes; 4/4; 4/4; 4/4; yes

1932   4067;   WARE, Harvey Lee; 1932-Jan-23; yes; M; Kiowa; yes; 4/4; 4/4; 4/4; yes

1932   4105;   WAYSEPAPPY, Wynema; 1931-Sept-5; yes; F; Comanche; yes; 4/4; [?]; 1/2; yes

1932   953;   WHITE, Elmer Martin; 1932-Mar-5; yes; M; Kiowa; yes; W; 4/4; 1/2; yes

1932   3084;   WHITESHIELF, Rita Joyce; 1931- Dec-7; yes; F; Apache; yes; 4/4; 4/4; 4/4; yes

1932   4253;   YACKEYONNY, Eva Lois; 1932-Feb-29; yes; F; Comanche; yes; 4/4; 4/4; 4/4; yes

1932   4278;   YEAHQUO, Marion Paul; 1931-Feb-14; yes; M; Kiowa; yes; /4; 4/4; 4/4; yes

1932   4285;   YEAHQUO, Ruth; 1931- June-12; yes; F; Kiowa; yes; 4/4; 4/4; 4/4; yes

1932   1257;   YOUNGMAN, Rodinick[sic]; Dec-31-1931; yes; M; Comanche; yes; 4/4; 4/4; 4/4; yes

1932   4318;   ZOQUOE, Edna Mae; 1931-June-2; yes; F; Kiowa; yes; 1/2; 4/4; 3/4; yes

1932   2235;   ZUREYA, Otto; 1931-Aug-7; yes; M; Fort Sill Apache; yes; Mex; 4/4; 1/2; yes

KIOWA INDIAN AGENCY
Wichita Reservation
Oklahoma
1925

BIRTH ROLL
Wichita, Caddo, and Delaware
Indians

State __Oklahoma__ Reservation __Kio Wichita__ Agency or Jurisdiction __Kiowa__
Office of Indian Affairs Births Occurring Between the Dates of July 1, 1924 and
June 30, 1925 to Parents Enrolled at Jurisdiction

KEY: 1925 Census Roll Number; Name; Surname and Given; Date of Birth; Live Birth (Yes or No); Sex; Tribe; Ward (yes or no); Degree of Father's blood; Degree of Mother's blood; Degree of Child's blood; At jurisdiction where enrolled (yes or no); [If "no", where, if given]

1926   390;   BEAVER, Herbert Dennis; 1924-July-24; yes; M; Wichita; yes; 4/4;
                4/4; 4/4; yes

1925   390[sic]; BEAVER, Williard Wayne; 1925-May-5; yes; M; Wichita; yes; 4/4;
                4/4; 4/4; yes

1925   967;   CLARK, Bobbie Louise; 1925-Apr-10; yes; M; Wichita; yes; W; 4/4;
                1/2; yes

1925   649;   CLARK, Elmo; 1924-Dec-28; yes; M; Wichita; yes; W; F; 1/2; yes

1925   378;   DELAWARE, Teddy; 1925-Apr-25; yes; M; Wichita; yes; 4/4; 4/4;
                4/4; yes

1921   213;   DOWNING, Mary Louise; 1925-June-19; yes; F; Caddo; yes; 1/4;
                1/4; 1/4; [blank]; Oklahoma City, Okla.

1925   659;   FRENCH, Lawrence Al; 1925-Jan-9; yes; M; Wichita; yes; 4/4; 4/4;
                4/4; yes

1926   1185;   GUY, Frank; 1925-June-5; yes; M; Wichita; yes; 4/4; 4/4; 4/4; yes

1925   610;   INKANISH, Margaret Elizabeth; 1924-Aug-30; yes; F; Wichita; yes;
                4/4; 4/4; 4/4; yes

1925   607;   INKANISH, William; 1925-May-18; yes; M; Wichita; yes; 4/4; 4/4;
                4/4; yes

1926   560;   JORDAN, Walter James; 1925-Jan-13; yes; M; Wichita; yes; 4/4; 4/4;
                4/4; yes

1926   1263;   LING, Roy; 1924-Aug-20; yes; M; Wichita; yes; 1/2; W; 1/4; yes

1926   322;   LOPEZ, Frank; 1925-Apr-18; yes; M; Wichita; yes; Mex; 1/4; 1/8;
                yes

1926   310;   McLANE, Jackson, Jr; 1924-Dec-27; f[sic]; Wichita; yes; 1/4; W; 1/8;
                yes

1925   1205;   McLEMORE, Nina Vanita; 1925-Apr-28; yes; F; Wichita; yes; W;
                1/4; 1/8; yes

State ___Oklahoma___ Reservation ___Kio Wichita___ Agency or Jurisdiction ___Kiowa___
Office of Indian Affairs Births Occurring Between the Dates of July 1, 1924 and
June 30, 1925 to Parents Enrolled at Jurisdiction

KEY: 1925 Census Roll Number; Name; Surname and Given; Date of Birth; Live Birth (Yes or No); Sex; Tribe; Ward (yes or no); Degree of Father's blood; Degree of Mother's blood; Degree of Child's blood; At jurisdiction where enrolled (yes or no); [If "no", where, if given]

1925   234;   NIASTOR, Rudolph Medford; 1924-Aug-23; yes; M; Wichita; yes; 4/4; 4/4; 4/4; yes

1925   732;   PARTON, Florence; 1924-Aug-20; yes; F; Wichita; yes; 4/4; 4/4; 4/4; yes

1926   765;   SHEMANY, Jimmie, Jr; 1925-May-18; yes; M; Wichita; yes; 4/4; 4/4; 4/4; yes

1925   97;   STEPHENSON, Dudley Allen; 1924-Sept-1; yes; M; Wichita; yes; 4/4; 4/4; 4/4; yes

1926   623;   STURM, Merle Edgar; 1924-Sept-14; yes; M; Wichita; yes; 1/2; W; 1/4; yes

1926   301;   TAYLOR, Columbus Washington; 1924-Dec-7; yes; M; Wichita; yes; 4/4; 4/4; 4/4; yes

1925   223;   THOMAS, Preston Floyd; 1925-Apr-22; yes; M; Wichita; yes; 4/4; 4/4; 4/4; yes

1925   366;   WALKER, Elvin; 1924-Oct-28; yes; M; Wichita; yes; 4/4; 4/4; 4/4; yes

1926   1233;   WHITE, May Cornelius; 1924-Sept-18; yes; F; Wichita; yes; 4/4; 4/4; 4/4; yes

1926   839;   TOUWIN, Lewellyn; [?]-Feb-13; yes; F; Wichita; yes; 4/4; 4/4; 4/4; yes

KIOWA INDIAN AGENCY

Wichita Reservation

Oklahoma

1926

BIRTH ROLL
Wichita, Caddo, and Delaware
Indians

State __Oklahoma__ Reservation __Wichita__ Agency or Jurisdiction _Kiowa_
Office of Indian Affairs Births Occurring Between the Dates of July 1, 1925 and
June 30, 1926 to Parents Enrolled at Jurisdiction

KEY: 1926 Census Roll Number; Name; Surname and Given; Date of Birth; Live Birth (Yes or No); Sex; Tribe; Ward (yes or no); Degree of Father's blood; Degree of Mother's blood; Degree of Child's blood; At jurisdiction where enrolled (yes or no); [If "no", where, if given]

1926   803;   DECKER, Naomi; 1925-Oct-6; yes; Fem; Wichita; yes; 4/4; 4/4; 4/4; yes

1926   1042;   EDMONDS, Cordelia Louis; 1925-Nov-13; yes; Fem; Wichita; yes; 4/4; 4/4; 4/4; yes

1926   495;   EXENDINE, Cecelia Mae; 1926-May-6; yes; Fem; Wichita; yes; 4/4; 4/4; 4/4; yes

1926   492;   EXENDINE; Vera Joe; 1925-Aug-7; yes; Fem; Wichita; yes; 4/4; 4/4; 4/4; yes

1925   659;   FRENCH, Lawrence Al; 1925-Jan-9; yes; M; Wichita; yes; 4/4; 4/4; 4/4; yes

1925   104;   GABBARD, Otto Ray; 1926-May-10; yes; M; Wichita; yes; W; 4/4; 1/2; yes

1926   274;   HADDEN, Allen Buntin; 1925-Aug-31; yes; M; Wichita; yes; 1/2; W; 1/4; yes

1926   204;   HORSE CHIEF, Jeane; 1925-July-15; yes; F; yes; Wichita; yes; 4/4; 4/4; 4/4; yes

1926   203;   HORSE CHIEF, Joanne; 1925-July-15; yes; F; yes; Wichita; yes; 4/4; 4/4; 4/4; yes

1926   24;   HUNT, Marian Louise; 1926-Jan-5; yes; F; Wichita; yes; 4/4; 4/4; 4/4; yes

1926   1212;   McCAMPBELL, Joan; 1925-Sept-16; yes; F; Wichita; yes; 4/4; 4/4; 4/4; yes

1927   670;   MILLER, Gibbs Llewellyn; 1926; yes; M; Wichita; yes; 4/4; 4/4; 4/4; yes

1926   1025;   MILLER, Joyce Nadine; 1925-Sept-14; yes; F; Wichita; yes; 4/4; 4/4; 4/4; yes

1927   676;   MILLER, Laverne; 1926; yes; F; Wichita; yes; 4/4; 4/4; 4/4; yes

1926   1092;   PARTON, Frances Martin; 1926-May-4; yes; F; Wichita; yes; 4/4; 4/4; 4/4; yes

State __Oklahoma__ Reservation __Wichita__ Agency or Jurisdiction __Kiowa__
Office of Indian Affairs Births Occurring Between the Dates of July 1, 1925 and
June 30, 1926 to Parents Enrolled at Jurisdiction

KEY: 1926 Census Roll Number; Name; Surname and Given; Date of Birth; Live Birth (Yes or No); Sex; Tribe; Ward (yes or no); Degree of Father's blood; Degree of Mother's blood; Degree of Child's blood; At jurisdiction where enrolled (yes or no); [If "no", where, if given]

1926   401;   PARTON, Frederick; 1925-Sept-2; yes; M; Wichita; yes; 4/4; 4/4; 4/4; yes

1926   831;   PARTON, Verle Veldo; 1925-Dec-26; yes; M; Wichita; yes; 4/4; 4/4; 4/4; yes

1926   1177;   REIMER, Donald Eugene; 1925-Nov-19; yes; M; Wichita; yes; W; 1/2; 1/4; yes

1926   262;   STEVENS, Vivian Aileen; 1925-Dec-24; yes; F; Wichita; yes; 4/4; 4/4; 4/4; yes

1926   346;   SNAKE, Hollie Louise; 1925-Oct-7; yes; F; Wichita; yes; 4/4; 4/4; 4/4; yes

1926   576;   THOMAS, Josephine Ellen; 1926-Jan-6; yes; F; Wichita; yes; 4/4; 4/4; 4/4; yes

1926   575;   THOMAS, Wm Charlie; 1926-Jan-6; yes; M; Wichita; yes; 4/4; 4/4; 4/4; yes

~~1926   483;   WILLIAMS, Leroy Irwin; 1925-Oct-13; yes; M; Wichita; yes; 4/4; 4/4; 4/4; yes~~

1926   5160;   WILLIAMS, Alvin; 1926-May-28; yes; M; Caddo; yes; 4/4; 4/4; 4/4; yes

1926   787;   WILLIAMS, Baby; 1926-May-28; yes; M; Caddo; yes; 4/4; 4/4; 4/4; yes

1926   874;   WILLIAMS, Calvin Vernone; 1926-Jan-18; yes; M; Wichita; yes; 4/4; 4/4; 4/4; yes

1926   794;   WILLIAMS, Herman Myron; 1926-Jan-21; yes; M; Wichita; yes; 4/4; 4/4; 4/4; yes

1928   1195;   WILLIAMS, Ina; 1926-June-14; yes; F; Caddo; yes; 4/4; 4/4; 4/4; yes

1926   483;   WILLIAMS, Leroy Irwin; 1925-Oct-13; yes; M; Wichita; yes; 4/4; 4/4; 4/4; yes

1926   640;   WILSON, Elmer Eugene; 1926-Jan-5; yes; M; Wichita; yes; 4/4; 4/4; 4/4; yes

116

State ___Oklahoma___ Reservation ___Wichita___ Agency or Jurisdiction ___Kiowa___
Office of Indian Affairs Births Occurring Between the Dates of July 1, 1925 and
June 30, 1926 to Parents Enrolled at Jurisdiction

KEY: 1926 Census Roll Number; Name; Surname and Given; Date of Birth; Live Birth (Yes or No); Sex;
Tribe; Ward (yes or no); Degree of Father's blood; Degree of Mother's blood; Degree of Child's blood; At
jurisdiction where enrolled (yes or no); [If "no", where, if given]

1926   652;   WILSON, Gilman; 1925-July-28; yes; M; Wichita; yes; 4/4; 4/4; 4/4;
              yes

1926   646;   WELLER, Inez; 1925-Aug-18; yes; F; Wichita; yes; 4/4; 4/4; 4/4; yes

KIOWA INDIAN AGENCY

Wichita Reservation

Oklahoma

1927

BIRTH ROLL
Wichita, Caddo, and Delaware
Indians

State __Oklahoma__ Reservation __Wichita__ Agency or Jurisdiction __Kiowa__
Office of Indian Affairs Births Occurring Between the Dates of July 1, 1926 and
June 30, 1927 to Parents Enrolled at Jurisdiction

KEY: 1927 Census Roll Number; Name; Surname and Given; Date of Birth; Live Birth (Yes or No); Sex; Tribe; Ward (yes or no); Degree of Father's blood; Degree of Mother's blood; Degree of Child's blood; At jurisdiction where enrolled (yes or no); [If "no", where, if given]

1927   57;   ADUNKO, Donald; 1926; yes; M; Wichita; yes; 4/4; 4/4; 4/4; yes

See #
1927   49;   BARCINDABAR, Robert; 1927-4-27; yes; M; Caddo, yes; 4/4; 4/4; 4/4; yes

1929   211;   DOWNING, Lucretia Ann; 1927-5-15; yes; F; Caddo; yes; 1/4; W; 1/8; yes

See #
1927   241;   EDGE, Noah Lee; 1926; yes; M; Caddo; yes; 4/4; 4/4; 4/4; yes

1930   326;   GAREN, Yetine; 1926-7-13; yes; F; Caddo; yes; 1/2; W; 1/4; [no]; Oklahoma City, Okla

1931   372;   HADDEN, Vernon Lewis; 1927-5-28; yes; M; Wichita; yes; 1/2; W; 1/4; yes

1928   361;   HALFMOON, Irene Elizabeth; 1927-3-13; yes; F; Wichita; yes; 4/4; 4/4; 4/4; yes

1927   428;   HOAF, Vern Spencer; 1926; M; Wichita; yes; 4/4; 4/4; 4/4; yes

1927   387;   JOHNSON, Vincent Buntin; 1926-9-23; yes; M; Caddo; yes; 4/4; 4/4; 4/4; yes

1928   555;   LAMAR, May Pearl; 1927-5-19; yes; F; Wichita; yes; 4/4; 4/4; 4/4; yes

1928   558;   LAMAR; 1927-4-16; yes; F; Wichita; yes; 4/4; 4/4; 4/4; yes

1927   687;   LEE, Georgia; 1926-8-1; m[sic]; Caddo; yes; 4/4; 4/4; 4/4; yes

1927   604;   LONGHORN, Robert A; 1926; yes; M; Wichita; yes; 4/4; 4/4; 4/4; yes

1927   725;   LOPEZ, Wanda; 1927; yes; F; Wichita; yes; Mex; 4/4; 1/2; yes

See #
1927   611;   LORENTZ, Harriet Jean; 1927-5-2; yes; F; Wichita; yes; 4/4; 4/4; 4/4; yes

121

State __Oklahoma__ Reservation ___Wichita___ Agency or Jurisdiction _Kiowa_
Office of Indian Affairs Births Occurring Between the Dates of July 1, 1926 and
June 30, 1927 to Parents Enrolled at Jurisdiction

KEY: 1927 Census Roll Number; Name; Surname and Given; Date of Birth; Live Birth (Yes or No); Sex; Tribe; Ward (yes or no); Degree of Father's blood; Degree of Mother's blood; Degree of Child's blood; At jurisdiction where enrolled (yes or no); [If "no", where, if given]

1927   727;   OSBORNE, Frank, Jr; 1926-11-26; yes; M; Wichita; yes; 1/2; W; 1/4; yes

1927   768;   PARTON, Maroline; 1926; yes; F; Wichita; yes; 4/4; 4/4; 4/4; yes

1927   414;   SMARTT, Lois Mae; 1927-3-2; yes; F; Caddo, yes; W; 1/2; 1/4; yes

1927   212;   SNAKE, Robert; 1926-11-22; yes; M; Caddo; 4/4; 4/4; 4/4; yes

        See #
1927   319;   SHEGAHSHE, George; 1926-10-24; yes; M; Caddo; yes; 4/4; 4/4; 4/4; yes

1928   571;   SPENCER, Ada Belle; 1927-5-1; yes; F; Wichita; yes; 4/4; 4/4; 4/4; yes

1927   760;   SMITH, Delbert Buntin; 1926; yes; M; Caddo; yes; 4/4; 4/4; 4/4; yes

1927   868;   SMITH, Elmer; 1926-9-5; yes; M; Wichita; yes; 4/4; 4/4; 4/4; yes

1927   953;   STANDING, Lewellyn; 1926-7-4; yes; M; Wichita; yes; 4/4; 4/4; 4/4; yes

1927   970;   STEPHENSON, Vernon; 1926-10-10; yes; M; Wichita; yes; 4/4; 4/4; 4/4; yes

1927   996;   SUMPTER, Cerdis Willie; 1926; yes; M; Caddo; yes; 4/4; 4/4; 4/4; yes

1927   1282; TAYLOR, Mattie Lo8[sic]; 1926-11-19; yes; F; Wichita; yes; W; M; M & W; yes

1928   1089; TOHO, Nelson; 1926-11-8; yes; M; Caddo; yes; 4/4; 4/4; 4/4; yes

1927   1140; WHEELER, Hilda May; 1926; yes; F; Wichita; yes; W; 4/4; 1/2; yes

1927   255;   WHITE, Vera Earline; 1926; yes; F; Caddo; yes; W; 4/4; 1/2; yes

KIOWA INDIAN AGENCY

Wichita Reservation

Oklahoma

1928

BIRTH ROLL
Wichita, Caddo, and Delaware Indians

State __Oklahoma__ Reservation __Wichita__ Agency or Jurisdiction __Oklahoma__
Office of Indian Affairs Births Occurring Between the Dates of July 1, 1927 and
June 30, 1928 to Parents Enrolled at Jurisdiction

KEY: 1928 Census Roll Number; Name; Surname and Given; Date of Birth; Live Birth (Yes or No); Sex; Tribe; Ward (yes or no); Degree of Father's blood; Degree of Mother's blood; Degree of Child's blood; At jurisdiction where enrolled (yes or no); [If "no", where, if given]

1928   50;   BATES, Georgia; 1928-Jan-13; yes; F; Wichita; yes; 4/4; 4/4; 4/4; yes

1928   1242;   BROWN, Marlin; 1927-July-13; yes; M; Caddo; yes; 4/4; 4/4; 4/4; yes

1928   1243;   BROWN, Marvin; 1927-July-13; yes; M; Caddo; yes; 4/4; 4/4; 4/4; yes

1930   1485;   BEAVER, Manueal[sic]; 1928-Apr-3; yes; M; Caddo & Del; yes; 4/4; 4/4; 4/4; yes

1930   62;   BODOKA, Anna Laura; 1928-Jan-23; yes; F; Wichita; yes; 4/4; 4/4; 4/4; yes

1928   457;   HUNTER, Freddie; 1927-Aug-8; yes; M; Wichita; yes; 4/4; 4/4; 4/4; yes

1928   1291;   JACKSON, Michael; 1927-Dec-27; yes; M; Caddo; yes; W; 1/2; 1/4; yes

1928   522;   KEYS, Thomas N; 1927-Sept-6; yes; M; Caddo; yes; 4/4; 4/4; 4/4; yes

1928   693;   MOORE, Myra Clements; 1928-May-28; yes; F; Wichita; yes; 4/4; 4/4; 4/4; yes

1928   1006;   MYERS; 1928-Mar-9; yes; M; Wichita; yes; 1/4; 1/4; 1/4; yes

1929   778;   PARTON, John Victor; 1928-Feb-17; yes; M; Wichita; yes; 4/4; 4/4; 4/4; yes

        See #
1928   798;   PICKARD, Jerland Lois; 1928-July; yes; F; Wichita; yes; 4/4; 4/4; 4/4; yes

1928   819;   REEDER, Wanda Lea; 1927-July-31; yes; F; Caddo; 1/2; 4/4; 3/4; yes

1929   446;   SNAKE, Bessie Marie; 1928-June-14; yes; F; Wichita; yes; 4/4; 4/4; 4/4; yes

1929   904;   SHEMAMY, Ernestine Pearl; 1928-June-15; yes; F; Caddo; yes; 4/4; 4/4; 4/4; yes

State __Oklahoma__ Reservation __Wichita__ Agency or Jurisdiction __Oklahoma__
Office of Indian Affairs Births Occurring Between the Dates of July 1, 1927 and
June 30, 1928 to Parents Enrolled at Jurisdiction

KEY: 1928 Census Roll Number; Name; Surname and Given; Date of Birth; Live Birth (Yes or No); Sex; Tribe; Ward (yes or no); Degree of Father's blood; Degree of Mother's blood; Degree of Child's blood; At jurisdiction where enrolled (yes or no); [If "no", where, if given]

1928   984;   STURM, Bettie June; 1928-Feb-28; yes; F; Caddo; yes; 1/2; W; 1/4; yes

1928   989;   STURM, Percy Loyd; 1927-Dec-8; yes; M; Caddo; yes; 1/2; W; 1/4; yes

1928   1292;   SWIFT, Lavera Mae; 1928-May-8; yes; F; Wichita; yes; 4/4; 4/4; 4/4; yes

1928   1050;   THOMAS, Alena May; 1927-Sept-15; yes; F; Wichita; yes; 4/4; 4/4; 4/4; yes

1931   1120;   THOMAS, James Jefferson; 1929-Nov-14; yes; M; Caddo; yes; 1/4; 1/4; 1/4; yes

1928   1097;   TOUNWIN, Milton Tracy; 1927-July-17; yes; M; Caddo; yes; 4/4; 4/4; 4/4; yes

1930   5224;   WILLIAMS, Lethia Mary Ann; 1928-June-21; yes; F; Caddo; yes; 4/4; 4/4; 4/4; yes

1928   1112;   WARDEN; 1928-Mar-24; yes; F; Wichita; yes; 4/4; 3/4; 7/8; yes

1928   1123;   WELLER, Harriet; 1927-Oct-3; yes; F; Caddo; yes; 4/4; 4/4; 4/4; yes

1928   1229;   WILLIAMS, Roland Glenn; 1928-Feb-25; yes; M; Caddo; yes; 1/4; W; 1/8; yes

1931   1264;   WILIAMS[sic], Melvin; 1928-Mar-16; yes; M; Caddo; yes; 4/4; 4/4; 4/4; yes

1929   157;   WOLF, Stanford; 1927-Dec-21; yes; M; Wichita; yes; 4/4; 3/4; 7/8; yes

1931   214;   DOWNING, James Franklin; 1928-Sept-23; yes; M; Caddo; yes; 1/4; 1/4; 1/4; yes[sic]; Oklahoma City, Okla

126

KIOWA INDIAN AGENCY
Wichita Reservation
Oklahoma
1929

BIRTH ROLL
Wichita, Caddo, and Delaware
Indians

State ___Oklahoma___ Reservation ___Wichita___ Agency or Jurisdiction ___Kiowa___
Office of Indian Affairs Births Occurring Between the Dates of July 1, 1928 and
June 30, 1929 to Parents Enrolled at Jurisdiction

KEY: 1929 Census Roll Number; Name; Surname and Given; Date of Birth; Live Birth (Yes or No); Sex; Tribe; Ward (yes or no); Degree of Father's blood; Degree of Mother's blood; Degree of Child's blood; At jurisdiction where enrolled (yes or no); [If "no", where, if given]

1929   1033;   BEAVER, Myrtle Ann; 1928-July-30; yes; F; Wichita; yes; 4/4; 4/4; 4/4; yes

1930   5148;   BROWN, Nathan Merl; 1929-June-27; yes; M; Wichita; yes; 4/4; 4/4; 4/4; yes

1929   148;   CHISHOLM, Thelma Ruby; 1928-Sept-9; yes; F; Caddo & Wich; yes; 4/4; 4/4; 4/4; yes

1929   1182;   COFFEE, Wanadalien Ethelda; 1929-Jan-1; yes; F; Caddo; yes; 4/4; 4/4; 4/4; yes

1930   1221;   EXENDINE, Joseph Newton; 1928-Aug-7; yes; M; Delaware; yes; 1/2; W; 1/4; yes

1929   456;   HUNTER, Irene; 1928-Oct-13; yes; F; Caddo & Del; yes; 4/4; 4/4; 4/4; yes

1929   468;   INKANISH, George Francis; 1928-Oct-13; yes; M; Caddo; yes; 1/2; 1/2; 1/2; yes

1930   2184;   LANDRUM, Ed Burney; 1929-Mar-3; yes; M; Wichita; yes; 1/2; W; 1/4; yes

1929   740;   LAYTEN, Louise Nadine; 1928-Aug-23; yes; F; Caddo; yes; 1/2; W; 1/4; yes

1929   615;   LORENTZ, Billy Jean; 1929-Jan-27; yes; F; Wichita; yes; 4/4; 4/4; 4/4; yes

　　　See #
1929   607;   LORENTZ, Gilbert; 1930-Feb-14; F[sic]; Wichita; yes; 4/4; 4/4; 4/4; yes

1929   1190;   McDANIELS, Shirley May; 1928-Oct-14; yes; F; Caddo; yes; Mex; Mex; Mex; yes

1929   660;   MILLER, Orville Roayne; 1928-July-5; yes; M; Wichita; yes; 4/4; 4/4; 4/4; yes

1929   668;   MOONLIGHT, Deloris; 1928-Oct-23; yes; F; Caddo; yes; 4/4; 4/4; 4/4; yes

Office of Indian Affairs Births Occurring Between the Dates of July 1, 1928 and
June 30, 1929 to Parents Enrolled at Jurisdiction

KEY: 1929 Census Roll Number; Name; Surname and Given; Date of Birth; Live Birth (Yes or No); Sex; Tribe; Ward (yes or no); Degree of Father's blood; Degree of Mother's blood; Degree of Child's blood; At jurisdiction where enrolled (yes or no); [If "no", where, if given]

1929   1167;   ORMSTON, Georgeen Kathleen; 1928-Dec-6; yes; F; Caddo; yes;
                1/2; W; 1/16; yes

       See #
1929   800;   PICKARD, Jerland Louis; 1928-July; F[?]; Wichita; yes; 4/4; 4/4;
                4/4; yes

1929   971;   STEPHENSON, Myles Robert; 1929-Jan-14; yes; M; Wichita; yes;
                4/4; 4/4; 4/4; yes

1929   791;   TAINPEAH, Anna Katherine; 1929-Mar-1; yes; F; Wichita; yes; 4/4;
                4/4; 4/4; yes

1929   1206;   WILLIAMS, Ula; 1928-Aug-28; yes; F; Caddo; yes; 4/4; 4/4; 4/4; yes

KIOWA INDIAN AGENCY
Wichita Reservation
Oklahoma
1930

BIRTH ROLL
**Wichita, Caddo, and Delaware
Indians**

State __Oklahoma__ Reservation __Wichita__ Agency or Jurisdiction __Kiowa__
Office of Indian Affairs Births Occurring Between the Dates of July 1, 1929 and
June 30, 1930 to Parents Enrolled at Jurisdiction

KEY: 1930 Census Roll Number; Name; Surname and Given; Date of Birth; Live Birth (Yes or No); Sex; Tribe; Ward (yes or no); Degree of Father's blood; Degree of Mother's blood; Degree of Child's blood; At jurisdiction where enrolled (yes or no); [If "no", where, if given]

1930   436;   BEDOKO, Maurice M; 1929-Dec-2; yes; M; Caddo; yes; 4/4; 4/4; 4/4; yes

1930   1149;   ELKINS, Orbie Dale; 1929-Oct-16; yes; M; Caddo; yes; 1/2; W; 1/4; yes

1930   1441;   GUY, Richard Ellis; 1930-Feb-25; yes; M; Caddo; yes; 4/4; 4/4; 4/4; yes

1931   386;   HARRY, Clayton Edward; 1930-Jan-1; yes; M; Caddo & Del; yes; 4/4; 4/4; 4/4; yes

1930   1543;   HAZLETT, Boone D, Jr; 1929-Sept-18; yes; M; Caddo; yes; 1/2; W; 1/4; yes

1930   1163;   LAWRENCE, Arthur Bruce; 1929-July-17; yes; M; Wichita; yes; 4/4; 4/4; 4/4; yes

1930   2292;   LONGHAT, Eddie Franklin; 1929-Dec-19; yes; M; Wichita & Caddo; yes; 4/4; 4/4; 4/4; yes

1931   179;   McLEMORE, Henry James; 1930-June-22; yes; M; Caddo; yes; 1/4; 1/4; 1/4; yes

1931   352;   NICHOLS, Lyman Wm; 1930-Apr-1; yes; M; Caddo; yes; W; 4/4; 1/2; yes

1931   850;   REEDER, Algerinen Loney; 1930-Mar-23; yes; M; Caddo; yes; 1/2; 4/4; 3/4; yes

1931   971;   SMITH, Dorla Jean; 1930-Mar-23; yes; F; Caddo; yes; 4/4; W; 1/2; yes

1930   1565;   SMITH, Gwendolyn Serena; 1929-Nov-13; yes; F; Wichita; yes; 4/4; 4/4; 4/4; yes

1930   3890;   STANDING, David Morris; 1930-Feb-3; F[sic]; Wichita; yes; 4/4; 4/4; 4/4; yes

1931   662;   TAYLOR, Chas Curtis; 1930-Mar-4; yes; M; caddo[sic] & Del; yes; 1/2; W; 1/4; yes

State __Oklahoma__ Reservation ___Wichita___ Agency or Jurisdiction _Kiowa__
Office of Indian Affairs Births Occurring Between the Dates of July 1, 1929 and
June 30, 1930 to Parents Enrolled at Jurisdiction

KEY: 1930 Census Roll Number; Name; Surname and Given; Date of Birth; Live Birth (Yes or No); Sex; Tribe; Ward (yes or no); Degree of Father's blood; Degree of Mother's blood; Degree of Child's blood; At jurisdiction where enrolled (yes or no); [If "no", where, if given]

1931   1088;   THOMAS, Arthur Laverne; 1930-May-30; yes; M; Wichita & Del; yes; 4/4; 3/4; 7/8; yes

1931   1121;   THOMAS Geo Edward; 1939-Nov-14; yes; M; Caddo; yes; 1/4; [?]; 1/8; yes

1930   4566;   TOHO, Malford; 1929-July-2; yes; M; Caddo; yes; 4/4; 4/4; 4/4; yes

1931   1224;   WILLIAMS, Chas Ed; 1929-Nov-22; yes; M; Caddo; yes; 1/4; W; 1/8; yes

1931   2189;   WILLIAMS, Sharen; 1929-Dec-11; yes; F; Caddo; yes; 1/4; W; 1/8; yes

KIOWA INDIAN AGENCY
Wichita Reservation

Oklahoma

1931

BIRTH ROLL
Wichita, Caddo, and Delaware
Indians

State __Oklahoma__ Reservation __Wichita__ Agency or Jurisdiction __Kiowa__

Office of Indian Affairs Births Occurring Between the Dates of April 1, 1930 and March 31, 1931 to Parents Enrolled at Jurisdiction

1931   396;   BEAVER, Katherine Mae; 1920-Aug-7; yes; F; Caddo & Del; yes; 4/4; 4/4; 4/4; yes

1931   106;   BUTLER, Geraldine; 1931-Feb-2; yes; F; Caddo; yes; 1/2;1/2;1/2; yes

1931   120;   CAMPBELL, Mabel; 1930-Aug-25; yes; F; Wichita; yes; 4/4; 1/2; 3/4; yes

See #
1931   439;   DICE, Max Don; 1931-Feb-14; yes; M; Caddo & Del; yes; W; 4/4; 1/2; yes

1931   271;   EDWARDS, Pearl Marie; 1930-July-12; yes; F; Caddo; yes; 4/4; 4/4; 4/4; yes

1931   1079;   FRENCH, Irene; 1930-Apr-9; yes; F; Caddo; yes; 4/4; 4/4; 4/4; yes

1931   1084;   HUPP, Eddie V; 1930-Dec-27; yes; M; Delaware; yes; W; 4/4; 1/2; yes

See #
1931   639;   MARTIN, Colleen; 1931-Mar-17; yes; F; Caddo; yes; W; 4/4; 1/2; yes

1931   753;   McDANIELS, Dennis Ray; 1930-Dec-9; yes; M; Delaware; yes; W; 1/2; 1/4; yes

1931   179;   McLEMORE, Henry James; 1930-June-22; yes; M; Caddo; yes; 1/4; 1/4; 1/4; yes

1931   681;   MILLER, Amarydllis[sic]; 1930-Sept-12; yes; F; Wichita; yes; 4/4; 4/4; 4/4; yes

1931   721;   MURROW; 1930-Aug-28; yes; M; Caddo; yes; 4/4; 4/4; 4/4; yes

1931   352;   NICHOLS, Lyman William; 1930-Apr-1; yes; M; Caddo; yes; W; 4/4; 1/2; yes

See #
1931   1211;   ARMSTON, Agnes Dayton; 1930-Aug-13; yes; F; Caddo; yes; W; 1/4; 1/8; yes

State __Oklahoma__ Reservation __Wichita__ Agency or Jurisdiction __Kiowa__
Office of Indian Affairs Births Occurring Between the Dates of April 1, 1930 and
March 31, 1931 to Parents Enrolled at Jurisdiction

KEY: 1931 Census Roll Number; Name; Surname and Given; Date of Birth; Live Birth (Yes or No); Sex; Tribe; Ward (yes or no); Degree of Father's blood; Degree of Mother's blood; Degree of Child's blood; At jurisdiction where enrolled (yes or no); [If "no", where, if given]

1931   758;   OSBORNE, Chiquita; 1931-Feb-24; yes; F; Delaware; yes; 1/2; W; 1/4; yes

        See #
1931   739;   OSBORNE, Deuaine Beaver; 1931-Mar-18; yes; F; Delaware; yes; 1/2; W; 1/4; yes

1931   750;   OSBORNE, Lyle Marleine; 1930-Oct-1; yes; F; Delaware; yes; 1/2; W; 1/4; yes

1931   811;   PARTON, Armita Lois; 1930-Oct-8; yes; F; Caddo; yes; 4/4; 4/4; 4/4; yes

1931   803;   PARTON, Delphinia Fay; 1930-May-8; yes; F; Caddo; yes; 4/4; 4/4; 4/4; yes

1931   803;   PARTON, Deltha; 1931-Jan-15; yes; F; Caddo; yes; 4/4; 4/4; 4/4; yes

        See #
1931   1314;   SECARKSE, Vernon Nathan; 1931-Feb-15; yes; M; Caddo; yes; 4/4; 4/4; 4/4; yes

1931   936;   SHEMAMY, Vermona Joyce; 1930-Sept-15; yes; F; Caddo; yes; 4/4; 4/4; 4/4; yes

1931   1088;   THOMAS, Arthur Laverne; 1930-May-30; yes; M; Wichita; yes; 4/4; 3/4; 7/8; yes

1931   765;   THOMPSON; 1930-Dec-15; yes; M; Caddo; yes; W; 1/4; 1/8; yes

1931   1174;   WELLER, Lois Nevada; 1930-Dec-27; yes; F; Caddo; yes; 4/4; 4/4; 4/4; yes

        See #
1931   1267;   WEST, Herbert Clinton; 1930-Dec-22; yes; M; Caddo; yes; W; 1/4; 1/8; yes

1931   1256;   WILLIAMS, Harold Jerome; 1931-Mar-16; yes; M; Caddo; yes; 4/4; 4/4; 4/4; yes

1931   1311;   WILSON; 1931-Mar-25; yes; F; Caddo; yes; 4/4; 4/4; 4/4; yes

KIOWA INDIAN AGENCY
Wichita Reservation
Oklahoma
1932

BIRTH ROLL
Wichita, Caddo, and Delaware
Indians

State __Oklahoma__ Reservation ___Wichita___ Agency or Jurisdiction _Kiowa__
Office of Indian Affairs Births Occurring Between the Dates of April 1, 1931 and
March 31, 1932 to Parents Enrolled at Jurisdiction

KEY: 1932 Census Roll Number; Name; Surname and Given; Date of Birth; Live Birth (Yes or No); Sex; Tribe; Ward (yes or no); Degree of Father's blood; Degree of Mother's blood; Degree of Child's blood; At jurisdiction where enrolled (yes or no); [If "no", where, if given]

1932   33;   ARMSTRONG, Walter Richard; 1931-Dec-30; yes; M; Caddo; yes; 1/2; W; 1/4; yes

1932   49;   BARCINDEBAR, Jennie Lorene; 1931-Nov-20; yes; F; Caddo; yes; 4/4; 4/4; 4/4; yes

1932   80;   BOBB, Johnny Dean; 1931-Nov-20; yes; M; Delaware; yes; 3/4; 1/4; 3/8; yes

See #
1932   205;   CLARK; 1931-May-16; yes; M; Caddo; yes; 1/2; 1/2; 1/2; yes

1932   455;   ECKIWAUDAH, Catherine Marie; 1931-Oct-9; yes; F; Caddo; yes; 1/4; 1/4; 1/4; yes

1932   252;   EDMONDS, Melvina Grace; 1931-July-29; yes; F; Caddo; yes; 4/4; 4/4; 4/4; yes

1932   319;   FULTON, Donna Lee; 1931-Aug-24; yes; F; Wichita; yes; 4/4; 4/4; 4/4; yes

1932   115;   GABBARD, James Campbell; 1931-Nov-19; yes; M; Wichita; W; 4/4; 1/2; yes

1932   418;   HENDRIX, Norma Jean; 1931-May-3; yes; F; Caddo; yes; 1/2; 1/2; 1/2; yes

1932   429;   HENRY, Veryl Raymond; 1931-Sept-15; yes; M; Caddo; yes; 1/4; 4/4; 5/8; yes

1932   1054;   HINKLE, Moneta Fay; 1931-Apr-7; yes; F; Delaware; yes; W; 1/2; 1/4; yes

1932   1055;   HINKLE; Oletha Fay; 1931-Apr-7; yes; F; Delaware; yes; W; 1/2; 1/4; yes

1932   453;   HOAG, Berwin; 1931-May-25; yes; F; Caddo; yes; 4/4; 4/4; 4/4; yes

1932   1333;   ISBELL, Lavene[sic]; 1931-Aug-29; yes; F; Caddo; yes; W; 1/2; 1/4; yes

1932   457;   MARTINEZ, Viviana; 1931-Apr-20; yes; F; Delaware; yes; Mex; 4/4; 1/2; yes

State __Oklahoma__ Reservation ___Wichita___ Agency or Jurisdiction _Kiowa_

Office of Indian Affairs Births Occurring Between the Dates of April 1, 1931 and March 31, 1932 to Parents Enrolled at Jurisdiction

KEY: 1932 Census Roll Number; Name; Surname and Given; Date of Birth; Live Birth (Yes or No); Sex; Tribe; Ward (yes or no); Degree of Father's blood; Degree of Mother's blood; Degree of Child's blood; At jurisdiction where enrolled (yes or no); [If "no", where, if given]

1932 1086; McCOY, Lawrence McKinley; 1932-Feb-23; yes; M; Caddo; yes; W; 4/4; 1/2; yes

1932 692; MILLER, Leroy; 1932-Feb-20; yes; M; Wichita; yes; 4/4; 4/4; 4/4; yes

See #
1932 693; MILLER, Violet; 1931-Aug-21; yes; F; Wichita; yes; 4/4; 4/4; 4/4; yes

1932 707; MILLER, Thos Buntin; 1931-July-23; yes; M; Caddo; yes; 4/4; W; 1/2; yes

1932 838; PICKARD, Trusilla; 1931-Apr-27; yes; F; Wichita; yes; 4/4; 4/4; 4/4; yes

1932 845; PUNLEY, Arthur, Jr; 1931-Oct-1; yes; M; Wichita; yes; 3/4; 3/4; 3/4; yes

1932 862; REEDER, Patricia Louise; 1931-Sept-1; yes; F; Caddo; yes; 1/2; 1/2; 1/2; yes

1932 1045; SUMPTER, Gibson; 1931-June-17; yes; M; Caddo; yes; 1/2; 1/2; 1/2; yes

1932 123; WHITEFOX, Claudine Lee; 1932-Jan-4; yes; F; Wichita; yes; 4/4; 1/2; 3/4; yes

KIOWA INDIAN AGENCY
Kiowa Reservation
Oklahoma
1925

DEATH ROLL
**Kiowa, Comanche, Apache and
Fort Sill Apache Indians**

State __Oklahoma__ Reservation __Kiowa__ Agency or Jurisdiction __Kiowa__
Office of Indian Affairs Deaths Occurring Between the Dates of July 1, 1924 and
June 30, 1925 of Indians Enrolled at Jurisdiction

KEY: Year & Number on last Census Roll; Name; Surname and Given; Date of Death; Age at Death; Sex; Tribe; Ward (yes or no); Degree of Blood; Cause of Death; At jurisdiction where enrolled (yes or no); [If "no", where, if given]

1925   224;   AUGOAHDY, Webb; 1925-June-29; 52; Male; Kiowa; yes; Full; Diabetes; yes

1924   827;   AHDENGBY, White Buffalo; 1924-Aug-24; 72; Male; Kiowa; yes; Full; Not known; yes

1924   1409;   AHHAITTY, Cora; 1924-Aug-24; 20; Fem; Kiowa; Full; Tuberculosis; yes

1924   923;   AKENETO, Rose; 1925-Mar-13; 17; Fem; Kiowa; yes; Full; Tuberculosis; yes

1925   965;   ASAH, James; 1925-Jan-12; 61; Male; Kiowa; yes; Full; Inanition; yes

1924   1399;   ATONGKY; 1924-July-20; 77; Fem; Kiowa; yes; Full; Unknown; yes

1924   310;   AUCHCHIAH, Flora Bell; 1924-Feb-21; 1; Fem; Kiowa; yes; Full; Not known; yes

1924   1651;   AUDLEGUVEOTY, Joe; 1925-June-3; 13; Male; Kiowa; yes; Full; Tuberculosis; yes

1924   38;   BITCHART, Oliver; 1924-Dec-10; 53; Male; Apache & Wich; yes; Full; Pul. Tuberculosis; yes

1924   847;   BLACKSTAR, Adrain Ellsworth; 1925-Jan-21; 2; Male; Kiowa; yes; Full; Not known; yes

1925   1022;   BOHONEMAH, Martha; 1925-Jan-24; 79; Fem; Kiowa; yes; Full; General Debility; yes

See #
1925   173;   BOINTY, Baby; 1925-Apr-18; Few hours; Fem; Comanche; yes; Full; Premature birth; yes

See #
1925   1115;   BOSIN, Ida May; Sept-23-1924; 1/12; Fem; Kiowa; yes; Full; Unknown; yes

1925   1346;   BRACE, Lena; 1925-Apr-13; 19; Fem; Kiowa; yes; Full; Pulmonary T.B.; yes

State __Oklahoma__ Reservation __Kiowa__ Agency or Jurisdiction __Kiowa__
Office of Indian Affairs Deaths Occurring Between the Dates of July 1, 1924 and
June 30, 1925 of Indians Enrolled at Jurisdiction

KEY: Year & Number on last Census Roll; Name; Surname and Given; Date of Death; Age at Death; Sex; Tribe; Ward (yes or no); Degree of Blood; Cause of Death; At jurisdiction where enrolled (yes or no); [If "no", where, if given]

1924   524;   DOMEBO, Andy; 1924-Aug-23; 27; Male; Kiowa; yes; Full; Tuberculosis; yes

1925   319;   DOYAH, Julia; 1925-June-8; 14; Fem; Kiowa; yes; Full; TB throat; yes

1924   203;   ESADOOAH, George; 1925-Feb-15; 35; Male; Comanche; yes; Full; Unknown; yes

See #
1924   203;   ESADOOAH, Fred; 1925-Jan-17; 2 days; Male; Comanche; yes; Full; Inanition; yes

1924   849;   GEARY, Rudolph Frank; 1924-Feb-7; 1; Male; Kiowa; yes; Full; Unknown; yes

1924   108;   GUOEBODE; 1924-Sept-26; 73; Male; Kiowa; yes; Full; Hemiplegia; yes

See #
1925   993;   HIGHWALKER, Nettie; 1925-Apr-7; 1/12; Fem; Kiowa; yes; Full; Pneumonia; yes

1924   1301;   HYDE, Wade Hampton; 1924-Sept-14; 3; Male; Comanche; yes; Full; Not known; yes

See #
1924   444;   PAHDOCONY, Kenneth; 1925-Jan-24; 2/12; Male; Comanche; yes; Full; Unknown; yes

1924   353;   PARRIAECHIVIT, Iolene; 1924-July-10; 6; Fem; Comanche; yes; Full; Ilio Colitis; yes

1924   1085;   PEAHBO; 1924-July-10; 79; Fem; Comanche; yes; Full; Unknown; yes

See #
1925   1055;   PAYWETOWAUP, Pearl; 1924-Dec-5; few hours; Fem; Comanche; yes; Full; Unknown; yes

1924   499;   PERMMORAH; 1925-Mar-16; 68; Male; Comanche; yes; Full; Unknown; yes

State __Oklahoma__ Reservation __Kiowa__ Agency or Jurisdiction __Kiowa__
Office of Indian Affairs Deaths Occurring Between the Dates of July 1, 1924 and
June 30, 1925 of Indians Enrolled at Jurisdiction

KEY: Year & Number on last Census Roll; Name; Surname and Given; Date of Death; Age at Death; Sex; Tribe; Ward (yes or no); Degree of Blood; Cause of Death; At jurisdiction where enrolled (yes or no); [If "no", where, if given]

1924   277;   KAUNKOAHMAH, Diana; 1924-Dec-24; 44; Fem; Kiowa; yes; Full; Heart failure; yes

1925   1531;   KAUQUAYE, (Odle Paugh); 1925-May-12; 72; Male; Kiowa; yes; Full; Kidney and blood disease; yes

1924   340;   KAUTIHOODLE; 1924-Sept-25; 52; Fem; Kiowa; yes; Full; Cardical[sic] asthma; yes

1925   309;   MADDICOME; 1924-July-7; 63; Fem; Comanche; yes; Full; Unknown; yes

1924   1278;   MARTINEZ, Homer; 1925-June-3; 10; Male; Comanche; yes; Full; Hodgkins[sic] Disease; yes

1925   1347;   MONATOBAY, Geraldine; 1925-Feb-7; 2/12; Fem; Comanche; yes; Full; Unknown; yes

1924   1328;   MOWWAT, Harrietta; 1924-Nov-2; 7/12; Fem; Kiowa; yes; Full; Bronchial Penumonia[sic]; yes

1924   628;   NAUNIE, Florine; 1924-Sept-1; 2; Fem; Comanche; yes; Full; Unknown; yes

1924   344;   NINSEY; 1925-May-14; 81; Male; Comanche; yes; Full; Fractured hip; yes

See #
1925   189;   SATEPEAHTAW, Finis Brown; 1925-May-23; 2; Male; Kiowa; yes; Full; Jaundice; yes

1925   863;   SAUPETTY, Kelley; 1925-June-5; 9/12; Male; Comanche; yes; Full; Summer complaint; yes

1924   1132;   SAUMTY, Oscar; 1925-Jan-25; 17; Male; Kiowa; yes; Full; Pulmonary T.B.; yes

See #
1925   342;   SEAHMER, Burke; 1925-Jan-17; 15 das; Male; Comanche; yes; Full; Unknown; yes

State ___Oklahoma___ Reservation ___Kiowa___ Agency or Jurisdiction ___Kiowa___
Office of Indian Affairs Deaths Occurring Between the Dates of July 1, 1924 and
June 30, 1925 of Indians Enrolled at Jurisdiction

KEY: Year & Number on last Census Roll; Name; Surname and Given; Date of Death; Age at Death; Sex; Tribe; Ward (yes or no); Degree of Blood; Cause of Death; At jurisdiction where enrolled (yes or no); [If "no", where, if given]

	See #	
1925	103;	SPOTTED CROW, Susie; 1925-Jan-17; 2/12; Fem; Comanche; yes; Full; Unknown; yes
1925	315;	TAHYO; 1925-June-2; 69; Fem; Kiowa; yes; Full; Unknown; yes
1924	1244;	TANETONE; 1924-Oct-21; 72; Male; Kiowa; yes; Full; Unknown; yes
1924	350;	TETCHEMHAVIT, Libby; 1924-Dec-13; 33; Fem; Comanche; yes; Full; Pulmonary T.B.; yes
1924	610;	TETCHEM; 1924-Aug-24; 46; Fem; Comanche; yes; Full; Unknown; yes
1924	239;	TINETIAH, (Haunpo Martin); 1924-Aug-7; 37; Male; Kiowa; yes; Full; Tuberculosis; yes
1924	841;	TISSOYO, Alice; 1925-Mar-17; 45; Fem; Comanche; yes; Full; Unknown; yes
1924	659;	TIXSEY, Anna; 1925-Apr-28; 13; Fem; Comanche; yes; Full; Pulmonary T.B.; yes
1924	471;	TOCHEGAH; 1925-May-20; 79; Fem; Comanche; yes; Full; Unknown; yes
1925	See # 116;	TSOTAHSISKO, John; 1924-Nov-6; 1/12; Male; Apache; yes; Full; Unknown; yes
1925	See # 1030;	WALLACE, Winfred Wanda; 1924-Oct-14; 2/12; Fem; Comanche; yes; Full; Unknown; yes
1925	388;	WAYSEPAPPY, Rose; 1925-June-20; 14; Fem; Comanche; yes; Full; Tuberculosis; yes
1924	51;	WOODARD, Thos; 1924-Aug; 86; Male; Kiowa; yes; Full; Unknown; yes

State __Oklahoma__ Reservation __Kiowa__ Agency or Jurisdiction __Kiowa__
Office of Indian Affairs Deaths Occurring Between the Dates of July 1, 1924 and
June 30, 1925 of Indians Enrolled at Jurisdiction

KEY: Year & Number on last Census Roll; Name; Surname and Given; Date of Death; Age at Death; Sex; Tribe; Ward (yes or no); Degree of Blood; Cause of Death; At jurisdiction where enrolled (yes or no); [If "no", where, if given]

See #

1925   947;   YEAHOUO, Florene; 1925-May-13; 1/12; Kiowa; yes; Full; Convulsions; yes

KIOWA INDIAN AGENCY

Kiowa Reservation

Oklahoma

1926

DEATH ROLL
Kiowa, Comanche, Apache and
Fort Sill Apache Indians

State __Oklahoma__ Reservation __Kiowa__ Agency or Jurisdiction __Kiowa__
Office of Indian Affairs Deaths Occurring Between the Dates of July 1, 1925 and
June 30, 1926 of Indians Enrolled at Jurisdiction

KEY: Year & Number on last Census Roll; Name; Surname and Given; Date of Death; Age at Death; Sex; Tribe; Ward (yes or no); Degree of Blood; Cause of Death; At jurisdiction where enrolled (yes or no); [If "no", where, if given]

See #
1926 1410; AHHAITTY, Murray; 1926-Mar-9; 3; Male; Kiowa; yes; Full; Pneumonia; yes

1925 1428; AHHAITTY, Violet; 1925-Sept-10; 1; Fem; Kiowa; yes; Full; Hereditary liver; yes

See #
1926 463; AHTONE, Carolyn; 1925-Oct-16; Not known; Fem; Kiowa; yes; Full; Whooping cough; yes

1926 463; AHTONE, Clouse; 1925-Sept-19; Not known; Male; Kiowa; yes; Full; Not known; yes

1925 50; AHKEAHBO, Florence; 1925-July-20; 1; Fem; Kiowa; yes; Full; Malnutrition; yes

1925 561; APEKAUM, Dardenella; 1926-June-24; 3; Fem; Comanche; yes; Full; Summer complaint; yes

1926 802; ATAUMBI, Mary Louise; 1925-Aug-18; Not known; Fem; Kiowa; yes; Full; Not known; yes

See #
1926 1718; ATTOCKNIE, Theodore; 1926-Feb-23; 8 das; Male; Comanche; yes; Full; Not known; yes

1926 217; AUNKO, Amos; 1926-Mar-1; 1; Male; Kiowa; yes; Full; Pneumonia; yes

See #
1926 1239; AUGUOYAH, Virginia; 1926-May-29; 61; Fem; Kiowa; yes; Full; Not known; yes

1925 1617; BEARTRACK, Clay Clifton; 1925-Aug-8; 1; Male; Kiowa; yes; Full; Not known; yes

1925 169; BERRY, Joseph; 1926-Feb-26; 3; Male; yes; Apache; yes; Full; Flu & Pneumonia; yes

State __Oklahoma__ Reservation __Kiowa__ Agency or Jurisdiction __Kiowa__
Office of Indian Affairs Deaths Occurring Between the Dates of July 1, 1925 and
June 30, 1926 of Indians Enrolled at Jurisdiction

KEY: Year & Number on last Census Roll; Name; Surname and Given; Date of Death; Age at Death; Sex; Tribe; Ward (yes or no); Degree of Blood; Cause of Death; At jurisdiction where enrolled (yes or no); [If "no", where, if given]

See #
1926   167;   BERRY, Marian Eliza; 1926-Feb-28; 10 das; Fem; Apache; yes; Full; Flu; yes

1925   77;   BIZANARETA, Susie; 1925-Dec-10; 36; Fem; Apache; yes; Full; Not known; yes

See #
1926 1659;   BOSIN, Alvin Blackbear; 1925-Sept-21; 1/12; Male; Comanche; yes; Half; Not known; yes

See #
1926   531;   BURGESS, La Vera; 1925-Aug-16; 7 das; Fem; Comanche; yes; Full; Tetanus; yes

1925 1385;   BRACE, Edna; 1926-June-18; 18; Fem; Kiowa; yes; Full; Pulmonary T.B.; yes

1925 1054;   DAINGKAU, Dora; 1925-Sept-25; 16; Fem; Kiowa; yes; Full; Pulmonary T.B.; yes

1925 1540   DOYETONE; 1926-Feb-28; 68; Male; Kiowa; yes; Full; Pulmonary T.B.; yes

1925   71;   GOODAY, Fred; 1926-Jan-14; 2; Male; Apache & Wich; yes; Full; Pneumonia; yes

1925   847;   GOOMBI, Joseph; 1926-May-6; 27; Male; Kiowa; yes; Full; Not known; yes

1926   698;   GOOMDO, Lucius; 1926-Feb-7; 16; Male; Kiowa; yes; Full; Not known; yes

See #
1926   838;   HAITSHAN, Peggy Jean; 1926-Feb-4; 2; Fem; Kiowa; yes; Full; Not known; yes

1925   97;   HAUNPY, Madeline; 1925-Sept-27; 9/12; Fem; Kiowa; yes; Full; Infantile Paralysis; yes

State __Oklahoma__ Reservation __Kiowa__ Agency or Jurisdiction __Kiowa__
Office of Indian Affairs Deaths Occurring Between the Dates of July 1, 1925 and
June 30, 1926 of Indians Enrolled at Jurisdiction

KEY: Year & Number on last Census Roll; Name; Surname and Given; Date of Death; Age at Death; Sex; Tribe; Ward (yes or no); Degree of Blood; Cause of Death; At jurisdiction where enrolled (yes or no); [If "no", where, if given]

See #
1926 1766; HORSE, Wilbur; 1925-Feb-19; 5/12; Male; Kiowa; yes; Full; Not known; yes

1926 1442; KAHTAHWASSUWOOKY; 1926-Jan-23; 78; Fem; Comanche; yes; Full; Not known; yes

1925   94; KAKAY; 1925-Aug-26; 53; Fem; Comanche; yes; Full; Consumption; yes

1925 114; KASSANAVOID; Jan-2-1926; 45; Male; Comanche; yes; Full; Consumption; yes

1925 606; KAULAY, Charlie; 1926; 21; Male; Kiowa; yes; Full; Tuberculosis; yes

1925 1703; KAYEGAMAH, Carrie; 1926-Mar-16; 40; Fem; Kiowa; yes; Full; Flu; yes

1925 1185; KEAHKO (Ware), Harry; 1926-May-10; 62; Male; Kiowa; yes; Full; Not known; yes

1925 750; KODASEET, Donald; 1926-Mar-16; 16; Male; Kiowa; yes; Full; Gunshot wound; yes

1925 1388; KOSECHATA, Thomas; 1925-July-4; 18; Male; Comanche; yes; Full; Tuberculosis; yes

1929 109; KOSTZUTA, Geo Washington; 1926-Jan-6; 20; Male; Apache; yes; Full; Pulmonary T.B.; yes

1925 1442; KOTSSUMAH; 1926-Jan-17; 65; Full; Apache; yes; Full; Tuberculo sis; yes

677; MAHKENAHVITTY; 1925-Oct-8; 87; Fem; Comanche; yes; Full; Senility; yes

See #
1926 131; MAYNAHONAH, Hattie; 1925-Oct-31; 2; Fem; Apache; yes; Full; Pneumonia; yes

State __Oklahoma__ Reservation __Kiowa__ Agency or Jurisdiction __Kiowa__
Office of Indian Affairs Deaths Occurring Between the Dates of July 1, 1925 and
June 30, 1926 of Indians Enrolled at Jurisdiction

KEY: Year & Number on last Census Roll; Name; Surname and Given; Date of Death; Age at Death; Sex; Tribe; Ward (yes or no); Degree of Blood; Cause of Death; At jurisdiction where enrolled (yes or no); [If "no", where, if given]

See #

1926 1459; MIHECOBY, Alma; 1925-Oct-29; 5 das; Fem; Comanche; yes; Full; Not known; yes

1925 505; MOBAY; 1926-Mar-14; 84; Fem; Kiowa; yes; Full; Senility; yes

1925 1409; MOPOPE, Charles; 1926-Feb-7; 1; Male; Kiowa; yes; Full; Pneumonia; yes

1925 584; NANEAH; 1926-Apr-10; 73; Full; Comanche; yes; Full; Not known; yes

1925 794; PAHDI, Leon; 1925-Dec-7; 12; Male; Comanche; yes; Full; Not known; yes

1925 260; PEKAH, Mollie; 1926-Jan-10; 10; Fem; Comanche; yes; Full; Not known; yes

1925 1056; PEPE; 1925-Aug-1; 56; Fem; Comanche; yes; Full; Not known; yes

1925 1225; PERSCHY, Ray; 1926-Jan-3; 14; Male; Comanche; yes; Full; Not known; yes

1925 764; PETSCHE; 1926-June-6; 68; Male; Comanche; yes; Full; Not known; yes

1925 109; PEHAUPATCHOH, Henry; 1925-July-11; 34; Male; Comanche; yes; Full; Killed by sheriff; yes

1925 867; PUEBLO, Corine; 1925-Oct-10; 11/12; Fem; Comanche; yes; Full; Not known; yes

1925 818; SANATETY; 1925-Sept-17; 47; Fem; Kiowa; yes; Full; Unknown; yes

1925 121; SANKADOTA, Mary; 1926-Mar-22; 19; Fem; Kiowa; yes; Full; Tuberculosis; yes

1925 1211; SAMONE, Henry; 1925-Nov-1; 23; Male; Comanche; yes; Full; Tuberculosis; yes

EXCLUSIVE OF STILLBIRTHS

State __Oklahoma__ Reservation __Kiowa__ Agency or Jurisdiction __Kiowa__

Office of Indian Affairs Deaths Occurring Between the Dates of July 1, 1925 and
June 30, 1926 of Indians Enrolled at Jurisdiction

KEY: Year & Number on last Census Roll; Name; Surname and Given; Date of Death; Age at Death; Sex; Tribe; Ward (yes or no); Degree of Blood; Cause of Death; At jurisdiction where enrolled (yes or no); [If "no", where, if given]

1925   1404;   SARGOWINNE, Jasper; 1925-Aug-18; 5; Male; Comanche; yes; Full; Not known; yes

1925   836;   SAUTY; 1925-Jan-26; 66; Fem; Kiowa; yes; Full; Not known; yes

1925   1099;   SAWUITHKY; 1926-Apr-1; 70; Fem; Comanche; yes; Full; Not known; yes

1925   190;   STARR, Mildred; 1926-Mar-6; 2; Fem; Apache; yes; Full; Indigestion; yes

         See #
1925   77;   STARR, Vincent; 1926-Mar-3; 7/12; Male; Apache; yes; Full; Pneumonia; yes

1925   107;   TABBYYER, Miles; 1926-Apr-5; 17; Male; Comanche; yes; Full; Pulmonary T.B.; yes

1925   1750;   TAHCUMAH; 1926-May-10; 86; Male; Comanche; yes; Full; Not known; yes

1925   5;   TAHTAHTIZEZ; 1926-May-1; 66; Fem; Apache; yes; Full; Not known; yes

1926   795;   TANETITE, Fletcher; 1926-Feb-3; 31; Male; Kiowa; yes; Full; Tuberculosis; yes

1925   1141;   TAPEDOME; 1925-Aug-13; 66; Male; Kiowa; yes; Full; Heart failure; yes

1925   573;   TEHAUNO; 1925-Dec-29; 46; Male; Comanche; yes; Full; Consumption; yes

         See #
1926   536;   TENEQUER, Baby; 1925-Oct-20; 1 da; Male; Comanche; yes; Full; Unknown; yes

         See #
1926   311;   TOBAH, Minnie; 1925-Aug-12; 1; Fem; Kiowa; yes; Full; Not known; yes

157

State __Oklahoma__ Reservation __Kiowa__ Agency or Jurisdiction __Kiowa__

Office of Indian Affairs Deaths Occurring Between the Dates of July 1, 1925 and June 30, 1926 of Indians Enrolled at Jurisdiction

---

KEY: Year & Number on last Census Roll; Name; Surname and Given; Date of Death; Age at Death; Sex; Tribe; Ward (yes or no); Degree of Blood; Cause of Death; At jurisdiction where enrolled (yes or no); [If "no", where, if given]

See #
1925 43; TOMAH, Milford; 1926-Mar-7; Not known; Male; Comanche; yes; Full; Not known; yes

1925 406; TOSEE; 1925-July-7; 76; Male; Comanche; yes; Full; Not known; yes

1925 1449; TOOAHPERMY (Mahseet), Jesse; 1926-June-10; 60; Male; Comanche; yes; Full; Pulmonary T.B.; yes

1925 49; TOWISCHY; 1926-Mar-5; 74; Male; Comanche; yes; Full; Blood poison; yes

1926 120; TSATAHSISKO, Lydia Ann; 1926; Not known; Fem; Apache; yes; Full; Not known; yes

See #
1926 121; TSATAHSISKO, Emma Bell; 1926-Mar-13; Fem; Apache; yes; Full; Bronchial pneumonia; yes

1925 199; TSCHYTSOE; 1926-June-12; 67; Male; Apache; yes; Full; Cancer; yes

1925 699; TSOCLEMAH (Aunko), Sadie; 1926-Mar-27; 38; Fem; Kiowa; yes; Full; Bronchial pneumonia; yes

1925 637; UKAPITTY, Beatrice Elizabeth; 1926-Apr-2; 3; Fem; Comanche; yes; Full; Pneumonia; yes

1925 1643; WACKMETOOAH, Judd; 1926-Jan-19; Not known; Male; Comanche; yes; Full; Consumption; yes

1926 485; WAHAHKINNEY, Charlie; 1926-Mar-9; Not known; Male; Comanche; yes; Full; Bronchial pneumonia; yes

1925 262; WERHEVAH, (Wermy), Samuel; 1926-June-10; Not known; Male; Comanche; yes; Full; Not known; yes

See #
1926 253; WERMY, Baby; 1926-May-18; few hours; Male; Comanche; yes; Full; Not known; yes

State __Oklahoma__ Reservation __Kiowa__ Agency or Jurisdiction __Kiowa__
Office of Indian Affairs Deaths Occurring Between the Dates of July 1, 1925 and
June 30, 1926 of Indians Enrolled at Jurisdiction

KEY: Year & Number on last Census Roll; Name; Surname and Given; Date of Death; Age at Death; Sex; Tribe; Ward (yes or no); Degree of Blood; Cause of Death; At jurisdiction where enrolled (yes or no); [If "no", where, if given]

1925   1185;   WOOSYPITI; 1926-Jan-30; Not known; Male; Comanche; yes; Full; Not known; yes

      See #
1926   512;   WOLF CHIEF, Addie; 1925-Oct-19; 1; Fem; Kiowa; yes; Full; Cholera; yes

1926   518;   YACKCHEBEAH, Jenice; 1926-Apr-2; 15; Fem; Comanche; yes; Full; Tuberculosis; yes

1925   708;   YAHPEAH, Leonard; 1925-July-15; 15; Male; Comanche; yes; Full; T.B. Meningitis; yes

1925   49;   ZUREGA, Thelma Jennie; Sept-22-1925; 1; Fem; Apache; yes; Not known; yes

KIOWA INDIAN AGENCY
Kiowa Reservation
Oklahoma
1927

DEATH ROLL
Kiowa, Comanche, Apache and
Fort Sill Apache Indians

State __Oklahoma__ Reservation __Kiowa__ Agency or Jurisdiction __Kiowa__
Office of Indian Affairs Deaths Occurring Between the Dates of July 1, 1926 and
June 30, 1927 of Indians Enrolled at Jurisdiction

KEY: Year & Number on last Census Roll; Name; Surname and Given; Date of Death; Age at Death; Sex; Tribe; Ward (yes or no); Degree of Blood; Cause of Death; At jurisdiction where enrolled (yes or no); [If "no", where, if given]

	See #	
1927	124;	AITSON, Etheline Mary; 1927-Jan-11; 1/12; Fem; Kiowa; yes; Full; Not known; yes
1927	See # 160;	APAUTY, Lewis; 1927-Feb-11; 1/12; Male; Kio & Com; yes; Full; Not known; yes
1927	1723;	ASAH, Moisie; 1926-June-4; 43; Fem; Kiowa; yes; Full; Not known; yes
1927	1208;	ASETAMY, John; 1927-Mar-5; 62; Male; Comanche; yes; Full; Volular[sic] heart lesion; yes
1927	See # 265;	ATETEWUTHTAKEVA; 1926-Aug-26; few hours; Fem; Comanche; yes; Full; Not known; yes
1927	See # 339;	AUTAUBO, Lycester; 1927-May-28; few hours; Male; Kiowa; yes; Full; Hemorrhage stomach; yes
1926	811;	BOLO, Mary; 1927-June-15; 49; Fem; Kiowa; yes; Full; Not known; yes
1926	1143;	BOYIDDLE; 1927-Feb; 67; Male; Kiowa; yes; Full; Not known; yes
1927	See # 2376;	CABLE, Orvella George; 1927-Mar-9; few hours; Male; Comanche; yes; Full; Not known; yes
1926;	1233;	CHAHKEAH, Earl; 1927-Apr-24; 16; Male; Kiowa; yes; Full; Ruptured appendix; yes
1928	543;	CHANDLER, Bud; 1927-Apr-11; 62; Male; Mexican; yes; Mexican; Not known; yes
1926	81;	CHEBAHTAH, Cleo; 1926-Sept-26; 9/12; Fem; Comanche; yes; Full; Indigestion; yes
1927	610;	CHICKAH; 1927-June-14; 86; Fem; Comanche; yes; Full; Stomach trouble; yes

State __Oklahoma__ Reservation __Kiowa__ Agency or Jurisdiction __Kiowa__
Office of Indian Affairs Deaths Occurring Between the Dates of July 1, 1926 and
June 30, 1927 of Indians Enrolled at Jurisdiction

KEY: Year & Number on last Census Roll; Name; Surname and Given; Date of Death; Age at Death; Sex; Tribe; Ward (yes or no); Degree of Blood; Cause of Death; At jurisdiction where enrolled (yes or no); [If "no", where, if given]

1926 1066; EMDOTO; 1927-Jan-29; 71; Male; Kiowa; yes; Full; Flu & pneumo
nia; yes

See #
1927 1089; HEATH, Leo; 1927-Jan-8; 3 das; Male; Comanche; yes; Full; Not
known; yes

1928 1099; HEMINOKEKY, Robert; 1927-Apr-22; 1; Male; Com & Apache;
yes; Full; Erysipelas; yes

See #
1927 1133; HOEKEAH, Pauline; 1926-Nov-3; 2 das; Fem; Kiowa; yes; Full; Not
known; yes

1928 1194; HUMMINGBIRD, Malcolm; 1927-Apr-2; 17; Male; Kiowa; yes;
Full; Not known; yes

1926   10; JOZHE, Julia Estine; 1926-Nov-10; 17; Fem; Apache & Wich;
yes; Full; Pulmonary T.B.; yes

1926 1353; KAULAY, Maude; 1927; 46; Fem; Kiowa; yes; Full; Not known; yes

1926   75; KAUNDY (Boots); 1927-Mar-22; 58; Male; Kiowa; yes; Full;
Pneumonia; yes

1926   33; KOMESTADDLE, Levena; 1926-Oct-22; 1; Fem; Kiowa; yes; Full;
Not known; yes

See #
1927 1454; KONAH, Estelline; 1926-Dec-21; 5/12; Fem; Kiowa; yes; Full; Not
known; yes

See #
1927 1588; LITTLE CHIEF, Lawrence Ralph; 1927-June-27; 5 das; Male;
Kiowa; yes; Full; Erysipelas[sic]; yes

See #
1927 1568; LITTLE CHIEF, Libbie; 1926-Jan-1; 1/12; Fem; Kiowa; yes; Full;
Not known; yes

1926 1426; LITTLE ELK, Gilbert; 1926; Not known; Male; Kiowa; yes; Full;
Not known; yes

State __Oklahoma__ Reservation __Kiowa__ Agency or Jurisdiction __Kiowa__
Office of Indian Affairs Deaths Occurring Between the Dates of July 1, 1926 and
June 30, 1927 of Indians Enrolled at Jurisdiction

KEY: Year & Number on last Census Roll; Name; Surname and Given; Date of Death; Age at Death; Sex; Tribe; Ward (yes or no); Degree of Blood; Cause of Death; At jurisdiction where enrolled (yes or no); [If "no", where, if given]

1926   10;   MAHCHETTWOOKKY, Bessie; 1927-Mar-3; 33; Fem; Comanche; yes; Tuberculosis; yes

        See #
1927   478;   MARTINEZ, James Bohart; 1926; 2; Male; Comanche; yes; Full; Not known; yes

1926   40;   NAHCOTCHER; 1926-Sept-5; 72; Fem; Apache; yes; Full; TB & old age; yes

1930[sic] 2774; NASHDELTE, Vincent Geo; 1927-Mar-26; Not known; Male; Apache; yes; Full; Not known; yes

1926   1335; NEVAQUAYA, Irene; 1927-Jan-15; 1½; Fem; Comanche; yes; Full; Not known; yes

1926   1448; NAHSUQUAS; 1927-Feb-8; 82; Male; Comanche; yes; Full; Not known; yes

1926   400;   NIYAH; 1927-May-4; 60; Fem; Comanche; yes; Full; Malignant uterus; yes

        See #
1927   2150; PAHDOPONY, Shell; 1927-Jan-31; 1/12; Fem; Comanche; yes; Full; Not known; yes

1926   46;   PAUMAHTY (Cora Frizzlehead); 1926-Dec-7; 45; Fem; Kiowa; yes; Full; Not known; yes

1926   1153; PERMAMSU, Jack; 1926-Nov-9; 73; Male; Comanche; yes; Full; Not known; yes

        See #
1927   2324   PERMAMSU, Juan; 1926-Dec-3; 4/12; Fem; Comanche; yes; Full; Inflamation[sic] of bowels & pneumonia; yes

1926   348;   POAUNT (Dominick); 1926-Aug-16; 31; Male; Kiowa; yes; Full; Not known; yes

1926   740;   POHACSUCUT, Betty Lou; 1926-Sept-11; 6/12; Fem; Comanche; yes; Full; Not known; yes

State __Oklahoma__ Reservation __Kiowa__ Agency or Jurisdiction __Kiowa__
Office of Indian Affairs Deaths Occurring Between the Dates of July 1, 1926 and
June 30, 1927 of Indians Enrolled at Jurisdiction

KEY: Year & Number on last Census Roll; Name; Surname and Given; Date of Death; Age at Death; Sex; Tribe; Ward (yes or no); Degree of Blood; Cause of Death; At jurisdiction where enrolled (yes or no); [If "no", where, if given]

1926   176;   PHOAWBITSY; 1926-Sept-27; 97; Fem; Comanche; yes; Full; Old age; yes

1927   2482;   POTIYO, Garnetta Ruth; 1927-June-30; 1; Kiowa; yes; Full; Acute anterior; yes

See #
1927   2507;   PUEBLO, Burnell; 1926-Aug-26; few hours; Male; Comanche; yes; Full; Not known; yes

1926   933;   QUERDIBITTY, Vernon; 1926-Aug-13; 5; Male; Comanche; yes; Full; Drowned; yes

See #
1927   176;   REYNO, Mary Rose; 1926-July-18; 1; Fem; Kiowa; yes; Full; Cholera Infantum[sic]; yes

1927   2641;   SANKODOTA; [blank]; 79; Male; Kiowa; yes; Full; Not known; yes

1930   3722;   SATOE, Virgil; 1927-June-10; 2; Male; Kiowa; yes; Full; Not known; yes

1927   1067;   SAU BEODLE; 1926-Dec-24; 80; Fem; Kiowa; yes; Full; Gall stones; yes

1926   869;   SAUPITTY; 1927-Feb-14; 65; Male; Comanche; yes; Full; Influenza; yes

1926   348;   SEAHMER, Jennie; 1926-Sept-18; 12; Fem; Comanche; yes; Full; Typhoid fever; yes

1927   2786;   STARR, David Alfred; 1927-Mar-3; 1; Male; Kiowa & Apache; yes; Full; Not known; yes

1927   2785;   STARR, Nellie Irene; 1927-Mar-4; 4; Fem; Kiowa & Apache; yes; Full; Not known; yes

1926   845;   SUTTON, Allen Morrison; 1926-Nov-27; 1; Male; Kiowa; yes; Full; Bronchial Pneumonia; yes

1926   1206;   TAHCUTINE; 1927-Jan-6; 67; Fem; Comanche; yes; Full; Not known; yes

State __Oklahoma__ Reservation __Kiowa__ Agency or Jurisdiction __Kiowa__
Office of Indian Affairs Deaths Occurring Between the Dates of July 1, 1926 and
June 30, 1927 of Indians Enrolled at Jurisdiction

KEY: Year & Number on last Census Roll; Name; Surname and Given; Date of Death; Age at Death; Sex; Tribe; Ward (yes or no); Degree of Blood; Cause of Death; At jurisdiction where enrolled (yes or no); [If "no", where, if given]

1926   45;   TAHMAHKERA, Houston; 1926-Aug-23; 8/12; Male; Comanche; yes; Full; Dysentery; yes

1926   1303;   TANA, Samuel Blair; 1926-Sept-10; 1; Male; Kiowa; yes; Full; Not known; yes

See #
1927   3165;   THOMPSON, Hute Bay; 1926-Oct-10; 1/12; Male; Kiowa; yes; Full; Pneumonia; yes

1926   1305;   TINEZENAYAH; 1926-Dec-29; 83; Fem; Kiowa; yes; Full; Old age & flu; yes

1926   316;   TOBAH, Hilton; 1927-Feb-21; 16; Male; Kiowa; yes; Full; Not known; yes

1926   587;   TOEHAY, Henry; 1926-Aug-4; 24; Male; Kiowa; yes; Full; Not known; yes

1926   229;   TOFPI; 1927-Feb-17; 58; Male; Kiowa; yes; Full; Pulmonary T.B.; yes

1926   24;   TOHADDLE, Carrie; 1926-Dec-5; 47; Fem; Kiowa; yes; Full; Not known; yes

1926   247;   TOFPI, Elsie Mae; 1926-Sept-15; 9/12; Fem; Kiowa; yes; Full; Not known; yes

1926   861;   TOINTIGH, Eleanor; 1926-Nov-11; 1; Fem; Kiowa; yes; Full; Not known; yes

1927   3392;   TOOENAPPER, Morris; 1926-June-24;1; Male; Comanche; yes; Full; Not known; yes

See #
1927   3581;   TSOODLE, Ernest; 1927-Feb-10; 2; Male; Kiowa; yes; Full; Pneumonia; yes

1927   3480;   TSALOTE; 1927-Jan-6; 66; Male; Kiowa; yes; Full; Not known; yes

1926   576;   TSOWYAH; 1926-July-30; 76; Male; Comanche; yes; Full; Not known; yes

State ___Oklahoma___ Reservation ___Kiowa___ Agency or Jurisdiction ___Kiowa___

Office of Indian Affairs Deaths Occurring Between the Dates of July 1, 1926 and June 30, 1927 of Indians Enrolled at Jurisdiction

KEY: Year & Number on last Census Roll; Name; Surname and Given; Date of Death; Age at Death; Sex; Tribe; Ward (yes or no); Degree of Blood; Cause of Death; At jurisdiction where enrolled (yes or no); [If "no", where, if given]

1927 3171; TIDDACK, Layton; 1927-May; 2; Male; Comanche; yes; Full; Not known; yes

1927 1255; UTAH; 1927-Mar-26; 45; Fem; Comanche; yes; Full; Cancer; yes

1926 1374; YELLOWFISH, Samuel; 1927-Mar-1; 19; Male; Comanche; yes; Full; Burns; yes

1930 4451; YEAHQUO, Samuel Tiedle; 1926-July-3; 2; Male; Kiowa; yes; Full; Not known; yes

KIOWA INDIAN AGENCY

Kiowa Reservation

Oklahoma

1928

DEATH ROLL
Kiowa, Comanche, Apache and Fort Sill Apache Indians

EXCLUSIVE OF STILLBIRTHS
State __Oklahoma__ Reservation __Kiowa__ Agency or Jurisdiction __Kiowa__
Office of Indian Affairs Deaths Occurring Between the Dates of July 1, 1927 and
June 30, 1928 of Indians Enrolled at Jurisdiction

KEY: Year & Number on last Census Roll; Name; Surname and Given; Date of Death; Age at Death; Sex; Tribe; Ward (yes or no); Degree of Blood; Cause of Death; At jurisdiction where enrolled (yes or no); [If "no", where, if given]

1928   2;   ADLEPINGQUOE (Topfi), Harold; 1928-June-22; 37; Male; Kiowa; yes; Full; Not known; yes

1928   42;   AHDASY, Page; 1928-Apr-20; 4; Male; Comanche; yes; Full; Not known; yes

1927   72;   AHKEAHBO, Maxine; 1928-Mar-28; 2; Fem; Kiowa; yes; Full; Diphtheria; yes

1927   1810;   AHPEAHTO, Charlie; 1928-May-23; 20; Male; Kiowa; yes; Full; Pulmonary T.B.; yes

See #
1928   108;   AHTON, Flora; 1927-Apr-21; 8/12; Fem; Kiowa; yes; Full; Not known; yes

See #
1928   126;   AITSON, Leta May; Apr-10-1928; 1; Fem; Kiowa; yes; Full; Not known; yes

1927   1341;   AITSON, Gertrude; 1928; 17; Fem; Kiowa; yes; Full; Not known; yes

1927   132;   AKO, Mildred; 1928-Apr-6; 2; Fem; Kiowa; yes; Full; Pneumonia; yes

1930   5347;   ARKEKETA, Johanna C; 1928-Jan-13; 1; Fem; Kiowa; yes; 1/4; Not known; yes

See #
1927   280;   AUCHICHIA, James Allison; Mar-13-1928; 6/12; Male; Kiowa; yes; Full; Pneumonia; yes

1927   184;   AUNGUVE, Verl; 1927-Sept-21; 1; Fem; Kiowa; yes; Full; Not known; yes

1927   183;   AUNGUVE, Dean; 1928-Jan-11; 4; Male; Kiowa; yes; Full; Diptheria[sic]; yes

1930   2974;   AUNKO, Dorothy Herwana; 1928-June-10; 2; Fem; Kiowa; yes; Full; Not known; yes

171

State __Oklahoma__ Reservation __Kiowa__ Agency or Jurisdiction __Kiowa__
Office of Indian Affairs Deaths Occurring Between the Dates of July 1, 1927 and
June 30, 1928 of Indians Enrolled at Jurisdiction

KEY: Year & Number on last Census Roll; Name; Surname and Given; Date of Death; Age at Death; Sex; Tribe; Ward (yes or no); Degree of Blood; Cause of Death; At jurisdiction where enrolled (yes or no); [If "no", where, if given]

1928   342;   AUTAUBO, Julia; 1928-Sept-13; 4/12; Fem; Kiowa; yes; Full;
Not known; yes

1927   413;   BOINTY, Jack; 1927-Nov-8; 59; Male; Kiowa; yes; Full;
Ereysipelas[sic]; yes

1927   147;   BOTONE, Vivian; 1928-Apr-8; 2; Fem; Kiowa; yes; Full;
Pneumonia; yes

1927   2066;   CAT, Fred; 1928; 18; Male; Kiowa; yes; Full; Not known; yes

1928   610;   CHOCKPOYAH; 1928-June-15; 78; Fem; Comanche; yes; Full;
Senility; yes

1927   649;   CODAPONY; 1928-May-8; 57; Male; Comanche; yes; Full;
Stomach Trouble; yes

        See #
1928   666;   CODYMAH; Sept-3-1927; Few hrs; Male; Comanche; yes; Full;
Not known; yes

1927   589;   COOSEWON, Kate; 1927-Aug-28; 37; Fem; Comanche; yes; Full;
Not known; yes

1927   3012;   COMANCHE; Phelix; 1928; 2; Male; Apache; yes; Full; Not known;
yes

1927   724;   COX, Emmett; 1927-Dec-17; 76; Male; Comanche; yes; 1/4;
Apoplexy; yes

1927   738;   COZAD (Brown), Belle; 1925-Feb-3; 35; Fem; Kiowa; yes; 1/4;
Tuberculosis; yes

1927   822;   DOMEBO, Charlie; 1927-Sept-13; 52; Male; Kiowa; yes; Full;
Not known; yes

1928   898;   EMTADDLE, Clyde; 1927-Dec-21; 19 das; Male; Kio & Apache;
yes; Full; Not known; yes

1927   918;   ERKABITTY (Pedahny Kate); 1927-Aug-11; 41; Fem; Comanche;
yes; Full; Acute Nephritis; yes

State __Oklahoma__ Reservation __Kiowa__ Agency or Jurisdiction __Kiowa__
Office of Indian Affairs Deaths Occurring Between the Dates of July 1, 1927 and
June 30, 1928 of Indians Enrolled at Jurisdiction

KEY: Year & Number on last Census Roll; Name; Surname and Given; Date of Death; Age at Death; Sex; Tribe; Ward (yes or no); Degree of Blood; Cause of Death; At jurisdiction where enrolled (yes or no); [If "no", where, if given]

1928   555;   GEARY, Geo Klera; 1927-Nov-21; few hrs; Male; Kiowa; yes; Full; Not known; yes

1927   3394;   GEIONETY, Margaret; 1928-Apr-19; 25; Fem; Kiowa; yes; Full; Pneumonia; yes

1928   988;   GONZALES, Ramon Palmer; 1928-Jan-9; 1; Male; Comanche; yes; 1/4; Not known; yes

1928   981;   GOOMDO, Eva; 1928-June-15; 34; Fem; Kiowa; yes; 1/2; Acute Nephritis; yes

1927   1032;   GWOOMAU, Mabel; 1928-Feb-25; 32; Fem; Kiowa; yes; Full; Pulmonary T.B.; yes

1927   982;   HADLEY, Martha; 1928-Apr-6; 2; Fem; Kiowa; yes; Full; Diphtheria; yes

1931   266;   HAMILTON, Diana; 1928-Jan-7; 2; Fem; Kiowa; yes; Full; Not known; yes

1929   1064;   HAUNPY, Marcus; 1928-Apr-22; 2; Male; Kiowa; yes; Full; Not known; yes

1927   1379;   HENRY, Frank Vincent; 1927-July-31; 1; Male; Kiowa; yes; Full; Meningitis; yes

1930   1684;   HOVAKAH, Jewell; 1928-Feb-21; 1; Fem; Kiowa; yes; Full; Not known; yes

1928   898;   HUMMINGBIRD, Clyde; 1927-Dec-21; 19 das; Male; Kiowa & Apache; yes; Full; Not known; yes

1927   1198;   HUMMINGBIRD, Rudolph; 1928-Mar-26; 1; Male; Kiowa; yes; Full; Pneumonia; yes

1927   1192;   HUMMINGBIRD, Vern; 1927-Oct-25; 2; Male; Kiowa; yes; Full; Tuberculosis; yes

1927   1225;   JONES, Nellie; 1927-Nov-1; 59; Fem; Kiowa; yes; 1/4; Goiter Operation; yes

State __Oklahoma__ Reservation __Kiowa__ Agency or Jurisdiction __Kiowa__
Office of Indian Affairs Deaths Occurring Between the Dates of July 1, 1927 and
June 30, 1928 of Indians Enrolled at Jurisdiction

KEY: Year & Number on last Census Roll; Name; Surname and Given; Date of Death; Age at Death; Sex; Tribe; Ward (yes or no); Degree of Blood; Cause of Death; At jurisdiction where enrolled (yes or no); [If "no", where, if given]

1928   1302;   KAUDLEKAULE, Naoma; 1927; Fem; Kiowa; yes; Full; Not known; yes

1928   598;   KAULAITY, Parton; 1928-Mar or May-14; 1; Male; Kiowa; yes; Full; Not known; yes

1927   1344;   KAUTOBONE; 1927-Nov-28; 70; Fem; Kiowa; yes; Full; Not known; yes

1928   3184;   KASSANAVOID, Lillian; 1928-June-13; 7/12; Fem; Comanche; yes; Full; Pneumonia; yes

1928   1424;   KLATHCHALLAH, Raymond; 1928-Feb-4; 6/12; Male; Kiowa; yes; Full; Not known; yes

1927   902;   KODASEET, James; 1927-Sept-29; 9; Male; Kiowa; yes; 1/2; Not known; yes

1927   3026;   KODASEET, Thelma Joyce; 1928-May-15; 2; Fem; Kiowa; yes; 1/2; Pneumonia; yes

1927   1458;   KOONKAHGAHCHY (Apache John); 1927-Dec-3; 84; Male; Apache; yes; Full; Not known; yes

       See #
1928   2246;   LEFTHAND, Evaline; 1928-Feb-14; 3/12; Fem; Kiowa; yes; Full; Not known; yes

1929   1593;   LITTLECHIEF, Caroline; 1927-July; 2; Fem; Kiowa; yes; Full; Not known; yes

1927   1589;   LONEWOLF, Webster; 1928-Feb-21; 46; Male; Kiowa; yes; Full; Not known; yes

1927   1774;   MACHO, Joseph; 1927-Sept-16; 28; Male; Comanche; yes; Full; Typhoid; yes

       See #
1928   1732;   MAUSAPE, Paul; 1927-Oct-6; 6 das; Male; Kiowa; yes; Full; Not known; yes

1927   3553;   MOAFPOPE; 1928; 65; Fem; Kiowa; yes; Full; Not known; yes

State __Oklahoma__ Reservation __Kiowa__ Agency or Jurisdiction __Kiowa__
Office of Indian Affairs Deaths Occurring Between the Dates of July 1, 1927 and
June 30, 1928 of Indians Enrolled at Jurisdiction

KEY: Year & Number on last Census Roll; Name; Surname and Given; Date of Death; Age at Death; Sex; Tribe; Ward (yes or no); Degree of Blood; Cause of Death; At jurisdiction where enrolled (yes or no); [If "no", where, if given]

1927   1830;   MOPOPE, Grover Lee; 1927-Sept-21; 1; Male; Kiowa; yes; Full; Pneumonia; yes

1927   1837;   MOPOPE, Alverdine; 1927-Aug-26; 10/12; Fem; Kiowa & Apache; yes; 1/2; Syphilis; yes

1927   1838;   MOTAH; [Blank]; 57; Male; Comanche; yes; Full; Not known; yes

1927   1944;   NEHI; 1928-Feb-29; 66; Male; Comanche; yes; Full; Pneumonia; yes

1927   2012;   NEMARAQUO, Ellen; 1928-Jan-14; 22; Fem; Comanche; yes; Full; Pneumonia; yes

1927   1985;   NEWOOKAHKOI, James; 1927-Nov-5; 24; Male; Comanche; yes; Full; Tuberculosis; yes

See #
1928   2024;   NIYAH; 1928-Feb-10; 9 das; Fem; Comanche; yes; Full; Severe cold & flu; yes

1928   2042;   ODLEPAHOYOTE, John Wm; 1928-June-21; 2; Male; Kiowa; yes; Full; Not known; yes

1928   2094;   OYEBI, Etheline; 1928; 8; Fem; Kiowa; yes; Full; Not known; yes

1927   2196;   PARRIAECKIVIT; [Blank]; 85; Male; Comanche; yes; Full; Not known; yes

1927   2100;   PAHCHEKA, Priscilla; 1927-Aug-14; 2; Fem; Comanche; yes; Full; Locked bowels; yes

1927   2137;   PAHDONGKEI, Rudolph; 1927-Aug-6; 5/12; Male; Kiowa; yes; Full; Diarrhea; yes

See #
1928   2167;   PAHDOPONY; 1927-Dec-27; few hrs; Fem; Comanche; yes; Full; Premature birth; yes

1927   2162;   PAHKOY, Lizzie; 1928-Feb-9; 56; Fem; Kiowa; yes; Full; Cerebral Hemorrhage; yes

State __Oklahoma__ Reservation __Kiowa__ Agency or Jurisdiction __Kiowa__
Office of Indian Affairs Deaths Occurring Between the Dates of July 1, 1927 and
June 30, 1928 of Indians Enrolled at Jurisdiction

KEY: Year & Number on last Census Roll; Name; Surname and Given; Date of Death; Age at Death; Sex; Tribe; Ward (yes or no); Degree of Blood; Cause of Death; At jurisdiction where enrolled (yes or no); [If "no", where, if given]

1927 2170; PAHOOKESY, Mary; [Blank]; 54; Fem; Comanche; yes; Full; Not known; yes

1927 2210; PASCHETO; [Blank]; 67; Male; Comanche; yes; Full; Not known; yes

1927 2164; PEWEWARDY, Geo Campbell; [Blank]; 2; Male; Kiowa; yes; Full; Not known; yes

1930 3347; POAUTY, Neoma Ruth; 1928-Apr-28; 1/12; Fem; Kiowa; yes; Full; Not known; yes

1927 2446; POOR BUFFALO, Duke; [Blank]; 53; Male; Kiowa; yes; Full; Not known; yes

1927 2526; QUERHERBITTY; 1928-Jan-26; 84; Fem; Comanche; yes; Full; Not known; yes

1927 2559; QUOINGUODLE; 1927-Oct-27; 58; Male; Kiowa; yes; Full; Pulmonary T.B.; yes

1927 2669; SATEPAUHOODLE, Abel; 1928-Mar-8; 57; Male; Kiowa; yes; Full; Killed by train; yes

1928 2725; SATOE, Mary Magdeline; 1928-May-29; 1; Fem; Kiowa; yes; Full; Not known; yes

1928 2746; SAUPITTY, Edgar; 1928-June-21; 24; Male; Comanche; yes; Full; Consumption; yes

1928 1961; SHORTNECK, Frances; 1928-June-21; 1; Fem; Kiowa; yes; Full; Not known; yes

1927 2628; STAR, Clarence; [Blank]; 3; Male; Apache; yes; Full; Not known; yes

See #
1928 3864; TABBYTITE, John Lawrence; 1928-Mar-13; 1; Fem; Kiowa; yes; Full; Not known; yes

State __Oklahoma__ Reservation __Kiowa__ Agency or Jurisdiction __Kiowa__
Office of Indian Affairs Deaths Occurring Between the Dates of July 1, 1927 and
June 30, 1928 of Indians Enrolled at Jurisdiction

KEY: Year & Number on last Census Roll; Name; Surname and Given; Date of Death; Age at Death; Sex; Tribe; Ward (yes or no); Degree of Blood; Cause of Death; At jurisdiction where enrolled (yes or no); [If "no", where, if given]

	See #	
1929	3088;	TAKEWAHPOOR, May Frances; 1928-June-12; 1/12; Fem; Comanche; yes; Full; Convulsions; yes
1927	3478;	TOPAUM, Emma; 1928-Jan-18; 24; Fem; Kiowa; yes; Full; Septi[sic] Meningitis; yes
1930	4707;	TOPAUM, Margaret; 1928-May-5; 1/12; Fem; Kiowa; yes; Full; Not known; yes
1927	3484;	TSALATE, Ellen; 1928-June-4; 14; Fem; Kiowa; yes; Full; Pulmonary T.B.; yes
1927	3593;	TSAAHAL; 1928-Apr-2; 51; Fem; Kiowa; yes; Full; Not known; yes

	See #	
1928	3518;	TSATAHSISKO, Flo; 1928-Mar-19; 1 das; Fem; Apache; yes; Full; Not known; yes
1929	3580;	TSATOKE, Madge Ellen; 1928; few hrs; Fem; Kiowa; yes; Full; Not known; yes
1928	2827;	TABBYTITE, Joe Beryle; [Blank]; Not known; f[sic]; Comanche; yes; Full; Not known; yes
1927	2816;	TABBYUWENIT (Wahahshboie); 1927-Oct-20; 39; Male; Comanche; yes; Full; Not known; yes
1928	1259;	TAH, Clifford Mitchell; 1927-July-8; 1; Male; Apache; yes; Full; Not known; yes
1928	2881;	TAHDOONHMPAH; 1928-Jan-21; 10 das; Fem; Comanche; yes; Full; Not known; yes
1927	3329;	TAHKAVA, Maud; [Blank]; 17; Fem; Comanche; yes; Full; Not known; yes

	See #	
1928	3043;	TAINPEAH, Ray; 1928-June-8; 6 das; Male; Kiowa; yes; Full; Syphilis; yes

State __Oklahoma__ Reservation __Kiowa__ Agency or Jurisdiction __Kiowa__
Office of Indian Affairs Deaths Occurring Between the Dates of July 1, 1927 and
June 30, 1928 of Indians Enrolled at Jurisdiction

KEY: Year & Number on last Census Roll; Name; Surname and Given; Date of Death; Age at Death; Sex; Tribe; Ward (yes or no); Degree of Blood; Cause of Death; At jurisdiction where enrolled (yes or no); [If "no", where, if given]

1928   3046;   TAKAUNGKY, Howard; 1928-June-15; 23; Male; Kiowa; yes; Full; Not known; yes

1927   3017;   TAKAUNGKY, Jim; 1928; 51; Male; Kiowa; yes; Full; Not known; yes

1927   2026;   TANEDOOAH, Helen; 1927-Nov-1; 2; Fem; Kiowa; yes; Full; Not known; yes

1928   3088;   TANETONE (Zoam), George; 1928-June-5; 38; Male; Kiowa; yes; Full; Septicemia; yes

1927   3103;   TARTSAH, Leta May; 1927-Oct-11; 1; Fem; Apache & Kiowa; yes; Full; Not known; yes

1927   3084;   TORCHPOKEADOOAH, May; 1927-Sept-7; 17; Fem; Comanche; yes; Full; Pulmonary T.B.; yes

1927   3112;   TAUDLEKAAKAUHOODLE; 1928-Jan-13; 71; Fem; Kiowa; yes; Full; Cancer stomach; yes

1927   3168;   TIDDARK, (Royce Pekah); 1927-Oct-19; 37; Male; Comanche; yes; Full; Not known; yes

1927   1331;   TOBAH, Stinson; 1927-May; 18; Male; Kiowa; yes; Full; Not known; yes

1927   536;   TOOISGAH, Costine; 1927-Dec-17; 12; Fem; Apache; yes; Full; Cerebro Spinal Meningitis; yes

1927   3446;   TOTITE, Thomas, Jr; 1928-May-5; 1 1/2; Male; Comanche; yes; Full; Measles & Pneumonia; yes

1928   300;   TSOHIO; 1928-June-14; 71; Fem; Kiowa; yes; Full; Not known; yes

1927   3642;   WAHWEEKWEAH; 1927-July-17; 74; Fem; Comanche; yes; Full; Not known; yes

See #
1928   3692;   WARE, Gerald Claudine; 1927-Dec-18; 3/12; Male; Kiowa; yes; Full; Lobar pneumonia; yes

State __Oklahoma__ Reservation __Kiowa__ Agency or Jurisdiction __Kiowa__
Office of Indian Affairs Deaths Occurring Between the Dates of July 1, 1927 and
June 30, 1928 of Indians Enrolled at Jurisdiction

KEY: Year & Number on last Census Roll; Name; Surname and Given; Date of Death; Age at Death; Sex; Tribe; Ward (yes or no); Degree of Blood; Cause of Death; At jurisdiction where enrolled (yes or no); [If "no", where, if given]

See #
1928 3719; WAYSEPAPPY; 1927-July-3; 1; Fem; Comanche; yes; Full;
Premature birth; yes

1927 3140; WEBB, Ruby Diamond; 1927-Oct-19; 11; Fem; Comanche; yes;
1/2; Typhoid; yes

1930 5068; WERHEVAHWERMY, Naoma; 1928-Apr-18; 1; Fem; Comanche;
yes; Full; Not known; yes

1927 3716; WETSELLIN (Apache Jim); 1928-Mar-27; 64; Fem; Apache; yes;
Full; Interstitial Nephritis; yes

1927 3300; WHITEFOX, Leonard; 1927-July-30; 2; Male; Kiowa & Apache; yes;
Full; Diarrhea; yes

1927 3728; WHITE HO SE[sic], James; 1927-July-1; 22; Male; Kiowa; yes; Full;
Not known; yes

1927 3756; WOODAHPEAP; 1928; 79; Male; Comanche; yes; Full; Not known;
yes

See #
1928 3813; WOOKSOOK, Edw Bill; 1928-Mar-2; 9/12; Male; Comanche; yes;
Full; Cerebral Spinal Meningitis; yes

1927 3768; WOOKSOOK, William; 1928; 29; Male; Comanche; yes; Full;
Not known; yes

1927 3861; YOUNIACUT, Forest; 1928-Jan-18; 2; Male; Comanche; yes; Full;
Not known; yes

1927 3864; ZATEKAUNKAUKOMAH, Charles; 1928; 20; Male; Kiowa; yes;
Full; Not known; yes

See #
1928 3903; ZOQUOE, Clifford; 1928-May-14; 1; Male; Kiowa; yes; Full;
Bronchial pneumonia; yes

KIOWA INDIAN AGENCY

Kiowa Reservation
Oklahoma
1929

DEATH ROLL
Kiowa, Comanche, Apache and
Fort Sill Apache Indians

State ___Oklahoma___ Reservation ___Kiowa___ Agency or Jurisdiction ___Kiowa___
Office of Indian Affairs Deaths Occurring Between the Dates of July 1, 1928 and
June 30, 1929 of Indians Enrolled at Jurisdiction

KEY: Year & Number on last Census Roll; Name; Surname and Given; Date of Death; Age at Death; Sex;
Tribe; Ward (yes or no); Degree of Blood; Cause of Death; At jurisdiction where enrolled (yes or no); [If "no",
where, if given]

	See #	
1929	37;	AHDOKOBO, Lamar; 1929-Feb-23; 14 das; Male; Kiowa; yes; 1/2; Pneumonia; yes
1930	36;	AHDOKOBO, Perry; 1929-Jan-3; 1 mo; Male; Kiowa; yes; Full; Not known; yes
1929	44;	AHDOSY, Willie; 1928-Dec-1; 49; Male; Comanche; yes; Full; Bronchial pneumonia; yes

	See #	
1929	69;	AHKEAHBO, Albert; 1928-Dec-28; 7/12; Male; Kiowa; yes; Full; Not known; yes
1928	9;	AGOPEMAH; 1928-Dec-4; 67; Fem; Kiowa; yes; Full; Paralysis Agitana[sic]; yes
1929	130;	AITSEN, Padberg; 1929-Jan-25; 4; Male; Kiowa; yes; Full; Bronchial pneumonia; yes
1929	164;	AMAUTY, Linn; 1928-Aug-19; 23; Male; Kiowa; yes; Full; Not known; yes
1929	169;	APAUTY, Joanna May; 1928-Sept-15; 3; Fem; Kiowa; yes; Full; Tonsilitis[sic]; yes
1929	342;	AUTAUBO, Julia; 1928-Sept-13; 4/12; Fem; Kiowa; yes; Full; Not known; yes
1928	1364;	BOONE, Frank; 1928-Nov-3; 10; Male; Kiowa; yes; Full; Typhoid fever; yes

	See #	
1929	2696;	BURNS, Hershel; 1928-July-22; few hrs; Male; Kiowa; yes; Full; Ilio colitis; yes

	See #	
1929	2089;	CAT, Dorian Nita; 1929-June-7; few hrs; Fem; Kiowa; yes; Full; Erysipelas; yes
1930	1374;	CHANEY, Gene Cecil; 1928-July-7; Not known; mm; Kiowa; yes; 1/2; Not known; yes

183

State __Oklahoma__ Reservation __Kiowa__ Agency or Jurisdiction __Kiowa__
Office of Indian Affairs Deaths Occurring Between the Dates of July 1, 1928 and
June 30, 1929 of Indians Enrolled at Jurisdiction

KEY: Year & Number on last Census Roll; Name; Surname and Given; Date of Death; Age at Death; Sex; Tribe; Ward (yes or no); Degree of Blood; Cause of Death; At jurisdiction where enrolled (yes or no); [If "no", where, if given]

1929   569;   CHATABIN; 1928-Oct-20; 84; Male; Kiowa; yes; Full; Old age; yes

1929   586;   CHEESCHAH; 1928-Dec-1; 95; Fem; Comanche; yes; Full; Not known; yes

1930   748;   CHIBITTY, Letha May; 1929-May-11; 11/12; Fem; Comanche; yes; Full; Not known; yes

1929   625;   CLARK, Albert, Jr; 1928-Sept-26; few hrs; Male; Comanche; yes; 1/4; Not known; yes

See #
1929   3083;   COMANCHE Thelma Mae; 1929-Jan-5; 6/12; Fem; Apache; yes; Full; Bronchial pneumonia; yes

See #
1929   761;   DAUKEI, Eva Lula; 1928-Nov-1; 12 das; Fem; Kiowa; yes; Full; Bronchial pneumonia; yes

See #
1929   724;   DAVIS, Joe Allen; 1928-Nov-14; 6 das; Male; Comanche; yes; 1/2; Morbus Caeruleus[sic]; yes

1929   841;   DAYEBI, Margie; 1928-Sept-21; 1; Fem; Kiowa; yes; Full; Ilio colitis; yes

1929   829;   DAYAH, Ray; 1928-July-1; 20; Male; Kiowa; yes; Full; Result of operation; yes

1929   875;   ECKIWAUDAH, Jonathan; 1929-Mar-6; 6; Male; Comanche; yes; 1/2; Not known; yes

1929   746;   EMTADDLE, Ernest; 1929-Jan-6; 19; Male; Kiowa; yes; Full; Not known; yes

1928   942;   FULLER, Lonnie Lee; 1928-Nov; 2; Male; Comanche; yes; 1/4; Not known; yes

See #
1929   943;   GEIMAUSADDLE, Catherine Belle; 1929-Jan-31; 2/12; Fem; Kiowa; yes; Full; Not known; yes

State __Oklahoma__ Reservation __Kiowa__ Agency or Jurisdiction __Kiowa__
Office of Indian Affairs Deaths Occurring Between the Dates of July 1, 1928 and
June 30, 1929 of Indians Enrolled at Jurisdiction

KEY: Year & Number on last Census Roll; Name; Surname and Given; Date of Death; Age at Death; Sex; Tribe; Ward (yes or no); Degree of Blood; Cause of Death; At jurisdiction where enrolled (yes or no); [If "no", where, if given]

See #
1929 964; GEIONITY, Phoebe; 1929-Jan-7; 6/12; Fem; Kiowa; yes; Full; Pneumonia; yes

1929 3333; GEIONITY, Moses; 1929-May-12; 2; Male; Kiowa; yes; Full; Not known; yes

1928 3265; HARRY, Mabel; 1929-Mar-22; 11; Fem; Comanche; yes; Full; Cerebral spinal meningitis; yes

1928 1160; HASTOSAVIT, Robert; 1928-Oct-8; 42; Male; Comanche; yes; Full; Typhoid; yes

1928 1851; HAVAKAH, May; 1928-Sept-15; 34; Fem; Kiowa; yes; Full; Pulmonary T.B.; yes

1928 1179; HAVAKAH, Tyler; 1928-Sept-5; 1; Male; Comanche; yes; Full; Summer complaint; yes

1928 1089; HEATH, Harry; 1929-Feb-14; 48; Male; Comanche; yes; Full; Pulmonary T.B.; yes

1928 1100; HEMINOKEKY, Edmond; 1929-Feb-2; 15 das; Male; Comanche & Apache; yes; Full; Not known; yes

1929 1115; HERNASY, Ora Belle; 1929-May-25; 1; Fem; Comanche; yes; Full; Pulmonary T.B.; yes

1928 1213; ICAAHVITTY, Ben; 1929-May-6; 71; Male; Comanche; yes; Full; Diabetes; yes

1928 1224; JONES, James N; 1929-Jan-5; 85; Male; White & Mexican; yes; [Blank]; Not known; yes

1928 1263; KARNO; 1929-Jan-11; 65; Male; Comanche; yes; Full; Pneumonia; yes

See #
1929 881; KODASEET, Ruth; 1928-Sept-18; 7 das; Fem; Kiowa; yes; Full; Not known; yes

185

State __Oklahoma__ Reservation __Kiowa__ Agency or Jurisdiction __Kiowa__

Office of Indian Affairs Deaths Occurring Between the Dates of July 1, 1928 and June 30, 1929 of Indians Enrolled at Jurisdiction

KEY: Year & Number on last Census Roll; Name; Surname and Given; Date of Death; Age at Death; Sex; Tribe; Ward (yes or no); Degree of Blood; Cause of Death; At jurisdiction where enrolled (yes or no); [If "no", where, if given]

1928   1459;   KOKOOM, Laverne; 1928-Aug-22; 3; Fem; Kiowa; yes; Full; Congested syphilis; yes

1928   1462;   KOMAH, Herring (Henry); 1928-Dec-3; 34; Male; Comanche; yes; Full; Alcoholism; yes

1928   3645;   KOMAIDLEY, Regina; 1929-Feb-8; 24; Fem; Apache; yes; Full; Eremia[sic]; yes

1929   1464;   KONAD, James; 1928-July-7; 24; Male; Kiowa; yes; Full; Not known; yes

         See #
1929   1763;   KOWENO, Robert John; 1929-Jan-12; 1/12; Male; Kiowa; yes; Full; Flu; yes

         See #
1929   1900;   KILLSFIRST, Loyd; 1929-Jan-5; 8/12; Male; Apache; yes; Full; Bronchial pneumonia; yes

1929   1615;   LOOKINGLASS, Sarah; 1929-June-17; 27; Fem; Comanche; yes; Full; Not known; yes

1929   1707;   MAUNAKEI, Curtiss[sic]; 1928-Nov-26; 18 das; Male; Kiowa; yes; Full; Hemophlis[sic]; yes

1928   1748;   MAYNAHONAH, Austin; 1928-July-14; 6/12; Male; Kiowa; yes; Full; Acute dysentery; yes

1930   5326;   MIHECOBY; 1928-Sept-8; [Blank]; Fem; Comanche; yes; Full; Not known; yes

1928   1819;   MONETATCHI, George; 1929-Feb-20; 18; Male; Comanche; yes; Full; Pulmonary T.B.; yes

1928   1852;   MOPOPE, Ethel; 1928-Dec-28; 16; Fem; Kiowa; yes; Full; Pulmonary T.B.; yes

1928   3070;   OMEHARTY; 1928-Dec-23; 75; Fem; Kiowa; yes; Full; Senility; yes

EXCULIVES[sic] OF STILLBIRTHS

State __Oklahoma__ Reservation __Kiowa__ Agency or Jurisdiction __Kiowa__

Office of Indian Affairs Deaths Occurring Between the Dates of July 1, 1928 and
June 30, 1929 of Indians Enrolled at Jurisdiction

KEY: Year & Number on last Census Roll; Name; Surname and Given; Date of Death; Age at Death; Sex; Tribe; Ward (yes or no); Degree of Blood; Cause of Death; At jurisdiction where enrolled (yes or no); [If "no", where, if given]

See #
1929   2132;   PAHCODDY, Mary Ann; 1929-Jan-6; 5 das; Fem; Comanche; yes; Full; Premature birth; yes

1929   200;   PAHDOCONY, Billie Allen; 1929-Jan-30; 8/12; Male; Comanche; yes; Full; Bronchial pneumonia; yes

1928   2307;   PEKAH, Mollie; 1929-Apr-1; 13; Fem; Comanche; yes; Full; Not known; yes

1928   2312;   PENAH; 1928-Oct-8; 69; Fem; Kiowa; yes; Full; Not known; yes

1929   2320;   PENNAH[sic], (Calico Jah); 1929-July-12; 69; Male; Comanche; yes; Full; Pulmonary T.B.; yes

1930   3298;   PEWO, Revina; 1928-Dec-15; [Blank]; Fem; Comanche; yes; Full; Not known; yes

See #
1928   2454;   POHACSUCUT, (Jack Permansu); 1928-Aug-18; 2/12; Male; Comanche; yes; Full; Ilio colitis; yes

See #
1929   2502;   PORTILLO, Isabel; 1928-Mar-4; 10/12; Fem; Comanche; yes; Full; Not known; yes

1928   2519;   POWO; 1928-Nov-10; 54; Male; Comanche; yes; Full; Dropsy; yes

1928   2536;   QUERDIBITTY; 1929-Jan-22; 56; Male; Kiowa; yes; Full; Bronchial pneumonia; yes

1928   2679;   SAPCUT, Vincent Russell; 1928-Nov-9; 3; Male; Comanche; yes; Full; Acute anterior poliomyelitis; yes

1928   2768;   SEYOYA, Margaret; 1929-Jan-8; 20; Fem; Comanche; yes; 1/4; Pulmonary T.B.; yes

1928   2781;   SITAHPATAH; 1928-Oct-20; 84; Male; Kiowa; yes; Full; Not known; yes

1928   2196;   SPOTTED CROW, Frank; 1928-July-3; 3; Male; Apache; yes; Full; Diarrhea & enteritis; yes

187

State __Oklahoma__ Reservation __Kiowa__ Agency or Jurisdiction __Kiowa__
Office of Indian Affairs Deaths Occurring Between the Dates of July 1, 1928 and
June 30, 1929 of Indians Enrolled at Jurisdiction

KEY: Year & Number on last Census Roll; Name; Surname and Given; Date of Death; Age at Death; Sex; Tribe; Ward (yes or no); Degree of Blood; Cause of Death; At jurisdiction where enrolled (yes or no); [If "no", where, if given]

1929   284;   TAHGATTSAN; 1928-Aug-27; 50; Fem; Kiowa; yes; Full; Acute indigestion; yes

1929   2973;   TAHLO, Ralston; 1929-May-22; 10/12; Male; Kiowa; yes; Full; Not known; yes

1928   3068;   TANEDOOAH, Katherine; 1929-Feb-15; 2; Fem; Kiowa; yes; Full; Bronchial pneumonia; yes

1928   3069;   TANEPEAHBY (Hummingbird); 1928-Oct; 85; Male; Kiowa; yes; Full; Not known; yes

1928   3071;   TANEQUODLE; 1928-Oct-9; 83; Male; Kiowa; yes; Full; Senility; yes

1928   3075;   TANEQUODLE, Peggy Lou; 1928-Nov-2; 1; Fem; Kiowa; yes; Full; Syphilis; yes

1928   3083;   TANEQUOOT, Austin; 1928-Aug-23; 29; Male; Kiowa; yes; Full; T.B. & liver trouble; yes

1928   3353;   TIDDACK, Edward; 1929-Feb-27; 9/12; Male; Comanche; yes; Full; Influenza; yes

1928   2339;   TIETAC, Ella; 1929-Feb-24; 30; Fem; Comanche; yes; Full; Lobar pneumonia; yes

1928   2932;   TOEMETY; 1929-Apr-19; 51; Fem; Kiowa; yes; Full; Killed in cyclone; yes

        See #
1929   3020;   TOPPAH, Magdelena; 1929-May-14; 1/12; Fem; Kiowa; yes; Full; Not known; yes

1928   3215;   TIGHKOBO, Campbell; 1928-Aug-29; 8; Male; Kiowa; yes; Full; Typhoid fever; yes

1928   3636;   TSOTIGH, Sadie Lue; 1929-Feb-27; 1; Fem; Apache & Kiowa; yes; Full; Not known; yes

1928   3525;   TOTITE, Thomas; 1929-Mar-22; 30; Male; Comanche; yes; Full; Consumption; yes

EXCULIVES[sic] OF STILLBIRTHS

State ___Oklahoma___ Reservation ___Kiowa___ Agency or Jurisdiction ___Kiowa___

Office of Indian Affairs Deaths Occurring Between the Dates of July 1, 1928 and
June 30, 1929 of Indians Enrolled at Jurisdiction

KEY: Year & Number on last Census Roll; Name; Surname and Given; Date of Death; Age at Death; Sex; Tribe; Ward (yes or no); Degree of Blood; Cause of Death; At jurisdiction where enrolled (yes or no); [If "no", where, if given]

See #

1929 3525; TOTITE, Clyde; 1929-May-11; 9/12; Male; Comanche; yes; Full; Paralytic stroke; yes

1928 3888; TOKESUITE; 1928-Sept-2; 69; Male; Comanche; yes; Full; Veneral[sic] disease; yes

1929 152; WAHKEHQUAH, Albert; 1929-May-2; 8; Male; Comanche; yes; Full; Septic Meningitis; yes

1928 2794; WARE, Irene; 1929-Feb-7; 18; Fem; Kiowa; yes; Full; Pulmonary T.B.; yes

189

KIOWA INDIAN AGENCY
Kiowa Reservation
Oklahoma
1930

DEATH ROLL
Kiowa, Comanche, Apache and
Fort Sill Apache Indians

State __Oklahoma__ Reservation __Kiowa__ Agency or Jurisdiction __Kiowa__
Office of Indian Affairs Deaths Occurring Between the Dates of July 1, 1929 and
June 30, 1930 of Indians Enrolled at Jurisdiction

KEY: Year & Number on last Census Roll; Name; Surname and Given; Date of Death; Age at Death; Sex; Tribe; Ward (yes or no); Degree of Blood; Cause of Death; At jurisdiction where enrolled (yes or no); [If "no", where, if given]

1930   403;   AYTOE; 1930-June-3; 62; M; Kiowa; yes; Full; Stomach & bowel trouble; yes

1930   565;   BROWN, Pauline; 1930-May-11; 14; F; Kiowa; yes; 1/4; Not known; [No]; Sasakwa, Okla.

1930   693;   CHALEPAH, Albert Clay; 1929-Aug-27; 3; M; Apache; yes; Full; Not known; yes

        See #
1930   697;   CHANUTE, Dollie Vivian; 1930-May-3; 1; F; Kiowa; yes; Full; T. B.; yes

1930   1313;   GEIOGAMAH, Stanley; 1930-May-6; 3; M; Kiowa; yes; Full; Not known; yes

        See #
1930   1460;   HAINTO; 1930-Apr-16; few hrs; F; Kiowa; yes; Full; few hrs; yes

1930   1486;   HARRY, May; 1930-June-12; 19; F; Comanche; yes; Full; Pulmonary T.B.; yes

1930   1708;   HUMMINGBIRD, Joseph; 1930-Apr-3; 49; M; Kiowa; yes; Full; Pulmonary T.B.; yes

1930   2123;   KOSECHATA, Cleo Lester; 1930-June-25; 3; F; Kiowa; yes; Full; Unknown; yes

1930   2354;   KARDSEY; 1930-Apr-16; 43; F; Comanche; yes; 1/4; Pneumonia; yes

1930   2673;   MOTHTERME, Jane; 1930-Apr-20; 34; F; Comanche; yes; Full; Unknown; yes

1930   2739;   NAHDAHYAKAH; 1930-May-15; 63; F; Comanche; yes; Full; Uremia; yes

        See #
1930   2747;   NAHNO; 1930-June-14; 1 day; F; Comanche; yes; Full; Hemophilia; yes

1930   2771;   NAPPYWAT; 1930-Apr-4; 88; M; Comanche; yes; Full; Old age & kidney trouble; yes

193

State __Oklahoma__ Reservation __Kiowa__ Agency or Jurisdiction __Kiowa__
Office of Indian Affairs Deaths Occurring Between the Dates of July 1, 1929 and
June 30, 1930 of Indians Enrolled at Jurisdiction

KEY: Year & Number on last Census Roll; Name; Surname and Given; Date of Death; Age at Death; Sex; Tribe; Ward (yes or no); Degree of Blood; Cause of Death; At jurisdiction where enrolled (yes or no); [If "no", where, if given]

1930   2348;   PARKER, Quannah; 1930-May-21; 16; M; Kiowa; yes; Full;
Pneumonia; yes

1931   2534;   PERMAMSU, Esther Ann; 1930-May-13; 2; F; Comanche; yes; Full;
Unknown; yes

1930   4122;   TAHMAHKERA; 1930-June-18; 55; M; Kiowa; yes; Full;
Diabetis[sic]; yes

1930   4191;   TAHSEQUAW, Albert; 1930-June-30; 32; M; Comanche; yes; Full;
Concussion brain; yes

1930   4687;   TOOAHMIPAH, Veokra; 1930-May-6; 5/12; F; Comanche; yes; Full;
Not known; yes

1930   4838;   TSATOWGKEAH, Mary; 1930-Apr-15; 50; F; Apache; yes; Full;
Not known; yes

1930   5361;   YACKESCHI, Les; 1930-Jan-13; 19; F; Comanche; yes; Full;
Not known; yes

KIOWA INDIAN AGENCY
Kiowa Reservation
Oklahoma
1931

DEATH ROLL
Kiowa, Comanche, Apache and
Fort Sill Apache Indians

State __Oklahoma__ Reservation __Kiowa__ Agency or Jurisdiction __Kiowa__

Office of Indian Affairs Deaths Occurring Between the Dates of April 1, 1930 and March 31, 1931 of Indians Enrolled at Jurisdiction

---

KEY: Year & Number on last Census Roll; Name; Surname and Given; Date of Death; Age at Death; Sex; Tribe; Ward (yes or no); Degree of Blood; Cause of Death; At jurisdiction where enrolled (yes or no); [If "no", where, if given]

1930   41;   AHDOAY, Samuel; 1931-Jan-28; 21; M; Comanche; yes; 4/4; Not known; yes

1931   67;   AHKEAHBO, Betty Lou; 1930-Oct-2; 1; F; Kiowa; yes; 4/4; Not known; yes

1931   101;   AHTONE, Nellie; 1931-Jan-1; 13 das; F; Kiowa; yes; 3/4; Not known; yes

1931   236;   ASEPERMY, Curtis Clayton; 1930- Nov-13; 3; M; Kiowa; yes; 4/4; Not known; yes

1931   333;   AUNKOY; 1931-Mar-28; 84; M; Kiowa; yes; Mex; Not known; yes

1931   335;   AUNQUOE; 1931-Mar-26; 55; M; Kiowa; yes; 4/4; Not known; yes

1930   403;   AYTOE; 1930-June-3; 63; F; Kiowa; yes; 4/4; Stomach and liver trouble; yes

1931   390;   BELATTERETA; 1930-Dec-20; 82; F; Kiowa; yes; 4/4; Not known; yes

1930   565;   BROWN, Pauline; 1930-May-11; 15; F; Kiowa; yes; 3/4; Not known; yes

See #
1930   710;   BULLBEAR, Cornelius; 1930-Oct-23; 15 das; M; Kiowa; yes; 4/4; Not known; yes

See #
1930   697;   CHANATE, Dollie Vivian; 1930-May-3; 1; F; Kiowa; yes; 4/4; Tuberculosis; yes

1931 2164;   CHANGO, Eva; 1931-Jan-24; 42; F; Apache; yes; 1/4; Carcinoma uterus; yes

1930 2335;   CHOCKPOYAH, Maud; 1930-Dec-31; 27; F; Apache; yes; 4/4; Don't know; yes

1930 4670;   COBAHTINE, Bettie; 1931-Jan-8; 24; F; Kiowa; yes; 4/4; Tuberculosis; yes

State __Oklahoma__ Reservation __Kiowa__ Agency or Jurisdiction __Kiowa__

Office of Indian Affairs Deaths Occurring Between the Dates of April 1, 1930 and March 31, 1931 of Indians Enrolled at Jurisdiction

KEY: Year & Number on last Census Roll; Name; Surname and Given; Date of Death; Age at Death; Sex; Tribe; Ward (yes or no); Degree of Blood; Cause of Death; At jurisdiction where enrolled (yes or no); [If "no", where, if given]

1931   See #
1931   3298;   COMANCHE, Alice; 1930-Dec-8; 1; F; Apache; yes; 4/4; Peupwia[sic] hemorrhage; yes

1930   4257;   EONEAH, Aliene; 1930-July-24; 9; F; Kiowa; yes; 4/4; Ruptured appendix; yes

1931   1041;   GEIOGAMAH, Carrie; 1931-Jan-10; 38; F; Kiowa; yes; 4/4; Not known; yes

1930   1313;   GEIOGAMAH, Stanley; 1930-May-6; 4; M; Kiowa; yes; 4/4; Not known; yes

    See #
1930   1460;   HAINTA; 1930-Apr-16; 5 mins; M; Kiowa; yes; 4/4; Not known, lived only a few minutes; yes

    See #
1930   1447;   HAKEAH, Perry Jack; 1930-Sept-3; 4/12; M; Kiowa; yes; 4/4; Broncho pneumonia; yes

1930   1486;   HARRY, May; 1930-June-12; 19; F; Comanche; yes; 4/4; Pulmonary T.B.; yes; Phoenix Sanatorium, AZ

1930   1721;   HUMMINGBIRD, Carroll; 1930-July-1; 6/12; F; Kiowa; yes; 4/4; Not known; yes

1930   1708;   HUNNINGBIRD[sic], Joseph; 1930-Apr-3; 50; M; Kiowa; yes; 4/4; Pulmonary T.B.; yes

1931   1322;   HUMMINGBIRD, Milne; 1931-Jan-13; 17; M; Kiowa; yes; 4/4; Not known; yes

1930   3610;   JOHNSON, Onida May; 1930-Aug-30; 5/12; F; Kiowa; yes; 1/4; Broncho pneumonia; yes

    See #
1930   2105;   KAPADDY, Thelma; 1931-Feb-1; 1/12; F; Comanche; yes; 4/4; Not known; yes

1930   2354;   KARDSEY; 1930-Apr-16; 43; F; Comanche; yes; 1/4; Pneumonia; yes

State __Oklahoma__ Reservation __Kiowa__ Agency or Jurisdiction __Kiowa__
Office of Indian Affairs Deaths Occurring Between the Dates of April 1, 1930 and
March 31, 1931 of Indians Enrolled at Jurisdiction

KEY: Year & Number on last Census Roll; Name; Surname and Given; Date of Death; Age at Death; Sex; Tribe; Ward (yes or no); Degree of Blood; Cause of Death; At jurisdiction where enrolled (yes or no); [If "no", where, if given]

1930   1975;   KEAHBONE, Betsy Rose; 1930-Nov-4; 15; F; Kiowa; yes; 4/4; Hereditary syphilis; yes

1930   1977;   KEAHBONE, Redford Aaron; 1930-Oct-27; 1; M; Kiowa; yes; 1/4; Acute Enteritis; yes

See #
1931   3292;   KLINEKALE, Mary; 1930-July-1; 4/12; F; Kiowa; yes; 4/4; Inamition[sic]; yes

1930   2057;   KOASSECHMY, Lita Jo; 1931-Feb-2; 1; F; Comanche; yes; 4/4; Not known; yes

1931   1563;   KOASSECHMY, Hope; 1931-June-23; 16; F; Comanche; yes; 4/4; Nepheritis[sic] acute; yes

1930   2093;   KOMAHTY, Hartley; 1930-Sept-20; 1; F; Kiowa; yes; 7/8; Not known; yes

1930   1376;   KOMTAHMEAH; 1930-Aug-15; 60; F; Kiowa; yes; 4/4; Not known; yes

1930   2123;   KOSECHATA, Cleo Lester; 1930-June-25; 3; F; Comanche; yes; 4/4; Not known; yes

1930   2196;   LEBARRE, Benjamin; 1930-July-12; 42; M; Comanche; yes; 1/2; Pneumonia; yes

1930   2264;   LOCO, Jaunita; 1931-Mar-23; 24; F; Fort Sill Apache; yes; 4/4; Pulmonary T.B.; yes

1931   1869;   MAUNKEE (Kiowa Bill); 1931-Jan-9; 72; M; Kiowa; yes; 4/4; Not known; yes

1930   2673;   MOTHTERME, Jane; 1930-Apr-29; 34; F; Comanche; yes; 4/4; Not known; yes

1930   2739;   NAHDAHYAKAH; 1930-May-15; 64; M; Comanche; yes; 4/4; Uremia; yes

See #
1930   2747;   NAHNO; 1930-June-14; 1 day; F; Comanche; yes; 3/4; Hemophilia; yes

Office of Indian Affairs Deaths Occurring Between the Dates of April 1, 1930 and
March 31, 1931 of Indians Enrolled at Jurisdiction

KEY: Year & Number on last Census Roll; Name; Surname and Given; Date of Death; Age at Death; Sex; Tribe; Ward (yes or no); Degree of Blood; Cause of Death; At jurisdiction where enrolled (yes or no); [If "no", where, if given]

1930   2771;   NAPPYWAT; 1930-Apr-4; 88; M; Comanche; yes; 4/4; Old age and Kidney trouble; yes

See #
1930   793;   OTIPPOBY, Wm Henry; 1931-Feb-17; 4/12; M; Comanche; yes; 7/8; Inanition, premature birth; yes

1930   2997;   PAHDOCO, Jesse; 1931-Jan-22; 41; M; Comanche; yes; 4/4; Pneumonia; yes

1930   2348;   PARKER, Quanah; 1930-May-21; 16; M; Comanche; yes; 1/4; Pneumonia; yes

1930   2812;   PARKER, Vera; 1930-Aug-17; 15; F; Comanche; yes; 5/8; Drowned; yes

See #
1930   3167;   PEBEAHSY, Runnel; 1930-Nov-2; 15 das; M; Comanche; yes; 4/4; Not known; yes

1931   2534;   PERMAMSU, Esther Ann; 1930-May-13; 2; F; Comanche; yes; 4/4; Not known; yes

1930   4085;   PESAHTETTAH, Nellie; 1931-Feb-20; 30; F; Comanche; yes; 4/4; Choleupsisis[sic]; yes

1930   1525;   PESEWONIT, Harry; 1930-Oct-25; 10; M; Comanche; yes; 4/4; Typhoid; yes

1931   2591;   PEWO, Gloria Etta; 1930-Nov-15; 1; F; Comanche; yes; 4/4; Not known; yes

1930   3341;   POAHWAY, Laverne; 1930-Nov-22; 10/12; F; Comanche & Kiowa; yes; 4/4; Not known; yes

1931   2740;   PUEBLO, Billie Malcolm; 1931-Jan-22; 3; M; Comanche; yes; 4/4; Not known; yes

1931   2752;   QUETONE; 1931-Feb-29; 82; M; Kiowa; yes; 1/4; Not known; yes

See #
1931   2897;   SAPCUT; 1931-Jan-19; 4 das; M; Comanche; yes; 4/4; Not known; yes

Office of Indian Affairs Deaths Occurring Between the Dates of April 1, 1930 and
March 31, 1931 of Indians Enrolled at Jurisdiction

KEY: Year & Number on last Census Roll; Name; Surname and Given; Date of Death; Age at Death; Sex;
Tribe; Ward (yes or no); Degree of Blood; Cause of Death; At jurisdiction where enrolled (yes or no); [If "no",
where, if given]

1930 3149; STUMBLING BEAR, Lavinia; 1931-Mar-18; 9/12; F; Kiowa; yes;
4/4; Chickenpox; yes

1930 4153; SUTTON, Catherine Pauline; 1930-Nov-11; 1; F; Kiowa; yes; 4/4;
Hereditary syphilis; yes

1930 4122; TAHMAHKERA, Markadera; 1930-June-18; 56; M; Comanche; yes;
4/4; Diabetes; yes

See #
1930 2890; TAHSEQUAW, Rudolph Alvin; 1931-Feb-13; 6/12; M; Comanche;
yes; 4/4; Pneumonia; yes

1930 4191; TAHSEQUAW, Albert; 1930-June-30; 33; f[sic]; Comanche; yes; 4/4;
Not known; yes

1930 4215; TAHTAHTY; 1930-Aug-29; 73; F; Comanche; yes; 4/4;
Myacardial Degeneratum[sic]; yes

See #
1931 3321; TANEDOOAH, Ruby; 1930-July-3; 1; F; Kiowa; yes; 4/4;
Not known; yes

1931 4247; TANEQUOOT, Edna; 1931-Feb-7; 27; F; Kiowa; yes; 4/4; Gallstone
& Appendicitis; yes

1930 4464; TIPPOTI, Hazel; 1931-Jan-29; 17; F; Comanche; yes; 4/4; Diabetes
mellitus; yes

1930 4687; TOOAHINPAH, Veakra; 1930-May-6; 7/12; F; Comanche; yes; 4/4;
Not known; yes

1930 4688; TOOAHINPAH, Page; 1930-Sept-12; 20; M; Comanche; yes; 4/4;
Pulmonary T.B.; yes

1930 4551; TOFPONETE; 1930-July-23; 62; F; Comanche; yes; 4/4;
Interstitial nephritis; yes

1930 4605; TOMAH, Jaunita Elenor[sic]; 1930-Oct-25; 9/12; F; Comanche; yes;
3/4; Fermantative[sic] diarrhea; yes

1930 4668; TONGKEAMHA, Corrine May; 1930-Aug-9; 1; F; Kiowa; yes; 4/4;
Iliocolitis[sic]; yes

State __Oklahoma__ Reservation __Kiowa__ Agency or Jurisdiction __Kiowa__
Office of Indian Affairs Deaths Occurring Between the Dates of April 1, 1930 and
March 31, 1931 of Indians Enrolled at Jurisdiction

KEY: Year & Number on last Census Roll; Name; Surname and Given; Date of Death; Age at Death; Sex; Tribe; Ward (yes or no); Degree of Blood; Cause of Death; At jurisdiction where enrolled (yes or no); [If "no", where, if given]

1930   4838;   TOATONGKEAH, Mary; 1930-Apr-15; 50; F; Apache; yes; 4/4;
Not known; yes

1930   794;   WAHERRAMMAH, Louise; 1930-Oct-25; 23; F; Comanche; yes;
4/4; Post operative shock; yes

See #
1931   4051;   WERMY, Billy Murphy; 1930-Nov-26; 6/12; M; Comanche; yes;
4/4; Pneumonia; yes

1930   5303;   WOODARD, Lizzie; 1930-Oct-24; 64; F; Kiowa; yes; 4/4;
Not known; yes

1930   5307;   WOOFPEBEHO; 1931-Jan-30; 81; M; Comanche; yes; 4/4;
Urema[sic] acute; yes

1931   4150;   WOOTHTOVO; 1931-Feb-6; 77; M; Comanche; yes; 4/4;
Not known; yes

1930   3460;   YACKEYONNY, Korene; 1930-Dec-2; 7; F; Comanche; yes; 4/4;
Diphtheria; yes

1930   5394;   YEAHQUO, Lizzie; 1930-Oct-7; 27; F; Kiowa; yes; 4/4; Don't know;
yes

1930   1632;   YOUNGMAN, Rosella Adella; 1930-Oct-31; 1; F; Comanche; yes;
4/4; Enterocolitis; yes

1930   5432;   ZOQUO, Hilton; 1930-Aug-22; 19; F; Kiowa; yes; 4/4; Not known;
yes

KIOWA INDIAN AGENCY
Kiowa Reservation
Oklahoma
1932

DEATH ROLL
Kiowa, Comanche, Apache and
Fort Sill Apache Indians

Office of Indian Affairs Deaths Occurring Between the Dates of April 1, 1931 and
March 31, 1932 of Indians Enrolled at Jurisdiction

KEY: Year & Number on last Census Roll; Name; Surname and Given; Date of Death; Age at Death; Sex;
Tribe; Ward (yes or no); Degree of Blood; Cause of Death; At jurisdiction where enrolled (yes or no); [If "no",
where, if given]

1931   120;   AHLEAH; 1931-Oct-1; 76; F; Kiowa; yes; 4/4; Tumor abdomen; yes,

1931   84;   AHPEAHTONE; 1931-Aug-7; 72; M; Kiowa; yes; 4/4; Not known;
yes

1931   94;   AHSAY; 1931-Apr-21; 68; M; Comanche; yes; 4/4; Hemorrhage
bowels; yes

1931   3175;   AHTAPETY, Richard; 1931-July-25; 18; M; Kiowa; yes; 4/4;
Not known; yes

       See #
1932   126;   AITSON, Mary; 1932-Jan-4; 1 day; F; Kiowa; yes; 7/8; Not known;
yes

1931   124;   AITSON, Forest; 1931-Oct-6; 2; M; Kiowa; yes; 7/8; Gastric
enteritis; yes

1931   125;   AITSON, Fred; 1931-July-18; 23; M; Kiowa; yes; 4/4; Pulmonary
T.B.; yes

       See #
1932   133;   AKO, David; 1931-June-19; 3 hrs; M; Kiowa; yes; 7/8; Not known;
yes

1931   228;   ASEPERMY; 1931-May-3; 62; M; Comanche; yes; 4/4; Not known;
yes

1931   308;   AUCHAHIAH, Thomas; 1931-June-3; 32; M; Kiowa; yes; 4/4;
Not known; yes

1931   334;   AUNPAUHE; 1932-Feb-17; 83; M; Kiowa; yes; 4/4; Not known; yes

1931   3311;   BEARTRACK, Lilliam[sic]; 1931-Dec-12; 5; F; Kiowa; yes; 4/4;
Lobar pneumonia; yes

1931   451;   BOONE, Martin; 1931-May-3; 21; M; Kiowa; yes; 4/4; Pulmonary
T.B.; yes

1931   514;   CHADDLEKOAH, Hazel; 1931-Aug-5; 38; F; Kiowa; yes; 4/4;
Septicemia puerperal; yes

State __Oklahoma__ Reservation __Kiowa__ Agency or Jurisdiction __Kiowa__
Office of Indian Affairs Deaths Occurring Between the Dates of April 1, 1931 and
March 31, 1932 of Indians Enrolled at Jurisdiction

KEY: Year & Number on last Census Roll; Name; Surname and Given; Date of Death; Age at Death; Sex; Tribe; Ward (yes or no); Degree of Blood; Cause of Death; At jurisdiction where enrolled (yes or no); [If "no", where, if given]

1931   1845;   CHAHORISTAN, Nannie; 1931-July-16; 49; F; Kiowa; yes; 4/4; Renal dropsy; yes

1931   606;   CHAYAH, (Mrs. Bones); 1931-Sept-8; 79; F; Comanche; yes; 4/4; Senility; yes

1931   688;   COATHTY, Emma; 1931-July-1; 42; F; Comanche; yes; 4/4; Uremia; yes

1931   827;   DAUKEI, Lois; 1931-Aug-19; 1; F; Kiowa; yes; 4/4; Dysentery; yes

1931   290;   ESAWOOTHTAKEQUA, Ida; 1932-Mar-15; 46; F; Comanche; yes; 4/4; Not known; yes

1931   3396;   FRANKLIN, Colonel Moore; 1931-June-5; 5/12; M; Kiowa; yes; 3/4; Pertussis; yes

1931   1189;   HAWZIPTA; 1931-Dec-12; 70; M; Kiowa; yes; 4/4; Not known; yes

See #
1932   1259;   HOAHWAH, Harvey; 1932-Jan-15; 1/12; M; Comanche; yes; 4/4; Bronchial pneumonia; yes

1931   690;   HOAHWAH, Morene; 1931-Aug-13; 18; F; Comanche; yes; 4/4; Tuberculosis; yes

1931   1252;   HOAUN, Gladys; 1931-Apr-14; 15; F; Kiowa; yes; 4/4; Uremia acute; yes

1931   574;   KEEHARTO; 1931-Aug-24; 57; F; Apache; yes; 4/4; Not known; yes

1931   1563;   KOASSECHANY, Hope; 1931-June-23; 17; F; Comanche; yes; 4/4; Nephritis acute; yes

1931   1586;   KOKOOM; 1932-Jan-11; 80; M; Kiowa; yes; 4/4; Not known; yes

1931   1717;   LEHMAN, Herman; 1932-Feb-2; 73; M; Comanche; yes; W; Centilas Dilatum Naya[sic]; yes

1931   1725;   LITTLECHIEF, Mike; 1931-July-23; 20; M; Kiowa; yes; 4/4; Pulmonary T.B.; yes

State __Oklahoma__ Reservation __Kiowa__ Agency or Jurisdiction __Kiowa__
Office of Indian Affairs Deaths Occurring Between the Dates of April 1, 1931 and
March 31, 1932 of Indians Enrolled at Jurisdiction

KEY: Year & Number on last Census Roll; Name; Surname and Given; Date of Death; Age at Death; Sex; Tribe; Ward (yes or no); Degree of Blood; Cause of Death; At jurisdiction where enrolled (yes or no); [If "no", where, if given]

1931   1757;   LONEWOLF, Otto; 1931-Aug-27; 24; M; Kiowa; yes; Negro; Killed by train; yes

1931   2988;   LUNA, Consuelo; [Blank]; 7; F; Comanche; yes; Mex; Injuries received by falling; yes

1931   593;   MITCHELL, Billy Lee; 1931-Apr-24; 1/12; M; Comanche; yes; 1/4; Bronchial pneumonia; yes

1931   1953;   MITHLO, Cynthia; 1931-July-12; 23; F; Fort Sill Apache; yes; 4/4; Pulmonary T.B.; yes

1931   2077;   MYERS, Randlett, Jr; 1931-May-25; 3; M; Comanche; yes; 1/2; Cerebro[sic] spinal Meningitis; yes

1931   2143;   NAUPETTY; 1932-Mar-31; 74; F; Comanche; yes; 4/4; Pneumonia lobar; yes

1931   2221;   NOHOCO; 1932-Jan-21; 65; F; Comanche; yes; 4/4; Not known; yes

1931   2250;   ONAHDY; 1931-Aug-1; 58; M; Comanche; yes; 4/4; Not known; yes

1931   2429;   PAUHAIR; 1931-Dec-5; 61; F; Kiowa; yes; 4/4; Mitral Insufficiency; yes

1931   2511;   PERDASOFPY, Billy Edward; 1931-Aug-21; 6/12; M; Comanche; yes; 4/4; Hereditary syphilis; yes

         See #
1931   2562;   PERMAMSU, Willa Dean; 1932-Jan-2; 4/12; F; Comanche; yes; 4/4; Lobar pneumonia; yes

1931   2539;   PERSHY; 1932-Jan-8; 67; M; Comanche; yes; 4/4; Not known; yes

1931   2541;   PERSCHY, Mary; 1931-Apr-22; 28; F; Comanche; yes; 4/4; Not known; yes

1931   2651;   POHACSUCUT, Henry; 1931-Dec-11; 51; M; Comanche; yes; 4/4; Lobar pneumonia; yes

1931   2725;   POWWETIPE; 1931-Apr-14; 64; M; Comanche; yes; 4/4; Tuberculosis; yes

Office of Indian Affairs Deaths Occurring Between the Dates of April 1, 1931 and
March 31, 1932 of Indians Enrolled at Jurisdiction

KEY: Year & Number on last Census Roll; Name; Surname and Given; Date of Death; Age at Death; Sex; Tribe; Ward (yes or no); Degree of Blood; Cause of Death; At jurisdiction where enrolled (yes or no); [If "no", where, if given]

1931   2856;   SAHLAHZAH, Lucy; 1932-Mar-18; 45; F; Apache; yes; 4/4; Pulmonary T.B.; yes

1931   2944;   SATOE, Bruce; 1931-Oct-27; 15; M; Kiowa; yes; 4/4; Pulmonary T.B.; yes

See #
1931   2974;   SATOE, Ensey; 1931-Oct-12; 1/12; M; Kiowa; yes; 4/4; Pneumonia; yes

1931   2149;   SHORTNECK, Roscoe; 1931-May-22; 1; M; Kiowa; yes; 4/4; Broncho pneumonia; yes

1931   3050;   SUANNY (Tim Mahseet); 1931-Oct-2; 55; M; Comanche; yes; 4/4; Not known; yes

1931   3102;   TAHBONE, Blanche; 1932-Feb-9; 21; M; Kiowa; yes; 4/4; Tuberculosis; yes

1931   3303;   TAKEWAHPOOR, George; 1931-Aug-8; 52; M; Kiowa; yes; 4/4; Anemia secondary; yes

1931   4247;   TANEQUOOT, Edna; 1931-Apr-17; 27; F; Kiowa; yes; 4/4; Not known; yes

1931   1030;   TOFPI, Laura; 1932-Jan-1; 28; F; Kiowa; yes; 4/4; Tuberculosis; yes

See #
1931   3677;   TONAHCOT, Evangeline; 1931-Nov-25; 22 das; F; Kiowa; yes; 4/4; Cold and leaking tube to heart; yes

1931   3632;   TONAHVITTY; 1931-Apr-8; 51; F; Kiowa; yes; 4/4; Apoplexy; yes

1931   3635;   TONARCY; 1931-June-28; 67; F; Comanche; yes; 4/4; Hemorrhage lungs; yes

1931   3663;   TONEPAHHATE; 1931-Aug-4; 23; F; Kiowa; yes; 4/4; Not known; yes

See #
1932   3811;   TOSSEE, Benneta; 1932-Jan-4; 6/12; F; Comanche; yes; 1/2; Ilio[sic] colitis; yes

State __Oklahoma__ Reservation __Kiowa__ Agency or Jurisdiction __Kiowa__
Office of Indian Affairs Deaths Occurring Between the Dates of April 1, 1931 and
March 31, 1932 of Indians Enrolled at Jurisdiction

1931   3817;   TSATAHSISKO, Cornelia; 1931-Aug-6; 1; F; Apache; yes; 4/4; Entero Collitis[sic] acute; yes

1931   3973;   WAHAHRACKAH, Herbert; 1931-Dec-8; 27; M; Comanche; yes; 4/4; Not known; yes

KIOWA INDIAN AGENCY
Wichita Reservation
Oklahoma
1925

DEATH ROLL
Wichita, Caddo, and Delaware
Indians

State __Oklahoma__ Reservation __Wichita__ Agency or Jurisdiction __Kiowa__
Office of Indian Affairs Deaths Occurring Between the Dates of July 1, 1925 and
June 30, 1926 of Indians Enrolled at Jurisdiction

KEY: Year & Number on last Census Roll; Name; Surname and Given; Date of Death; Age at Death; Sex; Tribe; Ward (yes or no); Degree of Blood; Cause of Death; At jurisdiction where enrolled (yes or no); [If "no", where, if given]

1925   188;   MILLER, Vera Belle; 1925-June-29; 2; Fem; Wichita; yes; Full; Bowel trouble; yes.

1924   850;   MOORE, Maryetto; 1925-May-6; 9; Male; Wichita; yes; Full; Run over by car; yes.

1924   816;   NUT TO TO (Yun nit); 1925-Mar-16; 50; Fem; Wichita; yes; Full; Unknown; yes.

1924   786;   PARTIN (Brown), Mollie; 1925-Jan-19; 51; Fem; Wichita; yes; Full; Malignant liver; yes.

1924   680;   SMARTT, Armen Leroy; 1924-Aug-9; 1; Fem; Wichita; yes; Full; Diabetes; yes.

1926   1028;   TOUNWIN, Lewellyn; 1925-Jan-30; 4/12; Fem; Wichita; yes; Full; Unknown; yes.

KIOWA INDIAN AGENCY
Wichita Reservation
Oklahoma
1926

DEATH ROLL
Wichita, Caddo, and Delaware Indians

State __Oklahoma__ Reservation __Wichita__ Agency or Jurisdiction __Kiowa__
Office of Indian Affairs Deaths Occurring Between the Dates of July 1, 1925 and
June 30, 1926 of Indians Enrolled at Jurisdiction

KEY: Year & Number on last Census Roll; Name; Surname and Given; Date of Death; Age at Death; Sex; Tribe; Ward (yes or no); Degree of Blood; Cause of Death; At jurisdiction where enrolled (yes or no); [If "no", where, if given]

1925   274;   CAMPBELL, Luther; 1926-Apr-4; 59; Male; Wichita; yes; Full; Not known; yes

1926   30;   DEAKSUNNEAHCUTTAHDISH; 1926-Jan-31; 77; Fem; Wichita; yes; Full; Old age; yes

1925   891;   DUNLAP, Lawrie; 1926-Jun-15; 53; Male; Wichita; yes; Full; Not known; yes

1925   65;   KAHDOSEAH; 1926-Jan-25; 67; Fem; Wichita; yes; Full; Old age; yes

1925   8;   LUTHER, William; 1926-Jan-20; 47; Male; Wichita; yes; Full; T.B. of bowels; yes

1925   120;   LORENTZ, Chas. Henry; 1926-May-27; 2; Male; Wichita; yes; Full; Deneral[sic] Peritonitis; yes

1925   234;   NIASTOR, Rudolph Medford; 1926-June-11; 2; Male; Wichita; yes; Full; Not known; yes

1925   25;   SEGAR, Waco Hunt; 1925-July-7; 2; Male; Wichita; yes; Full; Not known; yes

1925   911;   SQUIRREL; 1926-Apr-19; 63; Male; Wichita; yes; Full; Not known; yes

1925   42;   SWIFT, Charlie; 1925-Aug-24; 52; Male; Wichita; yes; Full; Not known; yes

1926   660;   TEWININ, Alice; 1926; 21; Fem; Caddo; yes; Full; Not known; yes

1925   235;   WAHASOS, Kitty; 1926-Mar-24; 68; Fem; Wichita; yes; Full; Not known; yes

1925   34;   WHEELER, Blanche; 1925-July-1; 11; Fem; Wichita; yes; Full; Tuberculosis ; yes

1926   520;   WHITEBEAD, Hannah; 1926-Apr-4; 8; Fem; Wichita; yes; Full; Not known; yes

KIOWA INDIAN AGENCY
Wichita Reservation
Oklahoma
1927

DEATH ROLL
Wichita, Caddo, and Delaware Indians

State __Oklahoma__ Reservation __Wichita__ Agency or Jurisdiction __Kiowa__
Office of Indian Affairs Deaths Occurring Between the Dates of July 1, 1926 and
June 30, 1927 of Indians Enrolled at Jurisdiction

KEY: Year & Number on last Census Roll; Name; Surname and Given; Date of Death; Age at Death; Sex; Tribe; Ward (yes or no); Degree of Blood; Cause of Death; At jurisdiction where enrolled (yes or no); [If "no", where, if given]

	See #	
1927	49;	BARCINDEBAR, Rabb; 1927-May-1; 5 das; Male; Caddo, yes; Full; Congenital malformation; yes

1926   236;   CALEY, Nellie; 1927-Jan-4; 3; Fem; Wichita; yes; Full; Not known; yes

1926   667;   CHAHPACHE; 1927-Jan-23; 68; Male; Caddo; yes; Full; Not known; yes

1929   264;   ELKINS, Emmit Maise; 1926-Dec-20; 17; Male; Caddo; yes; 1/4; Not known; yes

1926   196;   KODAKITS; 1927-Apr-3; 51; Fem; Wichita; yes; Full; Septicemia; yes

See #
1927   105;   LEONARD, Stratford; 1924-Nov-18; 2; Male; Wichita; yes; Full; Not known; yes

1926   975;   PENN, Bertha; 1927-May-12; 21; Fem; Caddo; yes; Full; Septicemia; yes

1926   255;   STEVENSON, Ula Frazier; 1926-Sept-17; 46; Fem; Wichita; yes; Full; Not known; yes

KIOWA INDIAN AGENCY
Wichita Reservation
Oklahoma
1928

DEATH ROLL
Wichita, Caddo, and Delaware
Indians

State __Oklahoma__ Reservation __Wichita__ Agency or Jurisdiction __Kiowa__
Office of Indian Affairs Deaths Occurring Between the Dates of July 1, 1927 and
June 30, 1928 of Indians Enrolled at Jurisdiction

KEY: Year & Number on last Census Roll; Name; Surname and Given; Date of Death; Age at Death; Sex; Tribe; Ward (yes or no); Degree of Blood; Cause of Death; At jurisdiction where enrolled (yes or no); [If "no", where, if given]

1927   27;   ARASPAR, Nicholas; 1927-12-7; 68; Male; Wichita; yes; Mexican; Not known; yes

1928   123;   CAMPBELL, Wilbur; 1928-6-17; 21; Male; Wichita; yes; Full; Gun shot wounds; yes

1927   187;   DAVIS, Ernest; 1928-1-14; 45; Male; Caddo; yes; Full; Ruptured appendix; yes

1927   296;   FRANK, Levi; 1928; 73; Male; Caddo; yes; Full; Not known; yes

1927   779;   HIMI, Mary; 1928; 67; Fem; Caddo; yes; Full; Not known; yes

1927   435;   HOWE, May; 1928; 45; Fem; Wichita; yes; Full; Not known; yes

1927   279;   LAWERNCE[sic], Eva Anita; 1927-8-23; 7; Fem; Wichita; yes; Full; Internal hemorrhage; yes

1927   566;   LEE, White; 1928-4-19; 58; Male; Wichita; yes; Full; Chronic intestinal nephritis; yes

See #
1928   613;   LORENTZ, Harriet; 1928-3-22; 1; m[sic]; Wichita; yes; Full; Tuberculosis; yes

1927   610;   LORENTZ, Henry (Everett); 1928; 35; Male; Wichita; yes; Full; Not known; yes

See #
1927   610;   LORENTZ, Lester; 1928-3-18; 2; Male; Wichita; yes; Full; Bronchial pneumonia; yes

1927   609;   LORENTZ, Pauline; 1928-4-17; 6; Fem; Wichita; yes; Full; Pulmonary T.B.; yes

1927   493;   MYERS, Mary; 1928-5-21; 39; Fem; Wichita; yes; Full; Gall bladder and liver trouble; yes

1928   641;   McLANE, Chas Patrick; 1928-1-8; 29; Male; Wichita; yes; 1/4; Not known; yes

State __Oklahoma__ Reservation __Wichita__ Agency or Jurisdiction __Kiowa__
Office of Indian Affairs Deaths Occurring Between the Dates of July 1, 1927 and
June 30, 1928 of Indians Enrolled at Jurisdiction

KEY: Year & Number on last Census Roll; Name; Surname and Given; Date of Death; Age at Death; Sex; Tribe; Ward (yes or no); Degree of Blood; Cause of Death; At jurisdiction where enrolled (yes or no); [If "no", where, if given]

1927   826;   REYNOLDS, Reuben Edward; 1928-1-2; 21; Male; Caddo; yes; Full; Gun shot wounds; yes

      See #

1927   315;   SHEGAHSHE, George; 1927-10-30; 1; Fem; Caddo; yes; Full; Not known; yes

1927   909;   SHEMAMY, Lydia Marie; 1928; 21; Fem; Caddo; yes; Full; Not known; yes

1927   917;   SHIRLEY, June; 1928; 93; Fem; Caddo; yes; Full; Not known; yes

1926   579;   TINHOOT; 1928; 93; Fem; Caddo; yes; Full; Not known; yes

1927   1082;   TOHO; 1928-3-29; 59; Male; Caddo; yes Full; Not known; yes,

1927   1216;   WILLIAMS, Thomas; 1927; 38; Male; Caddo; yes; Full; Not known; yes

1927   1250;   WILSON, Willie; 1927; 43; Male; Caddo; yes; Full; Not known; yes

1927   1274;   YUNHUNE; 1928; 68; Fem; Caddo; yes; Full; Not known; yes

KIOWA INDIAN AGENCY
Wichita Reservation
Oklahoma
1929

DEATH ROLL
Wichita, Caddo, and Delaware
Indians

State ___Oklahoma___ Reservation ___Wichita___ Agency or Jurisdiction ___Kiowa___
Office of Indian Affairs Deaths Occurring Between the Dates of July 1, 1928 and
June 30, 1929 of Indians Enrolled at Jurisdiction

KEY: Year & Number on last Census Roll; Name; Surname and Given; Date of Death; Age at Death; Sex; Tribe; Ward (yes or no); Degree of Blood; Cause of Death; At jurisdiction where enrolled (yes or no); [If "no", where, if given]

929   64;   BLACK (Tabbynanaca), Jonas; 1929-1-12; 60; Male; Comanche; yes; Full; Not known; yes

1928   163;   CONNER, Harris; 1929-4-18; 48; Male; Caddo; yes; Full; Not known; yes

1928   197;   DELAWARE, Lewis; 1928-10-7; 50; Male; Wichita; yes; Full; Not known; yes

1931   61;   GUY, Frank; 1929; 5; Male; Caddo; yes; Full; Not known; yes

1928   501;   KAHNOOSTY, Evelyn; 1929-5-6; 21; Fem; Wichita; yes; 1/2; Not known; yes

1929   525;   KIDDAHWADDY (Red Bird), Edward; 1929-6-16; 25; Male; Wichita; yes; Full; Not known; yes

1929   525[sic];   KIDDAHWADDY, Pearl; 1928-10-5; 18; Fem; Wichita; yes; Full; Peritonitis following typhoid; yes

1938   541;   KIOWA 1928-12-28; 71; Male; Wichita; yes; Full; Flu; yes

1928   552;   LAMAR, Albert; 1928-11-8; 41; Male; Wichita; yes; Full; Leakage heart; yes

     See #
1929   593;   LONGHAT; 1928-9-20; 1 da; Fem; Caddo; yes; Full; Premature birth; yes

     See #
192   607;   LORENTZ, Gilbert; 1929-1-2; 2/12; Male; Wichita; yes; Full; Bronchial pneumonia; yes

1928   717;   NED (Williams), Lizzie; 1929-3-20; 26; Fem; Wichita; yes; Full; Endocarditis; yes

1928   777;   PARTON, Johnson; 1928-7-6; 67; Male; Caddo; yes; Full; Not known; yes

     See #
1929   800;   PICKARD, Jerland (Lois); 1929-1-22; 6/12; Fem; Wichita; yes; Full; Pneumonia; yes

State __Oklahoma__ Reservation __Wichita__ Agency or Jurisdiction __Kiowa__
Office of Indian Affairs Deaths Occurring Between the Dates of July 1, 1928 and
June 30, 1929 of Indians Enrolled at Jurisdiction

KEY: Year & Number on last Census Roll; Name; Surname and Given; Date of Death; Age at Death; Sex; Tribe; Ward (yes or no); Degree of Blood; Cause of Death; At jurisdiction where enrolled (yes or no); [If "no", where, if given]

1928   855;   SAHKONO (Bates); 1928-12-27; 78; Male; Wichita; yes; Full;
Old age and flu; yes

1928   1043;   TEWININ, Lee; 1929-2-21; 30; Male; Caddo; yes; Full;
Sarcoma testicle; yes

1928   848;   WARDEN, Blanche; 1929-2-26; 42; Fem; Wichita; yes; Full;
Uremia; yes

1928   1113;   WASHINGTON, George; 1929-1-11; 76; Male; Wichita; yes;
Colored; Not known; yes

1929   1095;   WELLER, Pearl; 1928-10-4; 26; Fem; Caddo; yes; Full;
Not known; yes

1928   1146;   WHEELER, Margaret; 1929-2-13; 25; Fem; Wichita; yes; Full;
Bright's Disease; yes

1929   1299;   WITSTEKAH; 1929-6-26; 70; Fem; Wichita; yes; Full;
Not known; yes

1928   1290;   ZADOKO, Percy; 1929-4-24; 57; Male; Wichita; yes; Full;
Not known; yes

KIOWA INDIAN AGENCY
Wichita Reservation
Oklahoma
1931

DEATH ROLL
Wichita, Caddo, and Delaware
Indians

State __Oklahoma___ Reservation __Wichita__ Agency or Jurisdiction __Kiowa__

Office of Indian Affairs Deaths Occurring Between the Dates of April 1, 1930 and March 31, 1931 of Indians Enrolled at Jurisdiction

KEY: Year & Number on last Census Roll; Name; Surname and Given; Date of Death; Age at Death; Sex; Tribe; Ward (yes or no); Degree of Blood; Cause of Death; At jurisdiction where enrolled (yes or no); [If "no", where, if given]

1931   87;   BROWN, Helen; 1930-8-2; 26; F; Caddo, yes; Full; Not known; yes.

1931   88;   BROWN, Lucy; 1931-1-25; 48; F; Caddo; yes; 1/4; Not known; yes.

1931   136;   CARTER, Charlie; 1931-3-27; 46; M; Caddo; yes; Full; Lobar pneumonia; yes.

1931   160;   CHOWUNITSSE; 1930-12-10; 58; M; Caddo; yes; Full; Not known; yes.

1930   4314;   CHAWWAH; 1931-2-6; 68; F; Wichita; yes; Full; Chronic diarrhea; yes.

1931   291;   EXENDINE, Celia Mae; 1931-3-9; 15; F; Delaware; yes; 1/4; Not known; yes.

1931   1041;   HINKLE, Elmer Roy; 1930-5-20; 1; M; Delaware; yes; 1/4; Unknown; yes.

1931   148;   KANOOSTY, Mary; 1930-10-27; 19; F; Caddo; yes; Full; Unknown; yes.

1930   2227;   LEE, Spencer; 1930-7-31; 25; M; Wichita; yes; Full; Acute nephritis; yes.

1931   2498;   McLANE, Margaret; 1931-1-5; 57; F; Delaware; yes; 1/4; Not known; yes.

1930   5115;   WHITEBEAD, Harry; 1930-11-19; 59; M; Caddo; yes; Full; Not known; yes.

KIOWA INDIAN AGENCY
Wichita Reservation
Oklahoma
1932

DEATH ROLL
Wichita, Caddo, and Delaware
Indians

State __Oklahoma__ Reservation __Wichita__ Agency or Jurisdiction __Kiowa__
Office of Indian Affairs Deaths Occurring Between the Dates of April 1, 1931 and
March 31, 1932 of Indians Enrolled at Jurisdiction

1931   1;   ADAHNOE (Williams), Thomas; 1931-4-11; 66; M; Caddo; yes; 4/4; Not known; yes

1931 1071;   BEAVER, Kermit; 1931-4-14; 1; M; Caddo; yes; 4/4; Pertussis; yes

1931   129;   CAMPBELL, Mattie Florence; 1931-12-28; 31; F; Wichita; yes; 1/4; Pulmonary T.B.; yes

See #
1932   205;   CLARK; 1931-5-16; 1 hr; M; Caddo; yes; 1/4; Premature birth; yes

1931 1299;   EDGE, Groman; 1931-7-5; 9; M; Caddo; yes; 4/4; Not known; yes

1931   365;   GUY, Wm H; 1931-8-4; 48; M; Caddo; yes; 4/4; Gun shot wounds; yes

1931   497;   INKANISH, Mary; 1931-9-5; 61; F; Caddo; yes; 1/4; Not known; yes

1931   51;   LAMAR (Zollars), Marietta; 1931-8-25; 38; F; Wichita; yes; 4/4; Peritonitis, ruptured appendix; yes

See #
1931   693;   MILLER, Violet; 1931-8-22; 1 da; F; Wichita; yes; 4/4; Not known; yes

1931 1315;   PENN, William; 1931-4-25; 19; M; Caddo; yes; 4/4; Not known; yes

1931   630;   PICKARD, Lena Gladys; 1932-2-3; 52; F; Wichita; yes; 4/4; Cancer-breast; yes

1931 8-34[sic]; PRUNER, Hiram P; 1[sic]; 93; M; Caddo; yes; White; Not known; yes

1931 1322;   REEDER, Dixie; 1931-9-16; 21; F; Caddo; yes; 1/2; Septicemia; yes

1931   888;   ROSS, Wilfred; 1931-11-16; 19; M; Wichita; yes; 4/4; Not known; yes

1931 1076;   SHAW, Minnie; 1932-1-18; 57; F; Caddo; yes; 4/4; Not known; yes

1931 1049;   SUNHIN, Reeder; 1931-7-12; 67; F; Delaware; yes; 4/4; Septicemia and Rept. gall bladder; yes

State __Oklahoma__ Reservation __Wichita__ Agency or Jurisdiction __Kiowa__
Office of Indian Affairs Deaths Occurring Between the Dates of April 1, 1931 and
March 31, 1932 of Indians Enrolled at Jurisdiction

KEY: Year & Number on last Census Roll; Name; Surname and Given; Date of Death; Age at Death; Sex; Tribe; Ward (yes or no); Degree of Blood; Cause of Death; At jurisdiction where enrolled (yes or no); [If "no", where, if given]

1931   1085;   THOMAS, Harold; 1931-9-11; 22; M; Wichita; yes; 4/4; Pulmonary T.B.; yes

1931   923;   TINYOU; 1932-3-8; 68; F; Caddo; yes; 4/4; Not known; yes

www.ingramcontent.com/pod-product-compliance
Lightning Source LLC
Chambersburg PA
CBHW020248030426
42336CB00010B/668
* 9 7 8 1 6 4 9 6 8 1 6 2 1 *